RELIGION AND SCHOOLING IN CANADA

RELIGION AND SCHOOLING IN CANADA

The Long Road to Separation of Church and State

Robert Crocker

University of Ottawa Press
2022

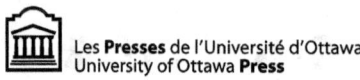
Les **Presses** de l'Université d'Ottawa
University of Ottawa **Press**

The University of Ottawa Press (UOP) is proud to be the oldest of the francophone university presses in Canada and the oldest bilingual university publisher in North America. Since 1936, UOP has been enriching intellectual and cultural discourse by producing peer-reviewed and award-winning books in the humanities and social sciences, in French and in English.

www.press.uOttawa.ca

Library and Archives Canada Cataloguing in Publication

Title: Religion and schooling in Canada : the long road to separation of Church and state / Robert Crocker, Professor Emeritus, Memorial University.
Names: Crocker, Robert K. (Robert Kirby), author.
Series: Education (University of Ottawa)
Description: Series statement: Education | Includes bibliographical references.
Identifiers: Canadiana (print) 20220161011 | Canadiana (ebook) 20220163464 |
    ISBN 9780776638171 (hardcover) | ISBN 9780776637815 (softcover) |
    ISBN 9780776638188 (PDF) | ISBN 9782760337824 (EPUB)
Subjects: LCSH: Church and education—Canada—History. | LCSH: Church schools—Canada—History. | LCSH: Religion in the public schools—Canada—History. | LCSH: Church and state—Canada—History.
Classification: LCC LC114 .C76 2022 | DDC 379.2/80971—dc23

Legal Deposit: Fourth Quarter 2022
Library and Archives Canada

© University of Ottawa Press 2022
All rights reserved.

No part of this publication may be reproduced or transmitted in any form or by any means, or stored in a database and retrieval system, without prior permission.

Production Team
Copy editing   Michael Waldin
Proofreading   Tanina Drvar
Typesetting   Nord Compo
Cover design   Lefrançois, agence marketing B2B

Cover Image
Yvon Gallant, *Collège Notre-Dame d'Acadie*

The University of Ottawa Press gratefully acknowledges the support extended to its publishing list by the Government of Canada, the Canada Council for the Arts, the Ontario Arts Council, the Social Sciences and Humanities Research Council and the Canadian Federation for the Humanities and Social Sciences through the Awards to Scholarly Publications Program, and by the University of Ottawa.

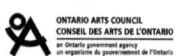  

Table of Contents

Preface vii
Acknowledgements xi
Introduction 1

1 **Philosophical and Legal Foundations** 11
  Separation of Church and State 13
  Freedom of Religion 14
  Secularism, Religious Pluralism,
  and Reasonable Accommodation 15
  Education as a Human Right 17
  Parent Rights versus State Control 18
  The Political Climate 21
  Economic Issues 22
  Models of Church / State Relationships 23
  Types of Denominational Schools in Canada 27

2 **Historical Context** 31
  Church Before State 31
  Confederation and Section 93 35
  Post-Confederation Consolidation and Expansion 42

3 **The 1982 Constitution and Impact of the Charter** 61
  Charter Challenges on Separate Schools 63
  Charter Cases on Parent Rights and Religion
  in Schools 68
  Lessons from the Charter Cases 75

4 **Constitutional Amendment: Newfoundland
  and Quebec** 77
  Newfoundland 78
  Quebec 93
  Lessons from Newfoundland and Quebec 100

5 **Catholic Schools in Canada** 105
  The Catholic Perspective 106
  The Decline of Religiosity and Church Influence 108

	Enrolments in Catholic Schools 110
	Are Catholic Schools Superior to Public Schools? 113
6	**Religion and Private Schools** 117
	The Ontario Commission on Private Schools 118
	Scope and Characteristics of Private Schools................ 120
	Private School Legislation 123
	Supreme Court Decisions on Private Schools 125
	Student Performance in Private Schools......................... 126
	The Policy Issue 127
7	**The Churches, the Federal Government, and Indigenous Education** 129
	The Colonial Era 130
	Confederation and the Indian Act.................................... 131
	Residential Schools.. 133
	Day Schools 135
	Doubts about the Residential School System 136
	The End of the Residential School System...................... 139
	Apologies, Litigation, and Resolution............................. 141
	Similarities and Differences in Indigenous and non-Indigenous Policies 146
8	**The Contemporary Debate**... 149
	Sex and Health Education 150
	Reasonable Accommodation and Quebec Bill 21........... 157
	Public Opinion Surveys.. 159
	Other Opinion Sources 162
	The Economic Argument.. 163
9	**The Way Forward** 167
	Status Quo versus Change 169
	A Framework for Change 173
	Models of Change.. 175
	Concluding Comments: Process and Implementation ... 189

Notes 195
Bibliography 211
Court Cases Cited 223

Preface

This book has been several years in the writing but close to a lifetime in the making. My early encounters with church and school were as a child attending a one-room United Church school in a small Newfoundland community. Most of my friends were Anglican, attending a three-room school just down the road. Catholics in a nearby community also had their own school. While Catholics were thought of as somewhat apart, even exotic, there was little animosity between Protestants and Catholics of the sort frequently heard of in earlier days.

School separation by religion was largely taken for granted at the time. Nevertheless, it always struck me as strange that my friends and I could do almost anything together except attend school. One attempt in the 1950s at combining the Anglican and United schools was aborted at the last minute because a few Anglican elders could not tolerate the prospect.

My own problem was solved when my parents decided, with good reason, that the Anglican school was a much better school. Even while decrying those responsible for keeping the schools separate, they sent me off to complete high school at the Anglican school. I became the envy of most of my classmates because I was the only student exempted from having to march off to church periodically or take confirmation lessons from the Anglican priest. Nevertheless, even though the Anglican ritual did seem a bit alien, it never occurred to me or my parents to seek exemption from the prayers that opened every school day.

A few years later, as a new university graduate, I had the privilege of working as a research assistant with the Royal Commission on Education in Newfoundland. A major issue on the agenda of that commission was the role of religious denominations in schooling. That job helped stimulate an academic career with the freedom to spend much of my time on policy-related research. Most of that research focused on matters having nothing to do with church and state. Nevertheless, that issue was never far from the surface through work with several commissions and task forces where it was necessary to navigate the limitations imposed by the constitutional status of denominational rights.

It was not until the early 1990s that I had reason to confront the issue much more directly. The occasion was an appointment as associate deputy minister of education, with responsibility for implementing a second royal commission report. That report was the first in Newfoundland to confront the denominational issue directly, as a matter of principle. For three years, I found myself immersed in the topic. I had much to learn about the role of church and state throughout Canada and particularly about the constitutional issues involved. Now, some twenty years later, there is time to reflect on what was learned during that period and to translate a life-long interest into an account of the role of church and state in Canadian education, the changes that have occurred since the 1982 constitution, and what the prospects for the future might be.

The intended audience for this book is academics, educational policy makers, and others interested in understanding the philosophical, legal, and practical issues underlying church/state relationships. I hope that the book will also appeal to those involved in advocacy, whatever side of the issue they may be on. Whether one favours abolition, expansion, or retention of denominational rights and religious activities in schools, the book is intended to help develop an understanding of what has brought us to where we are. I do have a point of view and some specific thoughts on future directions and will express these in the final chapter. However, this book is not intended as a polemic but as an attempt to present the issues in as full a manner as possible, recognizing that sincere and defensible positions exist on all sides.

I have relied largely on secondary sources for the brief historical account given in chapter 2. However, I consulted primary sources on particularly critical points. For example, Privy Council and Supreme Court cases, parliamentary debates, and provincial legislation were examined when available, even if well documented in historical accounts. The goal is not to duplicate the work of historians but to extend the historical discussion into the modern era and address the underlying philosophical issues of human rights, parent choice, freedom of religion, discrimination, and other areas not usually discussed in descriptive histories but critical to the modern debate.

Because of the impact of the Charter and the amending formula, I have placed greater emphasis on primary sources for the account of events since the 1980s. These sources include court decisions, parliamentary debates, legislation, royal commission reports, and government policy documents, along with academic literature related to these. The events leading to the constitutional amendments in

Newfoundland and Quebec in the 1990s were traced mainly through primary sources. The Newfoundland account differs somewhat from that for other provinces because I was able to rely to some extent on notes and recollections from my own involvement in the negotiations during the mid-1990s.

Throughout this book I have used the term "Catholic" as synonymous with "Roman Catholic." I have also used "Newfoundland" rather than "Newfoundland and Labrador" as the latter became the official name of the province only after most of the events recounted in this book had occurred. Finally, the term "Indian" has been used in some historical contexts, such as references to the Indian Act or to residential schools, where the more contemporary terms "Indigenous" or "First Nations" seem not to apply.

Acknowledgements

I wish to acknowledge the contributions of those who encouraged me to write this book and who contributed to its completion. Frank Riggs had the unenviable task of reading the first draft, which was far too long and certainly too disjointed. The late Ron Southcott also reviewed an early draft, giving the benefit of his long experience as a Catholic educator. Lloyd Brown, Jean Brown, and Alice Collins contributed their wisdom and experience to subsequent drafts. The late Chris Decker encouraged me both from the beginning of the Newfoundland reform project in the 1990s and more recently when it was unclear if I would ever finish the undertaking. The detailed comments provided by two anonymous reviewers were especially valuable in correcting errors of fact and interpretation and in pointing to some overlooked sources, especially around the early history and the chapter on Indigenous education.

I acknowledge the contributions of Caroline Boudreau, Mireille Piché, and Martin Llewellyn of the University of Ottawa Press in guiding me through the submission and review process.

As always, I am most grateful to my wife, Jan, for her encouragement throughout and for her meticulous editing of the many draft versions of the manuscript. I take full responsibility for any remaining errors or inadequacies.

Introduction

This book examines the historical relationship between church and state in Canadian education, the contemporary situation, and prospects for the future of this relationship. Its main emphasis is on legislative and legal developments since patriation of the constitution in 1982. The underlying thesis is that significant shifts have occurred in recent decades in societal views on human rights, religion, and schooling. These have already had a profound effect on the place of religion in schools and the place of sectarian schools within and outside the public school system. Issues such as freedom of religion, state neutrality on religion, education as a human right, parent rights, and the interest of the state in education are expected to require greater emphasis in debates over the future of education than they have in the past.

The status of sectarian schools has increasingly come under question, to the extent that the right of some Christian religious denominations to have their own schools, entrenched in the constitution at the time of confederation, have been extinguished in two provinces. However, they remain in place in three other provinces and in the territories. Although originally both Catholic and Protestant in character, these schools are now almost exclusively Catholic. This, along with increased secularism and greater diversity of religions in the population, has led many to challenge the privileged status of the Catholic church in education.

Under the British North America Act, Canada's original constitution, education was given as an area of provincial jurisdiction. Provincial powers were limited only by a single constraint, expressed in Section 93 of the constitution for Ontario and Quebec and in some variations of that section in the terms of union of several other provinces. These provisions were designed to protect any rights to separate schools held by Catholics and Protestants at the time of union. Since these rights, and the way they were exercised, varied from one province to another, the development of church/state relationships in education can only be understood by examining developments at a provincial level. Section 93 and its variants originally applied in six provinces: Ontario and Quebec from 1867, Manitoba from 1870, Alberta and Saskatchewan from 1905, and Newfoundland from 1949. Litigation and political action in the late nineteenth century effectively removed any right to separate denominational schools in Manitoba. Constitutional amendments in the 1990s had the same impact in Newfoundland and Quebec. Denominational rights are thus now applicable in only three provinces, Alberta, Ontario, and Saskatchewan and in the territories. The latter exist by federal statute and are not constitutionally protected.

The Charter of Rights and Freedoms, introduced on patriation of the constitution in 1982, has drawn explicit attention to human rights. The sections on freedom of religion and non-discrimination by religion are especially relevant to the place of religion in schools. The Charter has led the courts to take an expansive approach to issues of human rights. Laws seen as discriminatory or as impinging on individual religious freedom have consistently been overturned by the courts. Charter cases related to the conduct of religious activities or observances in public schools have resulted in a near prohibition of such activities, while allowing individual expressions of religion such as wearing religious symbols or private prayer.

On the other hand, challenges to the privileged status of sectarian schools have been completely unsuccessful. The main reason for this is Section 29 of the Charter: "Nothing in this Charter abrogates or derogates from any rights or privileges guaranteed by or under the Constitution of Canada in respect of denominational, separate or dissentient schools."[1] This explicitly precludes judicial action on matters affecting denominational rights. Section 29 is fundamentally in conflict with the religious freedom and non-discrimination sections of the Charter in that it protects laws and actions that would almost certainly be seen as discriminatory under these sections. The courts have taken the position that it is not within their mandate to resolve such constitutional contradictions. That is a matter for political action.

A full understanding of the contemporary status of sectarian schools requires a review of the history of such schools and the broader relationship of church and state. Three specific historical periods are of interest. The first is the confederation era between 1867 and 1905. During that time, all provinces other than Newfoundland became part of the union. The place of the churches in education, as it had developed during the colonial period, became formalized in legislation and in the constitution from 1867. The governing structures locked into place at confederation remained largely intact for more than a century.

The second critical period is the 1950s through the 1970s. During that time, royal commissions and other initiatives in several provinces set the stage for significant reforms to elementary and secondary education. Some of these reforms tested the limits of denominational protections but could not change the underlying constitutional structures. Constitutional protection for separate denominational schools remained in place in five provinces until the 1990s. Some form of denominational education also existed in four other provinces immediately following confederation. However, without constitutional protection these atrophied over time. Only British Columbia can be said to have had no official denominational presence from the time of confederation.

The period since 1982 is the one of most direct interest. The Charter has led to significant change in the place of religion in public schools. However, any impact on denominational schools has been blunted by Section 29. The most radical change has come, not from the Charter, but from the amending formula. In the 1990s, two provinces, Quebec and Newfoundland, determined that the continued existence of denominational schools was not sustainable. The reasons were different in each case: language in Quebec and economic constraints in Newfoundland. However, the desired outcome was the same: consolidation of school boards and schools across denominational lines. In both cases, it became clear after protracted negotiations that the desired result could not be achieved through consent of the affected denominations or through application of the Charter. These two provinces therefore took the more drastic route of constitutional amendment. This was made possible by the 1982 constitution because one part of the amending formula (Section 43) allows amendment on issues affecting a single province through resolutions approved by the legislature of that province and the Parliament of Canada. The circumstances leading up to the decisions to seek constitutional amendment in Newfoundland and Quebec, and the controversies engendered by these decisions, are explored in some detail as these have significant implications for what can be done in other jurisdictions.

In the early history of European settlement of Canada, Christian religious denominations were the primary supporters and providers of education for both settlers and Indigenous Peoples. Churches thus have a legitimate claim to having *been there first*. As the state became more active in supporting education, the prior claim of churches can be said to have set the stage for more than one hundred years of uneasy, and often conflicting, collaboration between church and state in elementary and secondary education. Critical events in the history of church/state relationships are examined to provide the context necessary to understand the persistence of separate schools in several provinces and their absence in others.

In modern times, the arrival of immigrants from many other parts of the world has led to religious and cultural plurality that extends well beyond the original Protestant/Catholic (and English/French) divide. Although only small minorities adhere to non-Christian religions, these groups, along with the rise of a significant conservative evangelical variety of Christianity, have led to a shift in the discourse over the place of religion in society, especially in education. Adding to the mix is the larger trend towards greater secularism in society. The Charter entrenches religious freedom and non-discrimination as fundamental rights. Over the past 35 years or so, the courts have rendered decisions that have clarified and expanded individual religious rights at the expense of collective and institutional rights. At the same time Section 29 of the Charter prevents the courts from ruling on the constitutional rights enjoyed by certain religious groups, particularly Catholics, that would be considered discriminatory under other sections of the Charter.

The denominational rights in question are those that were in place in each province immediately before union. These generally include the right to establish and govern schools, to non-discriminatory public funding of these schools, and to use religious criteria in student selection and teacher employment. Preserving these rights was part of what has been called the *historic compromise* necessary to bring about confederation. Without church support, the union would likely have been politically impossible at that time.

Before 1982, provinces on many occasions attempted to address the issue of denominational rights through legislation affecting control of school boards, taxation, school programs, and other aspects of schooling. This frequently resulted in litigation extending all the way to the Privy Council of the United Kingdom before 1949 and to the Supreme Court of Canada since that time. Almost all attempts to significantly shift control of the protected elements from church to state were rebuffed by the courts. An account of the most significant pieces of legislation and their fate in the courts is given in the relevant chapters.

It is unlikely that any attempt to limit religious rights through constitutional means could have succeeded prior to 1982 because the only recourse for constitutional amendment was to the Parliament of the United Kingdom, a step rarely taken. Since 1982, however, the level of constitutional attention to this issue has increased considerably. This is evidenced by the fact that four of the eleven constitutional amendments enacted since 1982 have been about denominational rights. Many other cases on the issue, especially those based on the Charter, have also reached the courts during the same period. This has resulted in several Supreme Court of Canada decisions which have clarified the constitutional position, upheld constitutional amendments in Newfoundland and Quebec, and restricted any attempt by other religions to attain protected status.

Constitutional cases have tended to be of three types: efforts to use the Charter to claim equal rights for other religious groups; challenges to religious activities and observances in public schools; and attempts to abolish, through constitutional amendment, the rights of the protected religions. Charter cases on religious activities have resulted in an almost total prohibition on such activities in non-denominational public schools, while allowing such activities in separate schools. On the other hand, the courts have rejected Charter challenges to existing denominational rights as well as claims to extend equal rights to other denominations. In the absence of constitutional protections, the trend would almost certainly be in the direction of complete secularization of public schools.

The constitutional amendment route has been more far-reaching. The amending formula has been used to extinguish denominational rights in the two provinces, Newfoundland and Quebec, where these had arguably been most strongly entrenched. The changes in both these provinces in the 1990s were driven, not by human rights or discrimination issues, but by compelling conditions on the ground. In Newfoundland, these conditions were mainly financial and demographic, having to do with the state of provincial finances and the difficulties in sustaining multiple school systems over a small and scattered population. In Quebec, the main issue was preservation of the French language and culture, along with a more fundamental secularization of Quebec society. Underlying philosophical issues such as equal treatment of all citizens, parental rights, harmonization across diversity, and religious discrimination were not the main driving forces in either case.

Similar circumstances have, until now, largely been absent in the three provinces where constitutionally protected separation by religion still exists. However, it is possible, even likely, that such circumstances will eventually occur. An example would be a desire of these provinces to restructure school boards or consolidate schools in a way that impinges on religious rights. Something close to this occurred in Alberta in the late 1990s when that province assumed major responsibility for school board funding. Rather than taking the route of constitutional amendment, the province decided to accommodate the historical right of separate school boards to retain the proceeds of local taxation.

More fundamentally, increased cultural diversity has created pressures in several different directions. On at least two occasions, Jewish parents have attempted to use the Charter to extend religious rights to that group. Some other individuals and small minority religious groups have attempted to invoke freedom of religion to claim an absolute right of parents over aspects of school programs. Recent events in both Ontario and Alberta, centring on religious opposition to provincial sex education programs and other aspects of school life, offer a case in point. To the extent that such opposition involves Catholic parents and leaders, it may impinge on existing constitutional protections. Where other religions are involved, this brings to the fore the issue of discrimination in favour of Catholics.

In recent times, the constitutional controversy centres on two main arguments. One side holds that the historic compromise on denominational rights is an immutable founding principle of confederation. Opposing this is the argument that special provisions for some religious groups to the exclusion of others is discriminatory and in conflict with the Charter. The historic compromise argument reflects an *originalist* interpretation of the constitution, which holds that the intent of the founders, as manifested in the original wording, must forever be respected. The discrimination argument is consistent with a *living tree* perspective, which holds that the constitution should be interpreted in light of societal changes. A reading of various Supreme Court decisions since 1982 indicates that the court has taken a living tree approach in most Charter cases, while taking an originalist position on denominational rights in education. Indeed, courts have little choice in this matter because of the special status given by Section 29.

Ideally, it should be relatively easy to expand rights but extremely difficult to restrict them. In reality, the opposite has occurred. Denominational rights have expanded only marginally over time, affecting only the denominations protected by the original provisions. For example, Catholic rights have been extended to secondary schools in Ontario and some accommodation of other religions has occurred through legislation providing public support to private schools in some other provinces. On the other hand, action on restricting rights has been quite radical. Use of the constitutional amending formula to extinguish denominational rights in two provinces has important implications for what could be done elsewhere if provincial governments were determined to do so.

Chapter 1 examines briefly the philosophical, legal, and political foundations of the relationship between church and state in education. Philosophically, the main issues centre around two areas of conflict: state accommodation of religious beliefs versus the doctrine of separation of church and state, and parent rights versus state responsibility for the education of children. The legal basis for education in Canada stems from the constitution—specifically, from education as a provincial responsibility limited only by Section 93 and its variants. Politically, provincial legislation on education reflects the usual influences of history, ideology, advocacy, language, availability of resources, and the like. Constitutional protections aside, conflict between religion and public policy is a frequent source of controversy.

Chapter 1 also looks briefly at church-state accommodations in selected other Western democracies. This illustrates that, even in many secular democracies, religion plays some part in education. Strict separation of church and state is found in public education in only a small number of countries, most notably the United States and France. Other variations range from specific influence of a state religion to systems that allow schools of a variety of religious persuasions to exist alongside a secular public system.

Chapter 2 presents a brief history of education from colonial times, through the confederation and post-confederation eras up to the 1980s. This is intended to provide some insight into the evolution from the churches as primary educational governing bodies to increased state financial support and eventual control.

Educational governance was the source of much controversy during the confederation debates. In the end the pre-confederation rights of Catholics and Protestants became constitutionally entrenched in some provinces but not others. The earliest post-confederation period, from 1867 to the late 1890s, saw major conflicts in New Brunswick and Manitoba settled with the effective abolition of denominational schools. However, the accession of Alberta and Saskatchewan to provincial status in 1905 brought back constitutional protections similar to those found in Ontario and Quebec. The question of denominational accommodations persisted up to 1949, when Newfoundland entered the union with protected rights not only for Catholics and Protestants but also for several specific Protestant denominations.

Chapter 3 brings the account into the modern era. This is defined as beginning in 1982, with patriation of the constitution and introduction of the Charter of Rights and Freedoms. As already indicated, the Charter has been used both to uphold protected denominational rights and to deny their extension to other denominations. It has also been used to limit the scope of religious activities in public schools. However, where the Charter has failed, the amending formula has succeeded in bringing an end to denominational education in Newfoundland and Quebec. In both these cases, long entrenched denominational rights were overturned almost overnight. The uniqueness of each of these provincial systems, and the complex and extreme circumstances leading to constitutional change, are addressed in detail in chapter 4.

Chapter 5 examines the contemporary state of denominational education in the three provinces, Ontario, Alberta, and Saskatchewan, where separate schools continue to enjoy constitutional protection. The focus is specifically on Catholic separate schools, since Protestant schools have, with a few minor exceptions, long since been absorbed into the public system in other provinces. Some characteristics of Catholic schools are described, and some of the controversial areas of interface between church and state jurisdiction are examined.

Private schooling was largely supplanted by public schooling in the nineteenth century, as education evolved from a privilege of the few to a public good. The more recent re-emergence of state support for private and independent schools is the subject of chapter 6. A few religious private schools, some highly prestigious, persist from the early era. However, recent years have seen slow growth in the number of private schools as some provinces have begun to provide partial public funding. The existence of such schools may be seen as a sort of safety valve, providing some scope for dissenters from public education. At the same time, these schools have proven to be controversial. Advocates tend to believe that such schools are an appropriate means of accommodating parent rights and that they should be funded on the same basis as public schools. Detractors take the opposite view: that these schools divert resources and fail to meet the cultural requirements of a diverse society. Some would argue that allowing public funding of religious private schools, or granting these the same status as Catholic schools, would be an appropriate way to resolve the discrimination inherent in the system of separate Catholic schools.

The federal government has historically played only a minor role in provincial education systems. Indigenous education is the only area in which constitutional responsibility rests with the federal government. Chapter 7 presents a brief account of the collaboration between the federal government and the churches in the education of Indigenous Peoples. This collaboration resulted in more persistent church influence in Indigenous education than in any of the provincial systems. Church support for federal assimilation policies and for establishment of the residential school system is an important chapter in church/state relationships. Although the last residential schools closed in the 1990s, the negative effect of federal policies and church practices in these schools on Indigenous culture are still being felt.

The last two chapters address the contemporary situation and the prospects for further change. Chapter 8 examines a range of issues surrounding the place of religion in schools. Diverse new controversies have arisen in the Charter era as non-traditional religions, as well as individuals, have attempted to use the Charter to gain rights, limit the ability of schools to engage with religiously controversial topics, or claim parental rights in the name of religion. Several Supreme Court cases are reviewed to shed light on the scope and limitations of parent rights and religious freedom versus secular public education.

This takes us back to the underlying philosophical issues and the constitutional provisions that either protect or restrict religiously based schools. The final chapter focuses mainly on Ontario, Alberta, and Saskatchewan. However, there are important implications for other provinces in possible models that allow for some religious accommodations. This book argues that change is needed to resolve underlying constitutional contradictions and to meet the needs of an increasingly diverse society. The main theme is that change should be driven by consideration of fundamental principles and by the rights and freedoms offered by the Charter, rather than waiting for some local crisis to emerge as was the case in Newfoundland and Quebec. The chapter concludes by examining competing arguments around maintaining the status quo, more broadly extending religious rights, or abrogation of these rights in favour of secular public schooling. It also outlines some conditions needed for change and ways to minimize disruption in the face of change.

CHAPTER 1

Philosophical and Legal Foundations

In common sense terms, religion may be thought of as a deeply held belief in a superior being or creator of the universe. The scope of such belief is wide, ranging from *deism,* a simple belief that such a being exists but does not interfere in the universe, to an all-encompassing belief in a personal God who guides and even determines all aspects of an individual's life. The latter concept leads to the view that religious beliefs override other values including those embodied in secular constitutions, laws, or institutions. In a theocracy, the supremacy of religious values extends to the political realm, whereby state laws follow directly from religious strictures.

Religion is conventionally thought of as a collective system of beliefs held by an identifiable group. An alternative conception is that religion is a private affair characterized by a deeply held set of individual beliefs, usually but not necessarily involving a deity. An example important for this discussion is a recent definition given by the Supreme Court of Canada. The case at hand, *Syndicat Northcrest v. Amselem,*[1] was one in which lower courts had called on experts in the Jewish religion to testify as to the legitimacy within that faith of practices being engaged in by a small group of Jews. The Supreme Court held that the beliefs of an individual cannot be determined by such experts or by any other collective. In arriving at this decision, the justices developed the following definition:

> Defined broadly, religion typically involves a particular and comprehensive system of faith and worship ... In essence, religion is about freely and deeply held personal convictions or beliefs connected to an individual's spiritual faith and integrally linked to one's self-definition and spiritual fulfillment, the practices of which allow individuals to foster a connection with the divine or with the subject or object of that spiritual faith.[2]

Historically most people have adhered to the strictures of some organized religious group. Organized religion, rather than the private sort, has been the major force in the interaction of religion and the broader society. However, religious groups have become increasingly splintered over time, to the point where individuals or small groups of dissenters are able to claim beliefs that depart from any form of orthodoxy. The privatization of religion thus may be thought of as arising from either profound or subtle variations of belief on the part of smaller and smaller collectives and the inability of established sects to accommodate such variation.

All the major world religions have played a large part in the affairs of state, and many political and legal systems have a basis in religious beliefs. From medieval to modern times, the Catholic church exerted a pervasive influence, extending to much of the world. Although this influence has waned, it remains significant in parts of South America, Africa, and Europe. Islam has become a dominant political force in many countries in the Middle East, Africa, and Asia. Even in secular democratic societies, religious groups can have a significant influence on governments through their voting power and their support of leaders adhering to their own belief systems.

Religious conflict can carry over to countries that have welcomed large numbers of immigrants. Indeed, in many countries, notably in Canada, religious conflict, and its manifestations in schooling, has been driven to a large extent by both colonization and later immigration. Individuals and groups fleeing religious persecution were instrumental in the founding of several states, including most of the colonies that went on to become the United States. Pakistan and Israel are notable twentieth-century examples of states founded on religion. In some countries, fundamentalist Christian denominations have become more prominent and influential over the past century, often expressing strong views on social issues. The historical Catholic/Protestant divide has been supplanted by broader divides within Christianity and between Christianity and other world religions.

In most developed countries, religious organizations have largely given way to the state in most public institutions. However, religion remains a strong influence in education in many countries. This is not surprising given the scope for influencing the beliefs of the next generation. Examples range from extreme indoctrination of religious beliefs to liberal education within a religious setting. Religious involvement has not been limited to elementary and secondary education. Many early universities were founded by religious orders, and some today retain either an explicit or implicit religious ambience.

Separation of Church and State

The doctrine of separation of church and state had its origin in seventeenth-century European Enlightenment philosophy. However, its most profound influence on political life occurred a century later, at the time of the American and French revolutions. James Madison and Thomas Jefferson, leading thinkers in the colony of Virginia, were dedicated realists who brought their perspective to the framing of the American Constitution. In France, Cartesian rationalism was a founding principle of the 1789 Revolution. Separation of church and state became one of the underlying themes in both these revolutionary states.

Other countries have adopted the same principle, some more assiduously than others. Some, such as Turkey or Ireland, are nominally secular but retain substantial religious influence in state affairs, including education. On the other hand, countries such as Britain and Sweden retain an established religion with some state support, while minimizing the role of that religion in the practical affairs of state, including education.

Although the doctrine of separation of church and state has, either explicitly or implicitly, become common in most Western democracies, this is by no means the case worldwide. The extreme contrasting case is the theocracy, in which there is little or no distinction between religion and state. Obvious examples are Iran and Saudi Arabia. Other modern versions are found in countries such as Israel and Pakistan, which were founded primarily as religious refuges and where the dominant religion continues to play a significant role in state affairs.

A version of theocracy, commonly known as "ultramontanism" has persisted within the leadership of the Catholic church. In its extreme form, this doctrine asserts the supremacy of religious authority over that of the state and rejects any compromise in situations where church doctrine comes into conflict with state law. In practice, deference to state authority is required because the means of enforcement available to churches, such as excommunication or ostracism, are less powerful than those, such as police and courts, available to the state. However, as perhaps best illustrated by the abortion debate, the expectation remains that Catholics will continue to advocate for change in state laws. To some, the supremacy of church doctrine is a key driver of the continued insistence of Catholics on having their own separate schools.

Ultramontanism was the dominant force in Quebec from the time of the conquest up to the 1950s. Quebec's Quiet Revolution of the 1960s may be framed as a decisive rejection of that doctrine, even though it took until the 1990s for this to affect sectarian schools. In other parts of Canada, it might be argued that oppression of the minority Catholic population may have been more of a factor than ultramontanism in the Catholic drive for separate schools around the time of confederation.

Freedom of Religion

Freedom of religion, another product of the Enlightenment, is closely related to the separation of church and state. At its core, freedom of religion includes the right to worship a supreme being, assemble for this purpose, publicly espouse religious belief, and even attempt to persuade others to a particular way of thinking. It also implies the freedom to do none of these. More specifically, freedom of religion implies state neutrality in religious matters. However, it does not necessarily preclude the existence of a state religion. In England and Sweden, among others, state religions continue to enjoy some level of state support. While this does not impinge on any of the fundamental freedoms outlined above, it also implies that not all religions have equal status. Allowing one religion into some aspects of the public sphere at least implicitly means state discrimination against other religions even if there is no explicit state interference in religious belief or practice.

In her recent book *Fighting over God*,[3] Buckingham traces in detail the emergence and development of freedom of religion in Canada. Her account begins with the Catholic/Protestant divide. The exclusion of religious minorities, and of Indigenous spirituality, is a recurring theme. The open discrimination against Jews, Jehovah's Witnesses, and other religions that existed until at least the mid-twentieth century, has gradually given way to increasingly explicit non-discrimination legislation, beginning with the Diefenbaker Bill of Rights and extending to the Charter of Rights and Freedoms and human rights legislation.

Buckingham challenges the conception of religion as a private affair, arguing that because individuals within groups such as Jehovah's Witnesses are firm adherents to their sect, the prospect of ostracism may have severe consequences. Buckingham argues that the courts are ill-prepared to deal with such issues because courts, while imposing settlements, cannot resolve the underlying tensions.[4] The law can help protect religious minorities from open discrimination, but it cannot suppress discriminatory opinion.

Secularism, Religious Pluralism, and Reasonable Accommodation

Much ongoing tension stems from two parallel but seemingly opposing trends in society: the rise of secularism and increased religious diversity. According to Taylor,[5] secularism is often thought of as being of two main types. The first is official secularity, essentially synonymous with separation of church and state. The second refers to a decline in religiosity among the population. Canadian society might now be considered as reflecting both forms. On the other hand, the United States, while adhering to a strict form of official secularity, exhibits a high level of religiosity among the population.

A third form of secularism, by Taylor's account, consists of a situation in which religious belief (specifically belief in God) is optional, existing among other fundamental belief systems. No more stigma is attached to espoused atheism than to open religious expression. In this situation, it is possible to have open debate about religion at the most fundamental level. Again, Canada and the United States may represent opposing systems. While avowed atheism is not a strong factor in Canadian political life, it is also true that a person's religion rarely arises as an issue in political discourse. On the other hand, religious, specifically Christian, belief remains a significant factor in American politics.

Increased religious diversity stems from both greater fragmentation among Christian denominations and shifting immigration patterns, which have brought to Canada many adherents of non-Christian religions. Greater religious diversity also accompanies increased racial and ethnic pluralism in society. To avoid any semblance of religious discrimination, state neutrality in religion is being manifested through court-imposed prohibitions around any form of officially sanctioned religious expression in public institutions. On the other hand, the right to individual religious expression, such as wearing religious symbols or engaging in individual prayer, is reinforced by Charter decisions.

This issue became so acute in Quebec in the early 2000s that the province was led to appoint a commission on what has come to be referred to as "reasonable accommodation." The Bouchard-Taylor report *Building the Future: A Time for Reconciliation*[6] made a plea to settle disputes through dialogue rather than litigation or legislation—a theme earlier developed by Taylor in *A Secular Age*.[7] In particular, the commission argued for a shift in thinking from multiculturalism (tolerance or acceptance of cultural differences) to interculturalism (integration of cultures). In the Quebec case, this required reconciling increased pluralism with the need to preserve a minority francophone society. The commission also enunciated a principle of open secularism, requiring a balance among four main components: freedom of conscience, equality of citizens, reciprocal autonomy of church and state, and state neutrality in matters of religion.

After a decade of controversy over the concept of reasonable accommodation, the provincial government finally settled on a law prohibiting certain public servants from wearing religious garb or overt religious symbols. The province has also used the notwithstanding section of the Charter to shield the law from Charter challenges. This law is having a profound effect on some teachers, particularly Muslim women, as it creates a fundamental conflict between religious practice and the work environment.

Accommodating religious diversity in schools may be thought of in two opposing ways. First, it might be argued that all religious denominations should be allowed to have their own separate schools or that some form of religious separation be provided in school programs. The opposite concept is that of unity through diversity. Under this view, diversity is best promoted through a common school system. While officially secular, this system could teach respect for all forms of diversity, not just religious, while also reflecting the common values of Canadian society. This view would hold that separation of schools by religion is more likely to promote division than unity, encouraging the development of societal enclaves that minimize contact with others.

Education as a Human Right

The evolution of education from a privilege of the few to mass elementary and secondary education had led to the concept of education as a universal human right. The United Nations Universal Declaration on Human Rights embodies this right in Article 26, which states in part:

1. Everyone has the right to education [. . .]
2. Education shall be directed to the full development of the human personality and to the strengthening of respect for human rights and fundamental freedoms [. . .]
3. Parents have a prior right to choose the kind of education that shall be given to their children.[8]

Similar statements are found in the 1959 United Nations Declaration on the Rights of the Child and are elaborated in the Convention on the Rights of the Child. Article 29 of the latter elaborates on these and gives further elements. These include the development of respect for parents, cultural identity, language and values, for the national values of the country in which the child is living, the country from which the child may originate, and for civilizations different from their own, preparation of the child for responsible life in a free society in the spirit of understanding, peace, tolerance, equality of sexes, and friendship among all peoples, ethnic, national and religious groups, and persons of Indigenous origin. That article also states that it should not be construed as to interfere with the liberty of individuals and bodies to establish and direct educational institutions and to the requirements that the education given in such institutions shall conform to such minimum standards as may be laid down by the state.[9]

It may be argued that some states honour these rights selectively or not at all, especially where some of these rights may be seen as threats to state power. Education is not always conducted in a liberating manner or in a spirit of tolerance, especially religious tolerance. Educational content is often mandated to ensure compliance with state or religious objectives. Even in liberal democratic states, it is not unusual to find some content to be either mandated or prohibited as a matter of state priorities rather than individual enlightenment. The precise scope and limitations of both individual and state rights in education is a matter of ongoing controversy the world over.

Parent Rights versus State Control

Interpreted strictly as stated, Article 26 of the Universal Declaration of Human Rights gives parents an absolute right to determine the form of education their children should receive. This would appear to include religious education in whatever form parents decide is appropriate but also the right to exclude topics that parents might find offensive.

If parent rights are absolute, then the state has no place in education other than perhaps to provide resources that parents can use to purchase the type of education they wish. However, the Convention on the Rights of the Child appears to modify the Universal Declaration by giving some broad goals towards which education should be directed. Interestingly, these include several statements about respect for human rights and freedoms but no statement about basic literacy or numeracy which most would consider the core components of education. Article 29 also states that the liberty to establish educational institutions can be subject to minimum standards set by the state. All this indicates that parent rights fall somewhere short of absolute. Indeed, it would be difficult to find a country that accords such an absolute right. In Canada, the Supreme Court has recently ruled against a parent who insisted on an absolute right to educate his own children as he saw fit.[10] Lower courts have done the same in other cases. Some of these cases are discussed more fully in later chapters.

If parental rights are not absolute, the debate shifts to the question: What are reasonable limitations on parental rights? A full spectrum of arguments may be found here. These range from minor infringements necessary to ensure that children attend school to complete abrogation of parental rights in favour of either state control or control by institutions such as churches. Over time, the balance has tended to shift in the direction of increased state control as states have contributed more resources and as the value of education for economic and social development has increased. As for church control, this may be thought of as parental deference to church doctrine in matters of education.

In practice, many more parents are likely to defer to state control of education than to insist on exercising any absolutist version of parental rights. Parent activism on behalf of their children's education is time-consuming and requires attention to many complex issues, particularly in the details of school programs. An example is home schooling, which is permitted in most Canadian provinces but is subject to many constraints and is practised by relatively few families. Nevertheless, this does not negate the principle. Arguments may still be advanced in favour of a high degree of parental choice of schools and programs. Indeed, the debate over denominational education in Canada is often framed as an issue of parental rights, especially as the influence of institutional churches has declined. The same is true for aspects of the curriculum that some parents or religious groups find objectionable. Sex education is one case in point, as is religious education itself. In some cases, this has extended to controversy over the teaching of biological evolution versus divine creation and to other areas considered to be false teachings by some religious fundamentalists.

In provinces where denominational separation of schools still exists, the issue extends to parts of the curriculum and to the overall ambience of the school. Indeed, the position of the Catholic church is that Catholicism must permeate all aspects of schooling and cannot be isolated into religious studies or similar courses.[11] The concept of permeation is the main reason the church has continued to insist on having its own schools. More broadly, this insistence stems from the ultramontane doctrine discussed earlier.

All publicly funded schools in Canada, whether denominational or not, are required to offer a state-mandated curriculum. Most provincial legislation includes provisions for students to opt out of specific programs on the request of parents. However, courts are now beginning to question whether this, itself, is discriminatory because it highlights differences. In some cases, denominational authorities, claiming to speak for their adherents, have made a public issue over program components they find objectionable.

The issue of parental control extends to provisions for specialized schools and private schools. Several variations exist on the theme of providing alternatives to regular public schooling. Among these are voucher programs, charter schools, and provisions for public funding of private schools. Some provinces do provide partial funding for independent schools. Specific provincial provisions, as they relate to the religious character of schools, are discussed in the relevant chapters.

Minority Rights

Most human rights declarations are fundamentally grounded in the rights of individuals rather than collectives. Nevertheless, many Western-style democracies provide exceptions or accommodations for disadvantaged minority groups based on ethnicity, religion, region, or other factors unique to the country. Indeed, many would see these exceptions as the mark of a mature society, one that is accepting of diversity. These exceptions help avoid a tendency towards the *tyranny of the majority* inherent in the strict application of the concept of majority rule.

Most of the rights conveyed by the Canadian Charter refer to "everyone," "persons," or "citizens" and not to groups or collectives. However, there are three notable exceptions to this emphasis. These are the affirmative action provisions in Section 15(2), the minority official language rights in Sections 16 through 23, and the reinforcement of denominational education rights in Section 29. The latter two are directly linked because of the historic intersection of language and religion in Canada.

It could not have been lost on the framers of the Charter that Section 29 conflicts with the religious freedom and non-discrimination sections of the Charter. Section 29 may be seen as reflecting an originalist interpretation of the constitution, remaining faithful to the historic compromise struck in 1867. Section 23, on the other hand, was a revolutionary move designed to create a new set of constitutional rights for the minority language group in each province.[12] Although Section 23 is subject to a "numbers warrant" clause, court rulings have required all provinces to establish minority language school boards and schools for very small numbers of rights holders. In Newfoundland, this led to a conflict of rights, requiring the province to establish several small French language schools at the same time as the province was endeavouring to persuade the denominations to relinquish their rights to establish small overlapping schools as they saw fit. The same conflict has required Ontario to establish four distinct education systems, accommodating both sets of rights. Quebec avoided the same requirement only by repealing Section 93 for that province.

It might be argued that there is a critical difference between expanding and restricting minority rights. One view is that, once gained, a minority right should not easily be rescinded. The opposing view is that societal change must be considered when the rare opportunity arises for constitutional change. Such a view would allow for either expansion or restriction of rights depending on circumstances. Politically, it is no doubt easier to grant new rights than to curtail existing rights. For example, the expansion of minority language rights might be interpreted as an effort to accommodate Quebec in the new constitution. The reasons for including Section 29 are less clear as denominational rights were already protected by Section 93. What has become clear from subsequent events is that, because of the structure of the amending formula and perhaps because of strong public support, minority language rights are now more firmly entrenched than those of religious denominations.

The Political Climate

All the previous issues underpin the political landscape within which the education system functions. However, education policy also reflects political ideology, advocacy and special interests, the economics of state support, and sometimes uniquely local issues such as duplication of services or school closings. While not foundational in themselves, these points deserve attention because attempts at educational reform, including those involving the role of churches, are often driven more by pragmatic considerations of what is politically possible and financially feasible than by the more fundamental principles discussed in this chapter.

Ideologically, conservative-leaning political parties tend to favour more traditional approaches to education, including less centralized control, a larger role for parents and families, and greater attention to religious and moral issues in schools. Those of a more liberal bent tend to support greater state control, greater attention to issues of social justice, and greater openness to non-traditional program topics. Many provincial governments and political parties have risen or fallen on this issue over the years. The most recent example is the 2007 Ontario election when a Progressive Conservative Party proposal to extend separate school funding to religions groups other than Catholics was soundly rejected. More generally, political parties have often weighed in on the controversies over sex and religious education, again mainly on ideological grounds. Nevertheless, most contemporary public controversy around these issues is driven by entities whose goals are not explicitly political, including the Catholic church, fundamentalist Christians, other religions, as well as seemingly ad hoc single-interest groups. The rise of internet-based communications tools, especially social media, has facilitated the activities of these groups to the point where their influence rivals those of the traditional media and political parties.

Economic Issues

The economics of education has been an area of concern at least since the end of the expansionary era of the 1950s to 1970s. Education is one of the costliest areas of provincial responsibility, second only to health care. The cost has shifted strongly from local authorities to provincial governments as many provinces have moved to more centralized funding and away from reliance on local property taxes. While few challenge the economic payoff of education for both individuals and society, governments have become more conscious of the need to control costs and are continually looking for ways to do so.

This is not the place for a detailed analysis of the cost structure of education. However, cost is one of the main points of contention in the debate over separate schools and how to accommodate minority religions. Many opponents of the system argue that the duplication of services inherent in maintaining either separate schools or partially funded private schools is a reason to question the existence of separate systems in any form. The counter-argument is that funding in support of dissenting minorities is part of the price of maintaining harmony in a diverse society. Funding for minority official language education is a case in point. There is no doubt that this adds some cost, especially where services must be provided to a small minority. That cost is now rarely questioned because the language rights provisions of the Charter now override considerations of cost. However, the cost of separate schools remains controversial.

The cost of maintaining overlapping denominational school systems was the main driving force behind the 1990s debate over denominational education in Newfoundland. A full account of this is given in chapter 4. Suffice it to say that the severe austerity of that time brought to the fore the additional cost of operating three large separate religious systems and several smaller ones in a province with a small, scattered, and declining school population. At a practical level, this manifested itself in half-empty schools, long-distance bussing, disproportionate capital funding, and other significant cost components. Although broader principles such as religion and parent rights were also part of the debate, there is little doubt that the issue was brought to a head by financial constraints.

The Newfoundland situation stands in contrast to that in Quebec. On the surface, the Quebec debate was primarily over language and culture. However, this itself was driven by the broader issue of secularism and the decline in influence of the Catholic church in Quebec politics. This was more clearly a case of a political debate being driven by philosophical principle. There is little to indicate that cost was a factor in the Quebec decision to amend the constitution to remove denominational rights.

Models of Church / State Relationships

In a recent article, Berglund[13] identifies four models of church / state relationships in education:

1. Cooperation between the state and religious institutions;
2. Parallel state or dominant religions;
3. One dominant state religion; and
4. Distinct separation between church and state.

Historically, the Canadian situation has been closer to the first. However, developments since adoption of the 1982 constitution show a clear trend towards the fourth model. As chapter 2 shows, state involvement in education originally took the form of support for schools operated by religious denominations. Common, state-mandated schools were later developments, though most of these retained some form of denominational influence until very recently and up to the present in some provinces.

Few states hold to a strict interpretation of the principle of separation of church and state as it applies to education. This section gives a few examples of how some countries have addressed the issue. The purpose is to set the stage for a more thorough discussion of future directions in Canada in the final chapter. The focus is on the contemporary situation in a few Western-style democracies with political systems similar to those in Canada and that may thus offer some lessons for Canada.

There is no formal separation of church and state in any of the parts of the United Kingdom.[14] In England, the Church of England is the established church, with formal links to the state in several areas. For example, the government approves senior church appointments and Anglican bishops sit in the House of Lords. The concepts of freedom of religion, non-discrimination by religion,[15] and the right to education have been codified in Acts of Parliament.[16] However, a section of the Human Rights Act allows religious schools to select students by religion and to engage in collective worship within a particular religion.

In England and Wales both the Church of England and the Roman Catholic Church operate large numbers of what are called "free" schools; as many as one-third by some accounts. Other religious groups may establish free schools, though their scale is much smaller. Known as "faith" schools, such schools are fully state supported and follow the national curriculum. However, faith schools may use religious criteria to admit students and employ teachers. In addition to state supported free schools, private fee-paying schools are allowed. Many such schools are religiously based.

In Scotland, most Protestant schools became state schools over time. However, other denominations are still able to establish separate schools. Catholic schools retain substantial autonomy. Local education authorities are required to set up a school for a particular denomination where numbers warrant. Such schools are subject to state inspection but are allowed to create an appropriate religious ambience and to hire teachers based on religious belief. Denominational schools may not discriminate on student admissions, though it seems to be assumed that parents choosing such schools accept their religious character.

Schools in Northern Ireland remain much more highly segregated than in other parts of the United Kingdom. Before the partition of Ireland in 1921, almost all schools were denominational, funded by the state but controlled by the churches. In the years following, most Protestant schools were transferred to state control while retaining a Protestant ambiance. Catholic schools continue to be fully state supported but remain under church control. More than half of all students attend Catholic schools. Catholic schools continue to teach religious education from a confessional standpoint, emphasizing Catholic teachings and values.

A new type of school, referred to as integrated schools, appeared in the 1980s. As the name implies, such schools are designed to promote a uniting of Protestant and Catholic students and teachers. The integrated school movement appears to be slow growing, currently serving only about 7 percent of students. Part of the difficulty is that such schools must be established by voluntary groups and little capital funding is provided by the state.

Turning to the United States, most people consider its constitution to be the classic example of official separation of church and state. This is embodied in the First Amendment: "Congress shall make no law respecting an establishment of religion, or prohibiting the free exercise thereof…"[17] Despite this, the place of religion in education has remained controversial throughout American history. Prayer and religious observances in public schools remained commonplace until the mid-twentieth century. A distinct Protestant bias was evident in these activities. In reaction, many Catholic parishes and religious orders established private schools. Commonly known as parochial schools, Catholic schools remain the dominant form of private schooling in the United States, though enrolment has declined substantially from its peak in the 1960s. The first amendment prohibition on established religion has always been used to prevent the extension of state funding to parochial schools. However, the issue remains controversial and is high on the political agenda in some states.

A series of Supreme Court decisions in the twentieth century resulted in the complete secularization of public schools in the United States. Despite these decisions, most polls indicate that a large majority disagree with the prohibition of religious activities in public schools.[18] Many see the prohibition as conflicting with another freedom protected by the first amendment, that of freedom of speech. Governments have responded to public sentiment by issuing statements to the effect that schools cannot prohibit students or teachers from engaging in private prayer or other religious activities in schools.[19]

Although France remains a predominately Catholic country, it is also one of the few countries in which formal separation of church and state exists. The leaders of the 1789 French Revolution were influenced by the French Enlightenment and were determined to secularize state institutions, including education. Nevertheless, the Napoleonic era saw an alternation between republic and monarchy, with corresponding oscillation in the relationships between church and state. A final break (the French *laïcité*) was achieved in 1905 with passage of a law mandating the separation of church and state and supporting individual religious freedom. This was further entrenched in the 1958 constitution: "France shall be an indivisible, secular, democratic and social Republic. It shall ensure the equality of all citizens before the law, without distinction of origin, race or religion. It shall respect all beliefs."[20]

The complete secularisation of French public schools has given rise to a relatively large private school system, attended by some 15 percent of students.[21] These schools are overwhelmingly Catholic. The

French private system differs from that in the United States in that most private schools are state contracted. These receive public funding, teach the national curriculum, and are subject to state inspection. Other mainly confessional schools receive no state support and rely entirely on fees and fundraising.

The contrast between France and Quebec is worthy of note. The French Revolution may be said to have bypassed Quebec because the colony had come under British control some 30 years earlier. The British did not suppress either the French language or the church. This allowed Quebec education to develop much as if the French Revolution had never occurred. Indeed, it took more than 200 years after separation of church and state in France for the concept of *laïcité* to gain a foothold in Quebec.

The Netherlands is one of a very few Western democracies in which a large-scale publicly funded denominational system continues to exist. The Dutch system is explicitly built around separation by denomination,[22] much as it was in Newfoundland prior to 1997. The right to full state support for denominational schooling came in 1917 through a constitutional amendment creating a combination of public secular schools and denominational schools, all of which receive equal state funding on a proportional basis.[23] Provisions in the Netherlands constitution allow for public education open to all, but also ensure that most schools are private and denominational.[24] More than 70 percent of Dutch students attend private-authority schools, with about half of the latter being Catholic, 40 percent Protestant, and 10 percent other (religious and non-religious).[25]

In the early colonial days in Australia, the Anglican church was effectively the state religion. Catholics, mainly of Irish descent, formed a small minority of the population. The Constitution Act of 1901 established freedom of religion. Section 116 of that constitution states that "The Commonwealth shall not make any law for establishing any religion, or for imposing any religious observance, or for prohibiting the free exercise of any religion, and no religious test shall be required as a qualification for any office or public trust under the Commonwealth."[26]

Education in Australia is constitutionally a responsibility of the states. However, Australian education is much more centralized than in Canada. The concept of local school boards and local tax assessment is largely alien to Australia. Also, the Australian federal government plays a much larger role in education than in Canada. In particular, the federal government provides supplementary funding for both state and independent schools. The Australian Education Act,[27] which has no counterpart in Canada, sets out the conditions of funding, including funding for religious schools.

The most important difference between Australian and Canadian school systems, as it affects the place of religion, is the distinction between government and non-government schools. In Australia all government schools are secular and are run directly by state departments of education. Government schools enrol about 65 percent of Australian elementary and secondary students, compared to more like 95 percent for public (including public separate) schools in Canada. Most non-government schools are religious in character, with about two-thirds of these being Catholic. The remainder are referred to as independent schools, with most being Anglican and the remainder of other Christian denominations, plus a few Jewish and Muslim schools.[28]

There was no public funding of non-government schools until the 1960s. However, the following decades have seen successive extensions of federal funding for such schools. According to a government document, this was mainly intended to support a struggling Catholic school sector.[29] However, there is some debate over whether these initiatives represented a shift in political ideology, a response to advocacy, or a means of relieving financial pressure on the public system by encouraging the expansion of schools that were supported mainly by private funds.

Federal funding for private religious schools has allowed such schools to flourish to a much greater extent in Australia than in Canada. The provisions for religious education are also different in that religious denominations are allowed access to schools where they can offer programs in keeping with their own beliefs. However, this is coming under increasing scrutiny as the number of such groups continues to proliferate.

Types of Denominational Schools in Canada

With the above models in mind, it is useful to note some variations in the types of denominational schools in Canada and the major shifts that have occurred. The historical precedents leading to these variations are explored in chapter 2.

School systems in Alberta, Ontario, and Saskatchewan are commonly referred to as public and separate. This distinction originated in early legislation under which the school of the majority denomination was considered the "common" school. The minority denomination was granted the right to establish a separate school for its own adherents. The assumption was that the distinction was between Catholics, on the one hand, and Protestants, collectively, on the other. No provision was made for non-Christian denominations. In reality, both types are public in that they are fully supported by public funds and operate under the same provincial programs and standards. Separate schools have specific rights to their own school boards and may use religious criteria to select students and employ teachers. In law, separate schools may be either Catholic or Protestant. Over time almost all Protestant schools became non-sectarian, though with vestiges of Protestantism remaining. Nevertheless, a very small number of Protestant separate schools can still be found in Ontario and Alberta.[30]

Prior to the 1997 constitutional amendment, the system in Quebec was somewhat more complex. In Montréal and Québec City, separate boards existed for both Catholics and Protestants. In other regions of the province, denominational schools were established on a principle of dissent. The school of the majority denomination was the common school, which students of all denominations could attend. In practice, these were almost universally Catholic. Members of the minority denomination could establish "dissentient" schools. The system is often described as "dual confessional" in that both types of school were sectarian, either Catholic or Protestant. Following the 1997 constitutional amendment, all public schools in Quebec are now non-sectarian.

In the absence of pre-confederation laws, schools in the three maritime provinces and in British Columbia were all legally non-sectarian. However, it was common for schools to exhibit Protestant or Catholic characteristics and to attract either Catholic or Protestant students. The denominations had no right to separate school boards or to select students or teachers on denominational grounds, even if this may have occurred in practice. Charter challenges in recent years have now removed virtually all traces of denominational identity.

At the time of union, the system in Manitoba was designed to be dual confessional as in Quebec. However, the situation was more fluid because denominational protection for that province extended to schools that existed *in practice* as well as in law at the time of confederation. Whether any public denominational schools existed in practice was a source of long-running controversy at the end of the nineteenth century. This led to litigation, federal vacillation, and even papal intervention before being settled by federal-provincial agreement in 1895. The result is that no public sectarian schools now exist in Manitoba.

Newfoundland was also a special case because, at the time of union in 1949, denominational rights were held individually rather than collectively by several Protestant denominations as well as by Catholics. After 1968, three Protestant denominations agreed to integrate their schools. Catholics, Pentecostals, and Seventh Day Adventists declined to participate in integration and continued to operate their own schools until the 1990s. Following the 1997 constitutional amendment, all public schools are now non-sectarian.

Legislation allowing separate schools is found in all three Canadian territories. Unlike in the provinces, these enjoy no constitutional protection but are embodied in federal legislation establishing self-government for the territories. Provisions are very similar to those in Alberta and Saskatchewan. The minority population in a community, whether Protestant or Catholic, may establish a separate school. Separate schools exist only in very small numbers in the Northwest Territories and Yukon. Schools in Nunavut are mainly focused on developing Inuit language and culture, and there is no reference to the current existence of any separate schools.

A few provinces provide partial support for private schools, many of which have a religious basis. Others allow such schools and provide some leeway in their religious activities but provide no public support. The status of these schools is discussed in more detail in chapter 6.

In a few instances, legislation has provided accommodation for small religious minorities. For example, schools in Hutterite and Mennonite communities are found in several provinces. These are public schools but reflect the language and cultural identities of the specific community. These offer examples of a model that is open to accommodating unique religious and cultural communities. However, this model seems not to be used as precedent for broader accommodation of other groups.

Finally, it is important to note the historical role of the churches in Indigenous schools. This issue is examined in some detail in chapter 7. Suffice it to say that Indigenous education is a federal responsibility. The various Christian denominations have historically played a large role in operating schools, under federal mandate. Their role in implementing federal assimilation policies represents an ignominious chapter in Canadian education. Since the 1970s, First Nations people have increasingly gained control of education on reserves. Statements about the denominational status of these schools indicate that this is a local decision and that efforts should be made to accommodate all. Most Indigenous students now attend provincial or territorial schools rather than on-reserve schools. However, it is not clear what proportion attend separate schools.

CHAPTER 2

Historical Context

This chapter gives a brief account of historical developments in the relationship between church and state from the colonial period to the time of patriation of the constitution in 1982. Its purpose is to help understand how denominational education emerged in different forms in different parts of the country, the underlying reasons for the protections offered in the British North America Act, and its refinement through public controversy, legislation, and litigation extending over more than a century.

Church Before State

The story of church and state in Canadian education begins with missionaries who accompanied the earliest explorers to North America. The explorers and settlers of New France were accompanied by members of Roman Catholic religious orders whose main mission was to spread the gospel and to "Frenchify" the Indigenous Peoples of the colony. Magnuson[1] gives a compelling account of the interactions between missionaries and natives, especially how differences in behaviours and customs contributed to the difficulties encountered by the Jesuits in carrying out their self-appointed mission of conversion. However, the missionaries also taught practical skills such as agriculture and carpentry. Basic literacy skills were taught only to the extent that they contributed to the primary mission.

On the British side, the earliest schools were founded by local initiatives, including the activities of school societies that were essentially offshoots of the Anglican church. These societies were particularly active in Nova Scotia (which at the time encompassed what is now New Brunswick and Prince Edward Island). Early colonial governors, such as Simcoe in Ontario and Selkirk in the Red River Colony, also took an interest in education. However, their early efforts were largely confined to providing modest state support for schools that remained under local and church control.

The British conquest of Quebec in 1759 led to the beginnings of Protestant, British-style education for the small number of British settlers, while the dominantly French Catholic population continued much as before. While there was some effort by the British authorities to anglicize the French population, this was no more successful in the long run than the earlier effort to Frenchify the Indigenous population. The irony that the conquest may have contributed to the perpetuation of sectarian education in Quebec long after it was abandoned in France has already been noted. Had Quebec remained a French colony, it is likely that it would have taken the path of France in establishing a secular education system at the end of the eighteenth century.

An influx of United Empire Loyalists into Upper Canada, Nova Scotia, and New Brunswick following the American Revolution shifted the balance significantly in favour of English settlers. The Loyalists were mainly Anglican. Catholic influence was almost non-existent until the first waves of Irish immigrants arrived. The Loyalists were generally disposed towards a non-sectarian form of education, with provision for religious instruction, obviously with a Protestant orientation. The strict separation of church and state that by then had taken hold in the United States did not follow that group to Canada.

Lord Durham's famous report on the future of Upper and Lower Canada led to the 1841 union between the two provinces.[2] As recommended in that report, the combined legislature of Upper and Lower Canada (formally known as Canada West and Canada East) attempted to establish a system of common schools. However, that legislation allowed "any number of dissentients (not necessarily Roman Catholics) in Township Schools to withdraw and form a school of their own."[3] The concept of dissent captured the principle of separation of schools by religion. Nevertheless, this proved to be unsatisfactory to the Upper Canada delegates, who soon realized that their desire for common schools was incompatible with the confessional system then in place in Lower Canada.

In Lower Canada, Québec City and Montréal had separate Catholic and Protestant school boards. Elsewhere, each district had a common school to which all students were entitled to attend. Adherents of the minority denomination were entitled to establish a separate school. In practice, all schools were denominational, with the common schools being primarily Catholic. The principle of dissent thus led to a dual denominational system.

In Upper Canada, it took several subsequent acts, as well as the administrative skills of Egerton Ryerson, who became Superintendent of Education in 1843, before the system took on its modern form. Ryerson's 1846 report, *A System of Public Elementary Instruction for Upper Canada*,[4] espoused the common school principle but raised no objection to separate schools for religious communities. Nevertheless, Ryerson was clearly of the view that common schools should be Protestant in orientation.

Throughout the 1850s, prominent Catholic leaders in Upper Canada continued to hold the position that separate Catholic schools should be the norm. The view was entrenched in legislation in 1863 with passage of what become known as the Scott Act. That act made key provisions for support of separate schools, including separate trustees, designation of school assessments, and the ability of boards to select students and hire teachers on religious grounds. The Scott Act was the last education act passed before the politicians turned their attention to the prospect of a broader confederation of the two parts of Canada with Nova Scotia and New Brunswick. Its provisions thus formed the basis for the post-confederation system in Ontario.

Although New France had its origin in what is now Nova Scotia, the French era was short-lived there. The expulsion of the Acadians and the arrival of pre-revolution American immigrants resulted in anti-Catholic sentiment in the colony. The first education act passed by the Nova Scotia legislature in 1766 was decidedly anti-Catholic, as reflected in the following statement: "and if any popish recusant, papist or person professing the popish religion, shall be so presumptive as to set up any school within this province, and be detected therein, such offender shall, for every such offence, suffer three months' imprisonment without bail or mainprize, and shall pay a fine to the King of ten pounds."[5]

Legislation in Nova Scotia has never recognized school separation by religion. However, this does not imply an absence of church influence. Relaxation of the early restrictions on Catholic education towards the end of the eighteenth century created an opportunity for Acadians to look for their own schools. By 1840, a de facto dual system of secular (in reality, Protestant) and sectarian schools had been established. An 1856 bill allowing for possible funding of separate schools failed. The resulting impasse seems to have led to a policy of turning a blind eye to the existence of separate Catholic schools, allowing them to be funded on the same basis as other schools.

The pre-confederation development of education in New Brunswick and Prince Edward Island was similar to that in Nova Scotia. However, New Brunswick's history was shaped to an extent by the presence of a larger Catholic population including Acadians who had retreated from Nova Scotia to northern parts of New Brunswick. As in Quebec, religion was intimately linked to language. By the 1850s, the Catholic population had increased to the point where it was possible for Catholic communities to establish schools reflecting their own religious character. During this period the legislature repeatedly defeated resolutions calling for discontinuation of aid to denominational schools. The Parish Schools Act of 1858 confirmed the religious basis of the schools, allowed bible reading, and specifically mandated the use of the Douay[6] version of the Bible for Roman Catholic students, without note or comment, on parent request.[7]

In Prince Edward Island the 1851 Free Schools Act made no explicit reference to sectarian schools. Its main religious provision was to authorize Bible reading at opening to those children whose parents desired it. The question of whether Bible reading should be compulsory or optional dominated discussion for several years after 1852, with Protestants the primary advocates of required Bible reading. A new government in 1859 strengthened the religion section of the act by adding the clause, "the introduction of the Bible in all schools is to be legally authorized."[8] There the issue remained until the confederation debates of the 1860s and entry of the island into the union in 1873.

Although the area west of Ontario was occupied mainly by Indigenous groups, including the Métis, the British appear to have assumed that all the vast territory known as Rupert's Land was a British colony. Governance of the European settlements in the region was effectively delegated to the Hudson's Bay Company after its 1821 merger with the North West Company. The company's interest in education was limited to providing modest support to schools established and run mainly by Anglican and Catholic missionaries. Conscious of church rivalry, the company was ecumenical in its approach, dividing its meagre support for education among the Catholic and the several Protestant churches active in the area.

By 1870, several mission schools, both Catholic and Protestant, had been established in areas beyond the Manitoba border. From these beginnings, the churches established claim to a large measure of control over education in the North-West Territories. The federal government, by signing treaties with several native bands, assumed responsibility for the education of Indian and Métis Peoples. That move had profound consequences for church/state relationships. The federal government itself had little interest in education. The early neglect of education by the Hudson's Bay Company was replaced by neglect on the part of the federal government, leaving the churches to fill the void. The federal government's policy of assimilation was adopted by the churches, which thereby became agents of that policy. Thus began a long and sorry history of church/state collaboration in the education of Indigenous people, a topic examined in greater detail in chapter 7.

Confederation and Section 93

During the confederation debates, it was critical in both Upper and Lower Canada to have the support of church leadership, both Catholic and Protestant, in advancing the confederation agenda. In Lower Canada, the influence of the Catholic church was so dominant that no possibility existed for schools to become non-sectarian. However, the interests of the Protestant minority were well protected through the principle of dissent. Upper Canada Catholics were equally adamant in demanding the same protections as their Lower Canada Protestant counterparts. Delegations from the Maritime provinces could afford to be less attentive to church leadership because of the small Catholic population and because there was no prior legislation protecting sectarian schools.

At the Quebec Conference of 1864, convened to work out the terms of confederation, education was identified as a provincial responsibility, with a crucial caveat:

> Resolution 43 (6)... saving the rights and privileges which the Protestant or Catholic minority in both Canadas may possess as to their Denominational Schools, at the time when the Union goes into operation.[9]

This resolution embodied the historic compromise required to bring about confederation. Without it, conventional wisdom is that the religious minorities in Ontario and Quebec would have had sufficient political influence to halt the entire project.

At the London Conference, in 1866, Resolution 43 (6) was reworked to become Section 93 of the British North America Act. That section reads as follows:

> 93. In and for each Province the Legislature may exclusively make Laws in relation to Education, subject and according to the following Provisions:
> (1) Nothing in any such Law shall prejudicially affect any Right or Privilege with respect to Denominational Schools which any Class of Persons have by Law in the Province at the Union;
> (2) All the Powers, Privileges, and Duties at the Union by Law conferred and imposed in Upper Canada on the Separate Schools and School Trustees of the Queen's Roman Catholic Subjects shall be and the same are hereby extended to the Dissentient Schools of the Queen's Protestant and Roman Catholic Subjects in Quebec;
> (3) Where in any Province a System of Separate or Dissentient Schools exists by Law at the Union or is thereafter established by the Legislature of the Province, an Appeal shall lie to the Governor General in Council from any Act or Decision of any Provincial Authority affecting any Right or Privilege of the Protestant or Roman Catholic Minority of the Queen's Subjects in relation to Education;
> (4) In case any such Provincial Law as from Time to Time seems to the Governor General in Council requisite for the due Execution of the Provisions of this Section is not made, or in case any Decision of the Governor General in Council on any Appeal under this Section is not duly executed by the proper Provincial Authority in that Behalf, then and in every such Case, and as far only as the Circumstances of each Case require, the Parliament of Canada may make remedial Laws for the due Execution of the Provisions of this Section and of any Decision of the Governor General in Council under this Section.[10]

Section 93 protected only those rights held *in law* at the time of union. This meant that separate schools in Ontario and the dual denominational system in Quebec were protected. In the absence of laws on sectarian schools, any such schools that existed in Nova Scotia and New Brunswick failed to enjoy constitutional protection.

Subsections 3 and 4 are critical but often overlooked aspects of Section 93. These subsections give the federal government its only role in education in the provinces—that of an avenue of appeal against provincial government actions perceived as impinging on Section 93 rights. Subsection 3 provides for appeal to the governor general in council (the federal cabinet) against any attempt by a province to change the rights of the protected denominations. Subsection 4 is even stronger, providing for appeal to the Parliament of Canada should the cabinet fail to act or the province fail to implement any cabinet directive on the matter. These subsections have been invoked on several occasions, most notably in New Brunswick and Manitoba in the 1890s and Quebec in the 1990s. While often interpreted as giving the federal government the role of guarantor of Section 93 rights, these subsections do not oblige the federal government to act on any such appeal. Only in the Manitoba case did the federal government show any inclination to intervene.

Why was the constitutional outcome for Nova Scotia and New Brunswick different from that for Ontario and Quebec? The relatively smaller Catholic populations and the absence of prior legislation were likely contributors. Also, the willingness of school authorities to turn a blind eye to the existence of schools with a Catholic ambience may have been a source of reassurance to the Catholic population. In any event, the large majorities of the Tupper and Tilley governments in these provinces allowed these governments to approve the union without running the risk that the project would fail over the separate school issue.

Although the first conference leading up to confederation took place in Charlottetown, Prince Edward Island initially rejected confederation. As far as can be determined, the issue of sectarian schools was not a pressing one at the time. Prince Edward Island entered the union without any pre-existing separate schools and with no direct reference to Section 93 in its Terms of Union. Nevertheless, the British North America Act applied to the province, leaving open the question of whether Section 93 might be applicable to any denominational schools that might later be established by law.

There was no pre-confederation history of public sectarian schools in the west-coast colonies when they combined to form British Columbia. This was likely because of its late settlement, the absence of any significant Catholic population, and vigorous advocacy by two newspaper editors, Amor de Cosmos in Victoria and John Robson in New Westminster. While this does not imply an absence of religion in schools, pre-confederation laws made no provision for separate denominational schools. The Terms of Union contained no reference to denominational schools and no direct reference to Section 93. Any denominational schools in existence at the time were private and not backed by any law that might create Section 93 protection. Indeed, the *Free Public School Act* of 1872 stated that "All Public Schools established under the provisions of this Act, shall be conducted upon strictly non-sectarian principles. The highest morality shall be inculcated, but no religious dogmas or creed shall be taught. All Judges, Clergymen, Members of the Legislature, and others interested in education, shall be school visitors."[11]

The situation in Manitoba on the eve of confederation was far more complex. The neglect of education by the Hudson's Bay Company had given the churches, especially the Catholic Church, a much stronger hold on education there than anywhere else except perhaps Quebec. The relatively larger Indigenous and Métis population added to the complexity. Although no sectarian schools existed in law at the time of confederation, many schools were de facto sectarian, particularly those operated by members of Catholic religious orders.

After the transfer of the North-West Territories to Canada, attempts to survey the land led the Métis under Louis Riel to form their own provisional government in defiance of both the company and the Canadian government. This, in turn, precipitated a rapid series of events, including armed uprising by Riel's group, its suppression by Canadian troops, and a negotiated settlement that saw Manitoba emerge as the fifth province of Canada.

The demand for separate schools became a critical element in the eventual settlement with the rebels. Riel's main concern was that the rights of the French-speaking inhabitants be protected. French rights were, of course, intimately linked to Catholic rights. Riel's provisional government drew up a list of rights, prominent among which was the equality of English and French and the right to denominational schools based on the dual system of Quebec. In the end, this demand was addressed through a more generic statement, enshrined as Section 22 of the Manitoba Act. That section was identical to subsections (1), (3) and (4) of Section 93, except for two words in subsection (1):

> 22(1) Nothing in any such Law shall prejudicially affect any right or privilege with respect to Denominational Schools which any class of persons have by Law *or practice* [author's emphasis] in the Province the Union.[12]

The two words "or practice" proved to be of critical importance. There were no laws in place governing denominational schools in Manitoba at the time of confederation. However, denominational schools certainly existed in practice. These two words became the constitutional sanction for a dual confessional system in Manitoba, similar to that in Quebec. As in other instances, religion and language were intertwined. Indeed, what became known as the "Manitoba schools question" was a dominant issue for more than two decades after the province joined the union, before being finally settled by a federal-provincial agreement in 1896. This issue is discussed in more detail in the next section.

A new phase of confederation in 1905 saw the western part of the North-West Territories divided to become two new provinces, Saskatchewan and Alberta. By then the churches had continued to expand their educational presence, due to neglect of the area on the part of the federal government and because of their missionary activities among the Indigenous Peoples. Several rounds of territorial legislation had provided for the majority denomination to set up schools and allowed the minority to establish separate schools. In 1901, in an effort to limit church control, the territorial assembly approved an ordinance establishing a department of education and giving the department "control and management of all kindergarten schools, public and separate schools, normal schools, teachers' institutes and the education of deaf, deaf mute and blind persons."[13] The main components of governance thus passed from the churches to the department. Nevertheless, the ordinance included several provisions respecting the formation of separate schools. These included the right of the minority denomination in any district, whether Protestant or Roman Catholic, to establish a separate school and exempting public school ratepayers from assessment for the separate school. The ordinance also limited religious instruction to the last half hour of the day and to reciting the Lord's Prayer at school opening. Although a fundamental right to separate schools was confirmed by this ordinance, effective control had passed to the government.

Having just lost the battle over Catholic schools in Manitoba, Catholic supporters mounted a strong campaign to strengthen the constitutional provisions for sectarian schools in the new provinces. The result was a provision creating a dual denominational system like that in Quebec but which had failed in Manitoba. This led to the resignation from the federal cabinet of Clifford Sifton, the Manitoba representative. He was only persuaded to return after being allowed to draft a new term consistent with the 1901 Ordinance and explicitly avoiding the *in practice* wording which had caused so much grief in Manitoba.

In the end, the Sifton proposal was incorporated as Section 17 of both the Saskatchewan and Alberta Acts. These were identical, reading as follows:

> **17.** (1) Section 93 of The British North America Act, 1867, shall apply to the said province, with the substitution for paragraph (1) of the said section 93, of the following paragraph:
> 1. "Nothing in any such law shall prejudicially affect any right or privilege with respect to separate schools which any class of persons have at the date of the passing of this Act, under the terms of chapters 29 and 30 of the Ordinances of the North-west Territories, passed in the year 1901, or with respect to religious instruction in any public or separate school as provided for in the said ordinances."
> 2. In the appropriation by the Legislature or distribution by the Government of the province of any moneys for the support of schools organized and carried on in accordance with the said chapter 29 or any Act passed in amendment thereof, or in substitution therefor, there shall be no discrimination against schools of any class described in the said chapter 29.
> 3. Where the expression "by law" is employed in paragraph 3 of the said section 93, it shall be held to mean the law as set out in the said chapters 29 and 30, and where the expression "at the Union" is employed, in the said paragraph 3, it shall be held to mean the date at which this Act comes into force.[14]

The entry of Newfoundland in 1949 represents the final act of confederation. The story of denominational education in Newfoundland is unique in many ways, and particularly because of the history of having separate schools for several Protestant denominations as well as for Catholics but no non-sectarian public schools. Although legislation in 1836 made no distinction between denominations, the reality was that the clergy remained the strongest force within the new school boards. In communities with more than one denomination, establishing new schools was inhibited by disputes among the denominations. Under the circumstances, any conflict between a relatively weak government and the powerful churches was almost certainly to be resolved in favour of the churches.

Subsequent acts helped entrench church control by allowing for proportional division of funding among the denominations and stipulating that all schools would belong to the majority denomination in the community. Any hope on the part of government that differences between Anglicans and Methodists would be minor enough to avoid further division was obviously misplaced. While both tended to favour common schools, neither could live with special status for Catholics. At this juncture, Newfoundland had established the beginnings of a system that precluded the existence of common schools. The proportional division of funding among the various Protestant denominations represents the fundamental difference between the development of denominational education in Newfoundland and that in other provinces. Specifically, the right to schools encompassed six groups: Catholic, Anglican, United Church, Salvation Army, Presbyterian, and Seventh Day Adventist. After confederation the same rights were extended to the Pentecostal Assemblies.

Though firmly entrenched, denominational rights enjoyed no constitutional protection in Newfoundland before 1949. The obstacles to non-denominational education were political, not constitutional. Catholic religious and political leaders were particularly adamant on this issue, perhaps because of their history of persecution but also no doubt because of the ultramontane doctrine under which Catholics felt justified in asserting an absolute right of the church to control the education of children. As in 1867, proponents of confederation were concerned that opposition by the churches could jeopardize the whole project.

This situation meant that neither Section 93 nor any of the variants in existence for other provinces fitted the Newfoundland situation at the time of confederation. Section 93 was therefore replaced by Term 17 of the Terms of Union.

> Term 17 (1949 version)
>
> In lieu of section ninety-three of the British North America Act 1867, the following Term shall apply in respect of the Province of Newfoundland:
>
> In and for the Province of Newfoundland the Legislature shall have exclusive authority to make laws in relation to education, but the Legislature will not have authority to make laws prejudicially affecting any right or privilege with respect to denominational schools, common (amalgamated) schools, or denominational colleges, that any class or classes of persons have by law in Newfoundland at the date of Union, and out of public funds of the Province of Newfoundland provided for education.
>
> (a) all such schools shall receive their share of such funds in accordance with scales determined on a non-discriminatory basis from time to time by the Legislature for all schools then being conducted under authority of the Legislature; and
>
> (b) all such colleges shall receive their share of any grant from time to time voted for all colleges then being conducted under authority of the Legislature, such grant being distributed on a non-discriminatory basis.[15]

With the addition of Newfoundland, sectarian schools were found in five provinces, with differences reflecting their different histories. Alberta, Ontario, and Saskatchewan had public and separate systems with the latter intended for the minority denomination in a community, whether Catholic or Protestant. Quebec had a dual denominational system, under which the majority denomination operated common schools and the minority denomination separate or *dissentient* schools. In Newfoundland, the system was multi-denominational, with no common public system. All these arrangements were locked into place by Section 93 of the BNA Act and its variants.

Post-Confederation Consolidation and Expansion

The status of sectarian education remained highly controversial in the years following confederation. Advocacy and protest, political ideology, legislation, and litigation all played their part in keeping the issue on the political agenda. Section 93 and its variants prevented any diminution of denominational rights. However, there was no comparable impediment to their expansion. Catholic church leaders were particularly active in advocating for the broadest possible interpretation of their rights. The trend during the period in question is best characterized as incremental expansion. Successive governments sometimes responded positively to expansionary pressure, primarily from Catholic agencies. This was frequently countered by litigation that consistently reaffirmed Section 93 rights while also more clearly establishing their limits.

It is impossible to do justice here to all the major events shaping the system between confederation and 1982. Nevertheless, brief comment on a few seminal events can help advance our understanding of how the system managed to survive the key transformative trends in Canadian society during the twentieth century.

An important case in Ontario arose in 1910 when the Department of Education, in response to concerns about the quality of education in French schools, formulated a regulation, known as Regulation 17, mandating the use of English in all schools, and limiting the use of French. Francophone opposition to this regulation came to a head in Ottawa, where the separate-school trustees refused to implement the regulation and closed the schools rather than obey an injunction. The government's response was to dismiss the trustees. Both Regulation 17 and the replacement of trustees found their way through the court system, ending up in the hands of the Judicial Committee of the Privy Council of the United Kingdom. That court ruled that the protected class of persons was based on religion and not language.[16] Whatever the reality of language differences on the ground, francophone Catholics were not separately protected under Section 93.

In Ontario, separation by religion was initially limited to elementary schools. Any Catholic secondary schools were private. Some expansion up to Grade 10 was tolerated in the early years. However, these moves were not thought to have constitutional protection. The key case was a claim in 1926 by the trustees of the Township of Tiny that they and other Catholic boards had a constitutional right to operate their own secondary schools. Perhaps not incidentally, the board in question was francophone where some leeway had been exercised in allowing secondary education in French. Ontario courts dismissed the claim, holding that secondary education was not a protected right under Section 93. The Supreme Court of Canada was divided on the case, which led to a final appeal to the Judiciary Committee of the Privy Council. That appeal also failed. Despite this, over the years some expansion into the lower secondary levels continued to be tolerated.

In 1945, the Ontario government appointed a Royal Commission on Education, chaired by Justice John Andrew Hope. In its final report, the Hope Commission noted that no other part of its work had absorbed so much time and proved as difficult as that of separate schools. The commission majority took the narrow position that the rights entrenched in 1867 must be honoured but that there was no requirement to expand these rights.[17] However, a minority of four could not be persuaded to accept that view. That group prepared a lengthy minority report, which argued that the early development of separate schools was based on irreconcilable differences between Catholics and others on the purposes of education and the role of parents and the church. In the end, the Ontario government ignored the parts of the Hope report dealing with the separate school issue.

In 1963, William Davis became minister of education, remaining in that portfolio until 1971 when he became premier. It is fair to say that Davis, both as minister and as premier, was responsible for greater change in education in Ontario than any other individual in the twentieth century. His influence may reasonably be compared to that of Egerton Ryerson a century earlier. Of the many initiatives taken during Davis's tenure, two stood out for their impact on separate schools; provincial funding and extending the right to separate schools to the secondary level.

By the 1960s, because of the limitations of local taxation, the provincial government was forced to assume an ever-greater proportion of funding for education. The immediate impact was to bring increased equality in funding between public and separate boards because differential formulas favouring poorer school districts tended to benefit separate schools. Greater funding allowed Catholic provincial education organizations to engage in renewed efforts to fund separate secondary schools.

In 1969, the Ontario Catholic School Trustees' Association submitted a brief to the government seeking the removal of the restrictions on public funding of separate secondary schools.[18] After waiting for close to two years, Premier Davis finally replied in 1971, firmly rejecting the proposal.[19] Dixon reports that, despite the desire of all party leaders to avoid having the status of separate secondary schools become an election issue in 1971, the matter was high on the minds of the public.[20] This led to a backlash against the Catholic position, which was widely seen as responsible for Davis's Progressive Conservatives winning a large majority in the election.

Meanwhile, the government had appointed yet another review committee. The report of that committee, commonly known as the *Hall-Dennis Report*,[21] is best known for its radical embrace of progressive education. Hall-Dennis had almost nothing to say about separate schools. However, the report endorsed the main principles of the United Nations Declaration on the Rights of the Child and particularly the statement that "Parents have a prior right to choose the kind of education that shall be given to their children."[22] That principle is widely used by supporters of separate schools as it holds out the promise of choice, even though this is inconsistent with the Catholic church's traditional insistence on its own primacy over that of parents. Again, despite wide support for the main thrust of the Hall-Dennis report, nothing was done to expand any parent rights provisions.

By the mid-1970s, the wave of enrolment increases following the baby boom generation had been rapidly replaced by a decline engendered by dramatically falling birth rates. A shortage of school facilities was rapidly replaced by a surplus. A review of secondary school programs in 1982 also resulted in a recommendation that Grade 13 be eliminated. Both these developments, by freeing facilities, provided an opportunity to revisit the separate secondary school issue. In June 1984, Premier Davis suddenly announced that he had changed his mind and that he was ready to extend separate school funding to the end of the secondary level. Although this came as a surprise to many, Dixon's[23] research indicates that the decision had been planned for some time and was not unexpected in Catholic education circles. It was not until after he retired did Davis explain why he had changed his mind, arguing that the meaning of Section 93 had, or should have, changed because completion of secondary education had now become the norm.

With the defeat of the government of Davis's successor, Frank Miller, in 1985 it fell to the Liberal government of Premier David Peterson to follow through on the Davis decision. A new bill, known as Bill 30, allowed, but did not require, a separate school board to offer secondary programs. Detailed transition arrangements were also made to protect teachers already under contract, subject to their agreement to respect the traditions of Catholic schools. Finally, to prevent any forced movement of students, the amendment provided for a secondary school student to elect to attend either a public or a separate school. The long battle for Catholic secondary schooling in Ontario had finally been won.

As for Quebec, the influence of the Catholic church became even stronger after 1867. The ultramontane doctrine effectively became the operating principle for the Quebec government. Its effects were especially pervasive in education. Although the province was formally responsible for education, administration of the system had been delegated to a Council of Public Instruction, which functioned independently of government. In 1869, that body was divided into two denominational committees. Eventually, these went their separate ways with the combined council effectively dissolving itself for lack of common interest or activity. In the first half of the twentieth century, church influence was all pervasive. The weakness of the state in education during that period is illustrated by the fact that there was no ministry of education in Quebec until 1965. Successive governments were periodically required to reaffirm the status quo, even to the point of making a virtue of the fact that Quebec had, uniquely, been spared the evils of secular, state-controlled education.

Variations from the French Catholic/English Protestant duality emerged over the years with successive waves of immigration. Beginning in the mid-nineteenth century, Irish immigration resulted in a small but growing English-speaking Catholic population. That population was accommodated to an extent by operating parallel English and French streams in the Catholic schools and eventually by separate English Catholic schools. English Catholics had no right to representation on the Catholic school boards or other governing bodies. However, they eventually acquired a degree of autonomy, opening secondary schools and establishing a separate examination board and separate inspectors.[24]

The status of the Jewish population, which had settled mainly in Montréal starting in the mid-nineteenth century, is an important case in point. No provision had been made for non-Christian denominations in any of the provinces before confederation or in its immediate aftermath. Although the Quebec Catholic system was in most localities nominally the common system, this was not the case in Montréal, which had a strict dual denominational division. Individuals were free to designate their property taxes to their board of choice. Jewish property owners generally directed their taxes to the Protestant board. However, following a dispute in 1886, many Jews decided to redirect their taxes to the Catholic board, in return for an agreement that 80 percent of the funds would be returned to the Jewish community to set up their own schools. In the aftermath, the Protestant School

Board of Greater Montreal found itself having to educate most Jewish students on much lower revenues than before.

The Jewish population was also concerned with its lack of representation on school governing bodies. This resulted in several court cases, which largely upheld the status quo. The whole issue came to a head in 1925 when the Quebec government referred to the courts a complex set of questions around the 1903 Act as it applied to Montréal and Québec City. The Quebec Court of Appeal declared the 1903 Act to be in violation of Section 93. However, it also ruled that the Montréal Protestant School Board was not required to accept Jewish students or hire Jewish teachers as a matter of right, though it may do so by grace.

Two Jewish citizens, Hirsch and Cohen, appealed this decision to the Supreme Court of Canada and subsequently to the Judicial Committee of the Privy Council. The Judicial Committee upheld the Supreme Court decision that the law violated Section 93.[25] However, it did observe that Section 93 did not prevent the Quebec legislature from passing laws to establish schools for religious groups other than Catholics and Protestants. Jews had the right to attend either Catholic or Protestant schools in Montréal, on the legally questionable but eminently practical grounds that these were common schools. However, they had no right to representation on either board.[26]

The dual system, with just sufficient accommodations for non-French Catholics and Jews to prevent further significant challenges to the constitutional order, remained in place until the early 1960s. By then, Quebec society had rapidly shifted from its rural, agrarian base to an urban industrial structure. In 1960, the population finally rose up against the conservatism of the Duplessis government and the Catholic church and elected a Liberal government under Jean Lesage. The train of events, commonly referred to as the Quiet Revolution, set in motion during the next six years was to profoundly change Quebec society, nowhere more so than in education.

The quarter-century from 1960 to the mid 1980s saw the complete overthrow of the church/state alliance that had prevailed since the days of New France. One of the first legislative initiatives of the Lesage government was a series of acts collectively referred to as the *Magna Carta of Education*.[27] The most far-reaching of these acts was the one establishing a royal commission of inquiry on education. While it might seem ironic that the person appointed to head the commission was a Catholic cleric, Msgr. Alphonse-Marie Parent, that appointment may have helped the commission avoid the fate of other attempts at change that had been thwarted by church opposition.

Though radical in other respects, the Parent Commission had to tread carefully around denominational rights. Its first report explicitly acknowledged the rights of Catholics and Protestants to confessional schools, while also pointing out that these rights were limited to schools in Montréal and Québec City and to the religious minority in other school districts.[28] The Parent Commission, like others of the time, in no way contemplated the possibility of constitutional change. Nevertheless, the commission held that the extensive autonomy enjoyed by the denominational committees of the Council of Education was not a constitutionally protected right but rather a consequence of government's laissez-faire approach to education. This set the stage for recommendations for a complete reworking of the provincial structure of education. Control by the denominational committees effectively passed to the new Ministry of Education. Provincial secondary schools were established, along with Collèges d'enseignement général et professionnel (cégeps), which included what would be the final year of secondary education in other provinces, and the beginnings of a provincial non-denominational university system.

By the mid-1960s the focus of the education debate in Quebec had shifted from religion to language. Over the next two decades, the denominational duality was left in place while successive governments wrestled with the emerging crisis over the rise of nationalism and the place of the French language in Quebec. As it happens, efforts to promote the French language in education were found to intersect with Section 93 rights at every turn. The final chapter of the church/state saga in Quebec education was only resolved when it became clear that the desire to turn Quebec into a secular French-speaking society was incompatible with the preservation of denominational rights. One set of rights had to be sacrificed to advance the other.

The next major step in the project to revive French was Bill 22, the Official Languages Act, introduced in 1974. The first section of this Bill made the radical declaration that "French is the official language of Quebec."[29] The most important implication of this was that French was mandated as the language of instruction. Obviously, its effect was felt particularly by the Protestant school boards, who could no longer give a choice in language of instruction and who consequently had to dramatically expand their French offerings.

The controversy over Bill 22 played a large part in the election of the separatist Parti Québécois in 1976. The key event for education in this period was the replacement of Bill 22 by the Charter of the French Language, commonly known as Bill 101. The new act allowed instruction in English only for Canadian citizens whose parents had received most of their elementary education in English.[30] The onus shifted from Francophones having to learn English to Anglophones and others (usually referred to as allophones) having to learn French. The traditional pattern of Francophones attending English schools for their economic advantage was soon reversed. Being mainly French, Catholic schools experienced less of an adjustment to the language laws than did Protestant schools.

Milner gives a detailed account of several incidents that showed both the continuing influence of the church on a segment of the population and an emerging divide within the Catholic community.[31] An example was an attempt by parents from Notre-Dame-des-Neiges School, a Catholic school in a suburb of Montréal, to save their school from closure by introducing measures intended to change its status to non-confessional. La Commission des écoles catholiques de Montréal bowed to pressure from church leaders and denied the request. The case found its way to the courts where Chief Justice Jules Deschênes ruled that the decision to change the status of the school was contrary to Section 93.[32] However, the judge also remarked that the increasingly pluralistic nature of Quebec society required some accommodation of groups not protected under Section 93. He then went on to make the radical suggestion that the province would be within its rights to establish a separate non-sectarian system of schools, a move recommended by the Parent Commission more than a decade earlier but never enacted.

Milner summarized the results of several polls conducted on the issue during this period.[33] The pollsters reported that language rather than religion was the main area of importance and that the preference for confessional schools was due to a mistaken belief that the existing system was based on language. In response to other questions, a majority showed a preference for pluralist or neutral schools.[34]

After winning the 1980 election, the Parti Québécois government's first major act was to prepare a white paper, titled in French *L'école Québécoise : Un école communautaire et responsable* and in English *The Quebec School: A Responsible Force in the Community*.[35] The white paper made the radical proposal that the school boards become non-denominational, with denominational characteristics to be determined at the school level. To avoid Section 93 challenges, Catholic and Protestant boards would continue to exist in Montréal and Québec City and dissident schools would still be allowed. Even though there was some support for the bill among Protestants, the Protestant school boards were determined to mount a challenge to its constitutionality. In any event, the bill was later amended to give back to school boards the power to determine the confessional status of the schools. This seemed to satisfy most of the critics, except for the Protestant school boards and the more extreme Catholic groups, both of which questioned the constitutionality of some of the bill's provisions on confessional schools.

As the new law was working its way through the legislature, the Supreme Court of Canada was hearing an appeal by the Quebec government against a Quebec court ruling on municipal taxation. Sections of that law limited the ability of school boards to raise local school taxes. In a unanimous decision, the Supreme Court upheld the ruling that the law was in violation of Section 93.[36] In doing so, it made several important points about the scope and limits of Section 93 as it applied to Quebec schools. First, the court again held that Section 93 is not so all-encompassing as to make the ministère de l'Éducation (Ministry of Education) subservient to the denominational school boards. The court also made an important observation about who constitutes the protected classes: "The school commissioners or trustees are not themselves a class of persons contemplated by s. 93(1) but they are the representatives of such a class for purposes of the management of denominational schools."[37] This ruling effectively stymied any effort to protect the French language by limiting denominational rights. However, by then the new constitutional regime was in place.[38] This set the stage for further challenges leading finally to the Quebec Section 93 amendment. Events leading up to that amendment are described in chapter 4.

Turning to New Brunswick, the Common Schools Act had declared all schools to be non-sectarian. MacNaughton remarks that, although the debate on the Common Schools Act took place a mere four years after confederation, she was unable to find any reference to Section 93 being used as an argument for protection of Catholic rights at the time.[39] However, it did not take long for some to realize that there might be a constitutional issue, including scope for federal intervention in the matter under subsections (3) and (4) of Section 93, as earlier described.

In a first attempt to reverse the act, the Catholic bishop appealed to the federal cabinet, arguing that Catholics did hold rights to their own schools under the 1858 act and that Subsection 93 (3) required that the federal government overturn the provincial legislation. The federal cabinet declined to intervene. Prime Minister John A. MacDonald doubted that the new constitution could survive federal interference in a matter that was expressly provincial. This led to a further appeal to Parliament under subsection 93(4). The new Parliament, under Liberal Prime Minister Alexander Mackenzie, asked the New Brunswick government to change its mind. However, it could not be persuaded to invoke Section 93(4) to disallow the legislation. Instead, it passed a resolution allocating funds to support an appeal to the Judicial Committee of the Privy Council.

The test case involved a Catholic ratepayer who had appealed unsuccessfully to the Supreme Court of New Brunswick against the town's property assessment. The appellant asked that this decision be reversed, contending that the "rights and privileges of the Roman Catholic inhabitants of the province as a class of persons, had been prejudicially affected by the Common Schools Act."[40] On July 17, 1874, the Judicial Committee dismissed the case. According to Sissons, a record preserved in the papers of John A. MacDonald showed that the justices took the position that whatever privilege Catholics enjoyed before confederation was not a legal right but an "accident which might have happened today and might have been reversed tomorrow."[41] This was an important judgment, frequently cited in the many subsequent cases over this issue in later years. However, far from settling the matter, this simply placed it back into the hands of the politicians.

Over the next twenty years, the arguments went back and forth. Significant events included a riot in the francophone community of Caraquet, which led to the death of one individual. In 1875, the matter again found its way to Parliament, this time, through a proposed amendment to the British North America Act recognizing separate or dissentient schools in New Brunswick. That effort also failed. However, provincial officials appeared to have looked the other way at a series of measures that amounted to de facto creation of sectarian schools at the local level.

The matter again came to a head in the early 1890s, this time in Bathurst, another predominantly Acadian community. The issue there centred around the opening of a Catholic boys' school taught by members of religious orders. Many students migrated to the new school, allowing its status to change from private to public. This led to a near-riot, reminiscent of the Caraquet riot twenty years earlier. The matter was finally referred to a commissioner who dismissed most of the complaints as exaggerated. However, he did point out some irregularities such as teaching Catholic religion during the noon hour, appointing an obviously unqualified Catholic as principal of the grammar school, and allowing the Catholic school buildings to be filled at the expense of the other schools.

In later years, it appears that the board of education afforded considerable discretion to local trustees. This gave Catholics great influence in areas where they could command a majority of the trustees. The situation appears to closely parallel that in Nova Scotia at the time. The main difference, aside from language, was in a narrow point of law. Whereas Nova Scotia legislation was silent on the matter of sectarian schools, the New Brunswick Act continued to explicitly define all schools as non-sectarian. The pattern in New Brunswick since the 1960s has been much the same as that for Nova Scotia. Almost all vestiges of the religious character of schools have disappeared, replaced by explicit separation by language.

As described earlier, Manitoba entered confederation with a slightly modified version of Section 93, protecting denominational schools that existed *in practice* as well as in law. The original intent was to create a dual denominational system as in Quebec. However, by the late 1880s both demographic change and suppression of the second Riel uprising resulted in a wave of anti-French sentiment. In 1889, the Manitoba Government announced that it planned to introduce legislation to abolish the dual school system and restrict the use of French.[42] This led to a test case, again over taxation. The case centred around the question of whether any Catholic schools existed in practice at the time of union. After the Manitoba courts dismissed the claim, the appellant took the case to the Supreme Court of Canada.[43] That court relied heavily on an affidavit submitted by Archbishop Taché, which held that all schools were denominational in practice if not in law at the time of confederation. In a ruling reversing the lower court decisions, the justices enunciated some principles of constitutional law that have held in subsequent cases. In particular, the court held that, by inserting the words "in practice" into Section 22 of the Manitoba Act, Parliament must have intended this to have a different meaning from the words in the original Section 93.

On appeal, the Judicial Committee of the Privy Council agreed with the Supreme Court of Canada that the words "in practice" were intended to create a distinction between what existed in law and the more fluid situation in Manitoba.[44] Although accepting that denominational schools did exist in Manitoba, the Judicial Committee declared that no denominational rights existed, either in law or in practice. It is noteworthy that the Supreme Court and the Judicial Committee differed only on a narrow point of law. The Judicial Committee held that, in the absence of any laws governing public schools, all schools prior to 1870 were private. This seems to imply that Section 22 of the Manitoba Act was redundant since no schools qualifying for protected status existed prior to confederation.

Unable to move either the courts or the provincial government, church authorities decided to try their luck with the federal government, as allowed by subsections 2 and 3 of Section 22. Not wishing to become bogged down as it had in the New Brunswick case, the federal government decided to refer the matter directly to the Supreme Court of Canada. The key question placed before the court was whether the decision of the Judicial Committee of the Privy Council in the *Barrett* and *Logan* cases dispose of or conclude the application for redress based on the contention that the rights of the Roman Catholic minority, which accrued to them after the union, under the statutes of the province, have been interfered with by the two statutes of 1890, complained of in the said petitions and memorials.[45] Without elaborating on the detail, the result, in a three to two split decision was that, though allowed, there was no requirement for federal intervention.

The split decision presented a further opening for appeal to the Judicial Committee. In its 1895 ruling, that court held that subsections 2 and 3 had to be considered as separate from subsection 1. If a provincial law is held by the courts to be *ultra vires* under subsection 1, then that is the end of the matter. On the other hand, if the provincial law is held to be valid, then having recourse to a second remedy, under subsections 2 or 3, would invite the province to ignore the federal decision. In any event, there was nothing in subsections 2 or 3 to direct the federal government to any specific form of action.[46]

Despite the Judicial Committee ruling, on March 21, 1895, the federal cabinet issued an Order in Council requiring the Manitoba government to amend its legislation to restore to the Catholic minority the right to build and manage schools and to a proportionate share of public funds allocated for education. In response, the Manitoba government did exactly what the Judicial Committee suggested might happen. It simply ignored the order. This led the federal government to present a bill to Parliament, restoring a Catholic school board and proposing to use interest from proceeds of the sale of federal lands in Manitoba should the Manitoba government continue to refuse funding for that board. However, by then, the government's mandate had run out. The Liberals under Wilfrid Laurier won the 1896 election with a decisive majority, winning even Quebec where the Catholic clergy had waged an active campaign in support of the Conservatives, based on the Manitoba schools issue.

With like-minded governments now in place in Ottawa and Winnipeg, the stage was finally set for a negotiated settlement. The Manitoba government now decided that some compromise was required after all. The final agreement, known ever since as the Laurier-Greenway compromise, did not provide for separate schools but allowed for thirty minutes of religious instruction by any Christian denomination after school hours, along with a few other provisions designed to satisfy particularly the French Catholic population.[47]

According to Skelton's account, most Catholics favoured the compromise, but the Catholic clergy and press were adamantly opposed.[48] The agreement did nothing to mollify those with the most extreme views on both sides. Archbishop Langevin went as far as to appeal to Pope Leo XIII who, following an investigation, issued an Encyclical Letter to the Canadian bishops in which he condemned the Manitoba law and reiterated the church position that Catholic children must first and foremost be educated in the faith.[49] Nevertheless, the Pope directed that Manitoba Catholics make use of the provisions granted to them while continuing to hold the faith and defer to the authority of the bishops.

In the end, neither protracted litigation, federal intervention, nor papal directive was successful in preserving separate Catholic schools in Manitoba. However, the lessons of Manitoba helped shape the terms of union for Saskatchewan and Alberta in 1905, ensuring that such schools continued to exist in these provinces.

Despite the identical wording of Term 17 of the Alberta and Saskatchewan Acts, the system evolved somewhat differently in these two provinces. The first Saskatchewan legislation in 1907 established secondary schools. In that act, there was no mention of separation by religion. Since there were no secondary schools in the province at the time of confederation, it seemed to have been assumed that these schools would not enjoy Term 17 protection. Nevertheless, the Catholic leadership had not given up on its mission to persevere in its demand for greater control of their schools.

Legislation passed in 1913 declared that, whenever a separate school was established, all adherents of the denomination of that school would be assessed as supporters of the school. A further section changed the method of apportioning corporate assessments, also in a way favourable to separate schools. This legislation led to protracted litigation over who should be considered a member of a class and whether the legislation went beyond what was required by Term 17. The constitutional question was whether the legislation amounted to discrimination against the majority denomination. Saskatchewan courts ruled that the legislation was constitutional on the reasoning that Term 17 applied specifically to the minority and not the majority denomination. On appeal, the Supreme Court of Canada proved to be hopelessly divided on both the constitutional question and the assessment issue. With four judges, a tie ensued, which had the effect of leaving the lower court rulings, and hence the legislation, intact.[50]

Two further cases related to the same issue eventually found their way to the Judicial Committee of the Privy Council, bypassing the Supreme Court of Canada.[51] In these cases, the Lords agreed that the law required all ratepayers who were members of the religious minority establishing a separate school to have their taxes allocated to that school. There was no provision for individual choice or opting out. With these rulings, the Saskatchewan system has remained largely intact for almost a century. Only recently did a new question emerge, having to do with whether the government is required to provide funding for non-Catholic students attending a Catholic school. That question is examined later.

Over the past century, the Catholic separate system in Alberta has become much stronger than that in Saskatchewan. This stems from the fact that religious secondary schools did exist in Alberta in 1905 and thus were protected under Term 17 of the Alberta Act. However, for the first forty years the Alberta separate school system grew very slowly. Most communities were too small to sustain two schools, and the rural tax base for Catholics was limited. The situation changed rapidly after the discovery of oil in 1947. Individual and corporate property assessments increased rapidly. The introduction of school construction grants followed by a provincially equalized property tax assessment system resulted in greater tax revenues for poorer districts.

These developments provided a substantial incentive to create new separate schools.

A royal commission appointed in 1957 addressed the separate school issue only briefly, remarking that there was considerable interest in the issue through briefs and public hearings. While acknowledging constitutional rights, the commission made a point of stating that the rights were limited, allowing the minority denomination "to establish a tax-supported denominational school in any school district where they constitute a religious minority as among persons of all other religions. Beyond this, their rights are identical to those of public school supporters, as specified in the Alberta School Act."[52]

A 1979 case initiated by the Calgary Public School Board raised the question of whether Term 17 of the Alberta Act prohibits actions prejudicial to the rights and privileges of the class that happens to operate the public schools. The specifics of the case were similar to those in Saskatchewan many years earlier; the distribution of corporate taxes and opting out of support for the separate school board. The trial judge ruled that Term 17(1) protects only the minority class while Term 17(2) prohibits discrimination against either class.[53] This was upheld by a unanimous decision of the Alberta Court of Appeal.[54]

The next major policy shift occurred in 1994. In that year, the Alberta government introduced a proposal to bring all funds raised in support of schools into a provincial pool and to distribute the funds on a per-student formula. This came under fire from separate school boards on the grounds that the framework interfered with their right to raise and expend funds locally. The government decided to accommodate these concerns by allowing separate school boards to opt out of the provision to remit funds to the province. That accommodation drew the attention of the public school boards, which contended that the opting out provision favoured separate boards. Despite having lost the earlier case, the Public School Boards Association of Alberta took up the case on behalf of its members.

The trial judge held the legislation to be invalid to the extent that it did not allow public boards to opt out of the funding scheme. On appeal, the Alberta Court of Appeal ruled that school boards, like municipal governments, enjoy only that level of autonomy granted by the province. The only exception is the limited rights granted separate schools under Term 17.[55] A further appeal to the Supreme Court of Canada resulted in unanimous rejection of all aspects of the appeal.[56] If anything, the Supreme Court was even more emphatic than the

Alberta Court that school boards enjoy no autonomy from the province. The rights enjoyed by Alberta separate schools are limited to the provision of religious education and do not include methods of funding.

With the entry of Newfoundland to the federation, a new variation on sectarian education was introduced. From 1949 to the 1990s, the multi-denominational system remained largely unchallenged. In practice, several significant developments served to change the face of the system. The first was the emergence and growth of schools of the Pentecostal Assemblies. That denomination had no schools prior to confederation, and hence held no constitutional right under Term 17 of the Newfoundland Terms of Union. However, a concentration of Pentecostal adherents in a few electoral districts led to a political climate under which recognizing yet another denomination was seen as preferable to challenging the whole structure. With a scattered, mainly rural, population, but with access to transportation and to per capita, rather than per-student, allocations for capital funding, the Pentecostal denomination was able, from a very modest beginning, to expand its school system substantially, including being allowed to establish its own school board.

In 1965, the provincial government appointed a royal commission on education.[57] That commission sought a legal opinion on whether the sectarian system could be changed and how this might be accomplished. That opinion reinforced the common understanding that the only way to significantly change the role of the churches was to amend Term 17. The commission therefore decided to limit its work on the denominational front to an attempt to restructure the Department of Education. Up to that time, the department had effectively been controlled by the churches through denominational superintendents. Though not explicitly stated, the understanding seemed to be that the existence of denominational officials in the department had no constitutional sanction. Under the proposed restructuring, the department was to be organized along functional lines, with religious rights decentralized to the denominational school boards.

To preserve some role for church authorities, and possibly to head off a constitutional challenge, the government accepted a proposal by the main denominations to establish new denominational committees outside of both the Department of Education and the school boards. These would be appointed by the churches and have their role limited to exercising constitutional rights. These rights remained sufficiently expansive to give these denominational committees continued control of school board membership, school construction, student selection, and teacher employment, in addition to religious education and other elements of the curriculum that might impinge on religion. Although the Department of Education was no longer denominational, its power was severely constrained by these provisions.

At around the same time, independent of the royal commission, the three largest Protestant denominations—Anglican, United Church, and Salvation Army—decided to integrate their systems at both the school board and the school level. This greatly facilitated the consolidation of schools and boards. Catholics, together with the two smaller Protestant groups, Pentecostal and Seventh Day Adventist, declined to participate in integration. The participating denominations did not relinquish their individual rights but decided to exercise these collectively through a single denominational committee.

In 1968, the Pentecostal leadership was persuaded to support the changes in the Department of Education by a promise from the provincial government to seek a constitutional amendment extending protection to that denomination. The province followed up on this promise through a resolution in the legislature. That effort stalled because the federal government was reluctant to proceed with the required petition to the Parliament of the United Kingdom for constitutional amendment. By the mid-1980s, however, the patriated constitution was in place. The amending formula provided an opening for constitutional amendment. It was perhaps no coincidence that the premier of the day, Brian Peckford, represented a district at the centre of concentration of the Pentecostal population. After winning an election in 1986 with that issue prominent in Pentecostal districts, the Newfoundland legislature passed a resolution asking the federal government to approve an amendment to Term 17. It appears from the record of parliamentary debates at the time that this amendment was approved federally with little debate other than expressions of support from all sides.[58]

Aside from it being the only instance in Canada in which denominational rights were expanded by constitutional amendment, the Pentecostal amendment was notable as the first test of Section 43 of the new constitution. That section allows constitutional provisions affecting only one province to be amended by approval of the legislature of that province and the federal government. The Pentecostal amendment was also the last significant move in the direction of expanding denominational rights in Newfoundland. Few at the time believed that the next few years would bring a momentous shift in the opposite direction. If the amending formula could be used to expand rights, it could also be used for the opposite purpose. A series of events in the early 1990s resulted in just that outcome. That story is taken up in chapter 4.

In summary, church/state relationships in education from 1867 to the 1980s may be considered as having developed in two directions. On the legal side, the Supreme Court of Canada and the Judicial Committee of the Privy Council affirmed denominational rights while, at the same time, establishing limits to these rights and rebuffing the efforts of church leaders to extend these rights. Overall, it may be argued that the courts have taken a narrow view of the extent of denominational rights vis-à-vis provincial powers. While bound by Section 93 and related provisions, the courts have shown no inclination to take an expansive view of the rights granted by these provisions.

On the legislative side, several instances can be found in which provinces have attempted to limit denominational rights in ways that have been declared unconstitutional. The Quebec language issue is the main case in point. On the other hand, where the province itself has expanded denominational rights, the courts have upheld the provincial power to do so, even though these moves were not required by Section 93. It remains an open question whether these actions have effectively created new constitutional rights or whether such decisions could be reversed by further provincial legislation. The Supreme Court decision in the Alberta case cited above suggests that the latter is likely to be true.

CHAPTER 3

The 1982 Constitution and Impact of the Charter

The British North America Act of 1867 created the independent nation of Canada. However, Canada's independence was limited in some important ways. Two of these are significant for our purposes. First, there was no provision for amending the constitution without recourse to the British Parliament. Second, although the BNA Act allowed the Parliament of Canada to establish a Supreme Court, the Judicial Committee of the United Kingdom Privy Council remained the court of last resort on Canadian constitutional matters until 1926.

When the constitution was finally brought home to Canada in 1982, most sections of the BNA Act remained unchanged. Specifically, Section 93 and its variants remained intact. There seems to have been little discussion of the issue of church and state or the place of separate schools. However, the new act contained two fundamental changes: the Charter of Rights and Freedoms, and the amending formula. These were destined to have a profound impact on state/church relationships in education. Although Section 29 of the Charter was clearly intended to preserve the denominational status quo, it may have been lost on the framers of the Charter that the amending formula was to have the opposite effect.

This chapter outlines the main provisions of the Charter related to denominational rights, religious freedom, and non-discrimination and examines the effect of the Charter on separate schools and the place of religion in schools. The impact of the amending formula is addressed in chapter 4.

Several sections of the Charter are pertinent to the issue of church and state. First, Section 2 sets out the fundamental freedoms enjoyed by Canadians, specifically "freedom of conscience and religion and freedom of thought, belief, opinion and expression."[1] Second, Section 15, generally referred to as the non-discrimination section, states that "every individual is equal before and under the law and has the right to the equal protection and equal benefit of the law without discrimination and, in particular, without discrimination based on race, national or ethnic origin, colour, religion, sex, age or mental or physical disability."[2] Finally, the issue of denominational schools is addressed directly in Section 29: "Nothing in this Charter abrogates or derogates from any rights or privileges guaranteed by or under the Constitution of Canada in respect of denominational, separate or dissentient schools."[3]

It is noteworthy that the preamble to the Charter explicitly acknowledges religion, but in the broadest possible terms: "Canada is founded upon principles that recognize the supremacy of God and the rule of law."[4] However, while the Charter goes on to outline in detail what is meant by the rule of law, there is no further reference to the supremacy of God or to religion as a founding principle. Indeed, the sections on freedom of religion and non-discrimination refer mainly to individuals and not to state institutions.

It should be immediately apparent that Section 29 is in fundamental conflict with both Sections 2 and 15. The protection for denominational schools is inherently discriminatory because it offers protection for schools of one religious sect that is not available to others. As for freedom of religion, that denomination is freer than others to promote its doctrines through an important public institution.

The final federal/provincial conference leading to patriation and the Charter was held in private, and no written record of the proceedings exists. Some of the actors have written their own, sometimes conflicting, accounts.[5,6] Scholars and journalists have also written extensively about the negotiations.[7] None of these make any significant reference to Section 29. Anything we can say about the reasons for including this section is speculative. It is possible that the negotiators fundamentally believed that the historic compromise remained valid and that there was a risk of Section 93 being overridden by the Charter. Also, at least some premiers may have feared sufficient backlash from denominational authorities to place the whole project in jeopardy—the same type of thinking used in 1867. It is worth noting that in Newfoundland the Pentecostal Assemblies were at the time actively promoting constitutional change to enshrine their education rights. Also in Ontario, the Catholic battle for rights to secondary schools was being actively fought. Both of these may have influenced the position of the respective premiers.

Charter Challenges on Separate Schools

Despite Section 29, there have been some Charter challenges to the existence of separate schools. An early case goes back to the Ontario decision to extend separate school funding to the secondary level. Two separate issues were at stake in this case. The first was whether Bill 30, the legislation implementing that decision, violated Section 93. By the time that case reached the courts in 1986, the Charter had come into effect. This raised the second question of whether the legislation violated Sections 2 and 15 of the Charter.

On February 18, 1986, the Ontario Court of Appeal, by a 3–2 majority, ruled Bill 30 constitutional.[8] The main majority argument was that the province could not limit Section 93 rights but was free to expand these rights. The two dissenting judges took the position that Bill 30 would have been a legitimate exercise of provincial power prior to the Charter. However, the Bill was now in conflict with Section 15 of the Charter because, by extending Catholic rights, it discriminated against other religions. Section 93 shelters from a discrimination argument only the laws that were in effect in 1867. Any later law that favoured one religion over others was subject to the Section 15 non-discrimination provision.

The split decision invited an appeal to the Supreme Court of Canada. That court ruled unanimously that there is no constitutional barrier to a province's power to expand denominational rights.[9] However, by the same reasoning, extension of rights through legislation can also be reversed by legislation. The court also ruled that, the *Tiny* case notwithstanding, Bill 30 could be construed as returning rights that had been held prior to confederation. Though the court did not say so directly, this seems also to imply that Bill 30 amounted to a restoration of pre-confederation rights and could thus not be rescinded by further legislation.

On the Charter question, the court issued the clear statement that the Charter cannot be used to repeal other provisions of the constitution. This is crucial as it holds that the Charter is not absolute in matters of discrimination if the issue at hand involves other sections of the constitution. Section 93 cannot be voided by Section 15 of the Charter. While this ruling appears to suggest that Charter Section 29 is redundant, it must be assumed that the framers of the Charter wanted to reinforce the principle of denominational rights, for whatever reason.

While going some way to clarify the rights of Catholics in the Charter era, the ruling did not explicitly address the broader issue of whether the existence of separate schools for Catholics amounts to discrimination against other religions. The first test case on this issue, known as *Adler versus Ontario* was launched by a group of Jewish parents who had been sending their children to private schools. This case began before the Ontario Superior Court in 1992.[10] The applicants also took the position that, in the Bill 30 ruling, the Supreme Court had not addressed the question of discrimination against other groups. They requested the court to issue a declaration that the non-funding of Jewish day school education in Ontario is unconstitutional and that parents of children in Jewish day schools are entitled to funding on the same basis as public and Catholic separate schools. The respondents countered that Charter Section 1 provides for reasonable limits on rights and freedoms that can be justified in a free and democratic society and that the right of provinces to legislate on education is also protected by the constitution.

In the ruling, the trial judge noted that the special status of Roman Catholic schools had been repeatedly upheld by the courts using the historic compromise argument. As for Section 1 of the Charter, the judge held that some issues are best left to the legislature, questioning whether the court should sanction what would be a radical departure to the funding formula. This was critical to the final ruling, in which the judge concluded that the rights of the claimants had indeed been infringed, but that the legislation in question was saved by the reasonable limits provision of Section 1 of the Charter.

The Ontario Court of Appeal upheld the decision. The matter was then appealed to the Supreme Court of Canada. The decision of that court was, in all important respects, the same as that of the lower courts. The Supreme Court again held that one section of the constitution cannot be used to negate another section. Specifically, the rights granted to Catholics under Section 93 cannot be extended to others by invoking either the religious freedom or the non-discrimination sections of the Charter. More specifically, the court held that "failure to act in order to facilitate the practice of religion cannot be considered state interference with freedom of religion. Moreover, the cost of sending their children to private religious schools is a natural cost of the appellants' religion and does not, therefore, constitute an infringement of their freedom of religion protected by s. 2(a) of the Charter."[11]

This ruling means that government inaction on funding for religiously based schools does not infringe on religious freedom. What might infringe is government action to fund some but not all other religions. Catholics are the sole exception because of their status under Section 93. This point is crucial because any government action to support, say, Jewish or Muslim schools could be challenged by any number of other groups claiming to be religious in nature. Extending such action to all religions raises the thorny issue of whether such claims are legitimate and thus over the definition of religion and who decides what is a religion. This issue will be examined in chapter 8.

The next significant case was also over discrimination against religions other than Catholicism. Arieh Waldman, the parent of a child enrolled in a Jewish private school, claimed religious discrimination by virtue of having to pay fees for private schooling as well as having to support the public school system through taxation, essentially the same claim as in the Adler case.

The *Bill 30* and *Adler* rulings had effectively closed the door on further access to Canadian courts. Waldman therefore took a different route, appealing directly to the United Nations Human Rights Committee. In a 1996 submission, Waldman invoked several articles of the United Nations Universal Declaration on Human Rights, particularly Article 26 (right to education), Article 2 (non-discrimination), and Article 18 (freedom of religion). Because the United Nations recognizes only sovereign states as respondents, the action was taken against Canada even though the issue at hand was specific to Ontario. Aside from other issues, this raised the question of the role of the federal government when matters of provincial jurisdiction spill over into the international arena. Waldman contended that the right to separate schools is essential to education and that denying this right to all but Catholics represented discrimination under Article 2 of the Human Rights Declaration. Finally, Waldman argued that the original argument for protecting Catholics from oppression by the Protestant majority is no longer valid and, indeed, should now be transferred to other religions.

In response, the Canadian representatives argued that the case was neither within the jurisdiction of the committee nor did it constitute a violation of Article 26. Differentiation in treatment based on reasonable and objective criteria does not amount to prohibited discrimination within the meaning of Article 2. These criteria were established at the time of confederation and were essential to bringing about the union. The Catholic system is not private but is a special component of the public system. The decision not to fund private schools in Ontario is not based on religion since non-religious private schools are also not funded. Failure to act to facilitate religious practice cannot be considered state interference with freedom of religion.

In its ruling, the committee noted that Canada did not show that the distinction made in 1867 remains valid or that Catholics are now victims of discrimination. The committee noted that the issue was not with the public system but with the exclusive nature of the Catholic system. A single secular system would not be discriminatory but, if any system based on religion is to be funded, then that funding should be available to all religions. Its final opinion was that Canada was in violation of Article 26 and was under obligation, as a party to the Human Rights Declaration, to provide a remedy that would eliminate the discrimination.[12]

The United Nations Covenant on Civil and Political Rights states that its provisions apply to all parts of federal states.[13] Nevertheless, in this case there is nothing the Government of Canada could do unilaterally because education is constitutionally within provincial jurisdiction. Even if it wished to do so, there is no way, without the consent of the affected province, for the federal government to enact legislation or change the constitution to remove the discrimination. As the Manitoba school question case showed, a province could simply ignore any federal directive on the matter.

The United Nations Human Rights Committee itself has no means of enforcement. The *Waldman* ruling has thus led to an impasse. On the one hand, Canada is obliged, by its ratification of the Covenant on Civil and Political Rights, to remedy any situation found discriminatory under the Universal Declaration on Human Rights. On the other, the federal government is powerless to act without the consent of the Government of Ontario. The issue can be resolved only by Ontario, either by removing funding for Catholic separate schools or by providing funding for schools of other religions. Up to now, successive governments in Ontario has shown no inclination to do either.

A 2017 judgment in a long-running case in Saskatchewan, commonly known as the *Theodore* case, bears on the question of how Catholic separate schools are funded. The dispute, between a public and a separate school board, involved the legality of funding for non-Catholics attending a Catholic school.[14] At issue was the decision of the public school board to close a school in a small rural community and bus its students to a more central location. The local Catholic school board decided to open a school to accommodate the small number of Catholic students in the school being closed. Many non-Catholic parents then decided to send their children to the Catholic school rather than taking a bus to the central public school. The public school board considered this to be a form of raiding, which not only undermined its decision but resulted in its per-student funding being redirected to the Catholic school. The constitutional issue at stake was whether funding for non-Catholic students attending Catholic schools is a constitutionally protected right. If not, does such funding violate Section 2 (religious freedom) or Section 15 (non-discrimination) of the Charter?

The case was recognized as not only affecting an individual school but all separate schools in Saskatchewan, Alberta, and Ontario. It is not unusual to find non-Catholic students in Catholic schools, for a variety of reasons. Disallowing funding to follow these students may be seen as a significant blow to the viability of these schools. One might argue that funding for Catholic students in public schools should offset this effect. However, the two are not parallel because Catholic students have a right to attend public schools while the opposite is not the case.

The arguments presented in the case ranged over the familiar history of religious freedom and of the rights protected under Section 93 and Term 17. It suffices to cite the main component of the trial judge's ruling. "The Constitution Act, 1867 does not provide a constitutional right to separate schools in Saskatchewan to receive provincial government funding respecting non-minority faith students because funding respecting non-minority faith students is not a denominational right of separate schools."[15] On that basis the judge also ruled that the funding of non-Catholic students in Catholic schools constitutes discrimination in violation of Sections 2 and 15 of the Charter. The sections of the Saskatchewan Education Act allowing such funding are therefore null and void.

This case caused ripples throughout Saskatchewan and beyond. The Saskatchewan premier first reacted to the ruling by declaring that the government would use the notwithstanding section (Section 33) of the Charter to nullify the court's decision. This override can extend for five years, after which it expires unless explicitly renewed. The notwithstanding section has been used rarely and only once before in education. In that case, discussed in the next chapter, Quebec used it to permit the continued existence of Catholic and Protestant schools even after it had removed the Section 93 rights of these groups.

The Saskatchewan government introduced legislation to implement its decision to use the notwithstanding section. However, that legislation was placed on hold pending the outcome of an appeal to the ruling. That judgment was rendered by the Saskatchewan Court of Appeal which overturned the trial judge's ruling.[16] On further appeal, the Supreme Court of Canada declined to hear the case, leaving the Saskatchewan Court of Appeal's ruling the final word on the constitutional issue. However, the broader question of the impact of recruitment of non-Catholic students into Catholic schools on the "catholicity" of Catholic schools remains controversial. That issue is further examined in chapter 5.

Charter Cases on Parent Rights and Religion in Schools

The *Adler* and *Waldman* cases demonstrate that the non-discriminatory provisions of the Charter cannot be used to override Section 93 rights. However, the Charter has been used in several other cases to address the broader question of the place of religion in public schools and the scope and limits of parent rights to educate their children as they see fit.

An Ontario case, known as *Zylberberg v. Sudbury Board of Education*, was an early test of the impact of the Charter on religious exercises in schools. Zylberberg, a Jewish parent, challenged the requirement that schools under the Sudbury (Public) Board of Education open each day with specified religious exercises. This was based on an Ontario regulation which stated: "A public school shall be opened or closed each school day with religious exercises consisting of the reading of the Scriptures or other suitable readings and the repeating of the Lord's Prayer or other suitable prayers."[17] Interestingly, this requirement reflects a Christian and, more specifically, Protestant bias that continues to exist in some public schools, even in the face of the much greater religious diversity of the Canadian population.

The case was heard in the Ontario Divisional Court in July 1986.[18] Two of the three judges dismissed the complaint. Both argued that the regulation did not compel anyone to participate. Any pressure to participate to avoid embarrassment is a minor infringement and thus a reasonable limitation of religious freedom under Section 1 of the Charter. One judge went as far as to argue that schools have an obligation to teach morality and that associating morality with God is a reasonable way to do this. The dissenting judge took the opposite stance: that any law requiring performance of religious exercises is an infringement on religious freedom even if it conforms to a person's own religion. On appeal, a five-judge panel of the Ontario Court of Appeal[19] overturned the original decision. The majority held that requiring a Christian prayer and Christian reading constitutes obvious discrimination against both people of other religions and non-believers. The right to claim exemption does not save the regulation because the regulation imposes a bias towards participation.

The *Zylberberg* decision was not appealed to the Supreme Court of Canada. The case has been widely cited in similar cases in both Ontario and other jurisdictions and serves as a landmark case on the impact of the Charter on religious activities in public institutions. By inference, it also shows that, in the absence of constitutional protections for separate schools, many of the practices found in these schools would be disallowed.

The *Zylberberg* ruling effectively prohibits the state from mandating religious exercises in public schools. However, other cases have served to expand the scope of individual religious practices in school settings. Perhaps the best known is *Multani v. Commission scolaire Marguerite-Bourgeoys*, commonly referred to as the kirpan case.[20] In that case, the parent, a member of the Sikh religion, challenged the school board's prohibition on his son's wearing of the Sikh ceremonial dagger. The board held that the kirpan is a weapon and refused to accept a compromise allowing it to be worn if sewn into the student's clothing. The parent then took the case to the Quebec Superior Court, alleging that the ban infringed on his religious freedom. That court overturned the ban, arguing that the kirpan is a non-trivial symbol of the Sikh faith, that its status is not the same as that of a knife or other weapon and that it posed virtually no danger. However, the court held that it must be secured to clothing in a way that removed any possibility of its use. The Quebec Court of Appeal overturned that decision, arguing that, although religious freedom was infringed, the ban on wearing the kirpan was reasonable under Section 1 of the Charter.[21]

This led the parent to further appeal to the Supreme Court of Canada.[22] That court agreed that the issue at hand was whether an infringement of religious freedom had occurred and, if so, whether it was reasonable under Section 1 of the Charter. In ruling that the prohibition on the kirpan was excessive, the majority held that schools allow other instruments such as scissors and baseball bats that could also be used as weapons even though that is not their intended use. The same argument could be made for the kirpan. In any event, the Charter provision on religious freedom overrides any minor risk posed by the kirpan. The court ruled that Section 1 of the Charter did not apply, and the ban was therefore declared null and void.

In a 2012 case, two Catholic parents, identified as S. L. and D. J. requested exemption from the Quebec Ethics, Religion and Culture course on the grounds that this course infringed their right to religious freedom. Specifically, the parents argued that the course promotes a relativistic view of religion, interfering with their right to pass on their Catholic faith to their children. The school board denied the request for exemption. The parents took their case to the Quebec Superior Court, which dismissed the parents' case. The Quebec Court of Appeal declined to hear an appeal.

The case then went to the Supreme Court of Canada. In their ruling, the justices argued that the sincerity of parents' belief, in itself, does not constitute grounds for a claim of infringement of rights. Exposing children to a variety of religions reflects the reality of a multicultural Canada from which children should not be sheltered. Presenting this reality is seen as part of the Quebec government's obligation with respect to public education. Parents remain free to transmit their own religious beliefs. The Supreme Court thus dismissed the parents' claim.[23]

Two other recent cases bear on the question of the limits of parental rights in education. In Ontario, a parent referred to as E. T., a member of the Greek Orthodox Church, requested that the Ontario Superior Court issue an order declaring the parent to be the final authority over the education of his children.[24] The applicant also sought an order that the parent be permitted to withdraw his children from lessons that conflicted with his religious beliefs. The applicant claimed that the absence of such accommodation violated his right to religious freedom and, more specifically, to the right to protect his children from false teachings.

The applicant presented a long list of topics in the school curriculum that he claimed were false teachings. Most of these were around sexual behaviour, but also included environmentalism, secular humanism, and values-neutral education. In dismissing the request for accommodation, the judge argued that the weight of legislation and judicial decisions favour inclusion over exclusion and that exposure of children to a variety of views is an essential component of education in a diverse society. The conclusion was that the applicant's desire for accommodation does not override other values conveyed by an inclusive school system. The judge also concluded that the substance of the case did not require a declaration that parental rights are paramount.

In *Bonitto v. Halifax Regional School Board*[25] a fundamentalist Christian parent sued the school board over its decision to prevent him from distributing religious literature on school property during school hours. According to court documents, the message being distributed was stark: anyone who does not accept Christ will go to hell. The parent held that the board's decision infringed on his Charter right to freedom of religious expression. In dismissing the plaintiff's application, the trial judge concluded that the infringement on the right of non-Christian students to be free of extreme Christian indoctrination outweighed the appellant's right to disseminate his own beliefs. The judge also held that the school is not a public place subject to constitutional protection of freedom of expression. On appeal to the Nova Scotia Court of Appeal, that tribunal unanimously agreed with all aspects of the trial judge's ruling.[26]

Some recent events in Alberta more directly illustrate the lingering effect of Christian religion in public schools. In 2011, the principal of Sturgeon Heights School in St. Albert suspended the traditional recitation of the Lord's Prayer after a complaint from a parent. The same thing happened at schools in Taber in 2013 and Busby in 2015. Section 50(1) (b) of the Alberta School Act in effect at the time explicitly allowed boards to "prescribe religious exercises for its students."[27] The *Zylberberg* case would appear to have established that this section is unconstitutional. The Supreme Court has also ruled that allowing students to sit out such exercises is not a sufficient remedy. On the other hand, Section 137 (2) of the 1901 Ordinance of the Northwest Territories, which defines the system in place at confederation, did explicitly allow "the board of any district to direct that the school be opened by the recitation of the Lord's Prayer."[28] It may thus be argued that this recitation is one of the areas protected under Section 17. A new Education Act, first passed in 2014 but not proclaimed until 2019, retains a similar provision. As far as can be determined, that provision has not been tested in court.

Another Alberta case gives some guidance on the limits on what can be done in private schools. In 1986, Thomas Larry Jones, pastor of a fundamentalist Christian church, refused to send his children to public schools, choosing instead to teach them and others in the church basement. The Alberta School Act allows an exemption for those attending a private school or engaged in home schooling. However, this requires certification by appropriate school board authorities that the standard of education being provided is equivalent to that in public schools. Jones refused to apply for the exemption and was consequently charged with truancy.

Jones argued that God, not the state, has final authority over the education of his children and that the sections of the School Act on exemptions and truancy violated his Charter right to freedom of religion—specifically, his right to educate his children as he pleased. The trial judge ruled in Jones's favour. However, the Alberta Court of Appeal reversed this decision, leading Jones to further appeal to the Supreme Court.

The Supreme Court agreed with the Alberta Court of Appeal and dismissed the case.[29] The majority argued that even if Section 7 of the Charter does include the right of parents to educate their children as they see fit, the School Act does not deprive them of that right. The act establishes a standard for education that school boards are delegated to enforce and that parents should be required to meet even if they decide to use an alternative to the public schools.

The most far-reaching feature of this decision is that the Supreme Court appears to be saying that the right of parents to educate their children as they see fit is not infringed by the existence of compulsory state standards. Since these are the very standards to which some parents object, the decision seems to say that parent rights are both absolute and limited. While these two views seem contradictory, this reasoning is consistent with the Universal Declaration on Human Rights and the Convention on the Rights of the Child, where the first section seems to say that parental rights are absolute but the second identifies some elements of education that, presumably, parents would not be permitted to override.

A second case of interest is that of *Loyola High School v. The Attorney General of Quebec*.[30] Loyola is a private English Catholic school in Montréal operated by the Jesuit Order. In 2010, the Quebec minister of education denied a request from the school for an exemption to allow it to teach Quebec's mandatory Ethics and Religious Culture (ERC) course from a Catholic perspective. This led Loyola and John Zucchi, the parent of a child at that school, to apply to the Quebec Superior Court to have the denial quashed. The appellants argued that the denial violated Section 2(a) of the Charter of Rights and Freedoms and of Section 3 of the Quebec Charter of Human Rights and Freedoms. This made the issue a matter of constitutional law.

The trial judge concluded that most of the reasons given by the minister in support of the decision were erroneous. The decision was therefore quashed on administrative grounds. However, the constitutional question was more far-reaching. It asked whether the minister's denial amounted to religious discrimination under either the Canadian or the Quebec Charters. The judge held that, as a corporation, Loyola was a legal person and could claim religious discrimination in the same manner as an individual. He also noted that the concept of prior right of parents is embedded in An Act respecting the Ministère de l'Éducation, du Loisir et du Sport. The judge held that the minister's decision placed Loyola in an untenable position. Either it had to teach its own program in violation of the act or teach the provincial ERC in violation of the teachings of the Catholic church. In requiring the latter, the minister was judged to be in violation of the school's freedom of religion under the Quebec Charter.

The attorney general of Quebec then took the case to the Quebec Court of Appeal. In December 2012, the appeal court overruled the decision holding that, in substituting his judgment for that of the minister, the trial judge had erred in overturning a legitimate exercise of ministerial discretion. The court did not take a definitive stance on the constitutional issue. However, it allowed the appeal on the grounds that the minister's decision was reasonable and did not require judicial intervention.[31]

The school then appealed to the Supreme Court of Canada. That case was decided in March 2015.[32] The majority held that the minister was not required to permit Loyola to teach about other religions from a Catholic perspective. To do so would require that other religions be seen as legitimate only to the extent that they are aligned with the tenets of Catholicism. On the other hand, preventing the school from teaching Catholicism from its own perspective does amount to a serious interference with religious freedom, while doing little to advance the state's interest in religious neutrality. The minister's decision must reflect a delicate balance between objectives of the state and the constitutional right to freedom of religion. In the court's view, that balance had not been achieved. The result was therefore a unanimous decision to allow the appeal and to order the minister to grant an exemption based on a compromise proposal presented by the school, whereby it would supplement the ERC course with material taught from a Catholic perspective.

That decision has been widely interpreted as one that strongly upholds the constitutional right of freedom of religion on the part of an institution with a religious focus. In fact, the decision was more nuanced. It actually set limits to the right of a school to follow its own religious path to the exclusion of other religions or contrary to the interest of the state in promoting a diverse society. Loyola was not given carte blanche to teach a mandated course solely from a Catholic perspective. The ruling suggests that freedom of religion is limited if exercised in a way that is discriminatory towards other religions.

On the surface, it might appear that the *Jones* and *Loyola* cases yield contradictory conclusions, with the first restricting parent rights to operate a private religious school and the second extending these rights in an established private school. However, the latter point defines the difference between the two cases. As a long-established school, Loyola presumably met ministry requirements for private schools, with the one exception of its non-compliance with the mandated ERC course. The *Loyola* ruling was much narrower than the *Jones* ruling, involving only the teaching of a specific course. Nevertheless, had the school not agreed to a compromise it might have had to make the difficult decision of whether to conform to ministry requirements or close.

One Charter case from New Brunswick is relevant to the broader issue of religion in schools.[33] In 1988, a Jewish parent complained to the New Brunswick Human Rights Board of Inquiry that a teacher, Malcolm Ross, had made derogatory comments about Jewish people during his off-duty time. The school board reprimanded Mr. Ross but took no other action. After contradictory rulings by the board of inquiry and the New Brunswick courts, the case reached the Supreme Court of Canada. Specifically, the issue before the court was the application of Sections 2 and 1 of the Charter. The court held that the original board of inquiry order violated Section 2, which protects Ross's writings and statements and his freedom of religion, which includes the right to criticize other religions. On the other hand, the court argued that the teacher's actions were discriminatory against Jews and created an atmosphere in the community that undermined his ability to perform his duties as a teacher. Evaluation of a teacher's conduct must be based on his position rather than on whether the conduct occurs inside or outside the classroom. Mr. Ross remained free to express his views but not within the limits of his duties as a teacher.[34]

Lessons from the Charter Cases

What lessons are to be learned from these Charter cases? First, it is clear from the *Adler* case that the non-discrimination provisions of the Charter cannot be used as a vehicle to challenge the existence of the primarily Catholic sectarian schools that are protected by Section 93 and its variants. The Supreme Court has made it clear that one constitutional provision cannot override another, even if the two are contradictory. Section 29 of the Charter makes it abundantly clear that the framers of the 1982 constitution wanted it that way. This has given the courts no discretion in this matter even as they have gradually expanded the scope of the non-discrimination provisions of the Charter, not only on issues of religion but also into non-stated areas such as homosexuality and same-sex marriage.

The second lesson is that the courts have taken an expansive view of individual religious freedom, including the right to individual religious expression in schools. However, they have taken the opposite stand on institutional expressions of religion such as opening prayers or religious exercises. Courts have even held that allowing exemptions from such activities is an insufficient remedy because their very existence amounts to pressure to participate. These decisions make it clear that, without the confederation era constitutional protections, reinforced by Section 29 of the Charter, any system of de facto sectarianism carried forward from the nineteenth century could not be maintained. The effect is to create two contradictory classes of public education systems in Canada, whereby sectarian schools are constitutionally protected in some provinces and constitutionally prohibited in others.

The third lesson relates to parent rights. The *Jones* case established that parents cannot use a religious freedom argument to claim an absolute right to educate their children as they see fit. In fact, parent rights may be substantially constrained by the state's authority to establish programs and standards. The same may be said about the two cases involving the Quebec Ethics, Religion and Culture Course. The Supreme Court has clearly held that the existence of a state-regulated system of education does not interfere with the ability of parents to convey their own religious beliefs to their children. The state has a right to set educational standards and to develop means for their enforcement. It also has a right to include in the school curriculum a course that treats religion as an academic subject and presents religion in a comparative manner. There are compelling reasons for the state to determine school programs and to ensure that all students follow these programs.

Although the question of parent choice is not entirely a matter of religion, the court cases illustrate that the conflict between parents and the state and the assertion of parent rights often centre on religion or on areas closely linked to religion. The issue of separate schools or other accommodations for religious groups has often been framed in terms of parent choice. Indeed, even the Catholic church has used that argument in defence of its own school system, despite its historic insistence that the church itself is the primary authority in education. The question to be addressed here is whether, and to what extent, parent choice in areas that impinge on religion should be respected and accommodated. While the court cases have settled some specific points, the courts have been constrained by Section 93 and Section 29 of the Charter from taking a more comprehensive view of the issue.

The fundamental contraction between Charter Section 29, on the one hand, and the non-discrimination provisions of the Charter, on the other, remains. This cannot be resolved by the courts. Many would argue that it is better to leave well enough alone and that philosophical consistency is not an absolute requirement in designing a school system, or even a constitution, as long as most people are well served by the system. On the other hand, controversy over sectarian education has never gone away in provinces where separate schools continue to exist. Controversy has ended only where no such schools existed at confederation and, importantly, in the two provinces where constitutional action has put an end to such schools. There is no evidence of any substantial effort to restore sectarian schools where they have been abolished. The reality is that only political action, including constitutional amendment if needed, can put the matter to rest. The next chapter describes how two provinces were led to take just that action.

CHAPTER 4

Constitutional Amendment: Newfoundland and Quebec

The previous chapter has shown that the Charter has had considerable impact on how religion is treated in public schools. However, it has had virtually no impact on the core structure of denominational education. The Supreme Court has made it clear that one section of the constitution cannot be used to override another, even if the sections are mutually contradictory. Resolving such contradictions is a political and not a judicial matter. Since the constitutional battles of the 1980s, neither federal nor provincial political leaders have shown any inclination to reopen the constitution to resolve this or any other issues left over from the patriation effort.

That is not to say that nothing can be done, however. Where the Charter has failed, the amending formula has presented an opportunity for change that few might have foreseen at the time. To understand how this has come about, it is important to point out that the amending formula was originally intended to put an end to the need to petition the Parliament of the United Kingdom for any change in the Canadian constitution. Although there was no disagreement on the goal, the structure of the amending formula was the subject of much debate during the patriation negotiations. This centred largely around the degree of consensus among the federal government and the provinces required for any amendment to take place.

The eventual compromise led to a three-part formula. Some issues, such as those affecting the Crown or the composition of the

Supreme Court, require unanimous consent of the federal government and the provinces. Most other issues require consent of the federal government and seven provinces representing at least 50 percent of the population. Finally, of most relevance here, the third part, embodied in Section 43, permits amendment with the consent of the federal government and any one province if the issue affects that province alone.

Prior to the Newfoundland and Quebec amendments discussed in this chapter, Section 43 was used on several occasions—for example, to declare New Brunswick a bilingual province and to allow construction of a bridge to Prince Edward Island replacing the constitutional requirement for the federal government to maintain a ferry service. More important for this discussion was its use to extend constitutional protections to schools of the Pentecostal Assemblies of Newfoundland. There is some irony in the fact that the Pentecostal amendment established a precedent for the more far-reaching changes in the opposite direction that are described here.

Newfoundland

By the late 1980s, denominational education was more firmly entrenched in Newfoundland than anywhere else in Canada. The Pentecostal constitutional amendment had just been passed with little debate. On the surface, things seemed calm and stable. However, underneath, fissures in the system were becoming ever more visible. Galway and Dibbon used the metaphor of "the perfect storm"[1] to describe a confluence of factors that prevailed in the early 1990s. These included out-migration, enrolment decline, the perilous state of the province's finances, low achievement, poor infrastructure, diminished church power, and loss of faith in denominational education. In particular, the Catholic church had been weakened by a series of scandals. A commission of inquiry documented the systemic nature of the abuses and the failure of the church hierarchy to hold those responsible to account.[2] The reputation of the church leadership had been severely compromised, and the archbishop of St. John's was forced to resign. Consequently, the Catholic hierarchy could no longer exert the level of political influence it had in the past. In addition, organizations such as the Newfoundland and Labrador Teachers' Association, the Newfoundland and Labrador Human Rights Association, the media, and a royal commission on employment and unemployment[3] had begun to add voices critical of denominational education.

In 1989 a Liberal government was elected. The new premier, Clyde Wells, was a prominent lawyer with expertise in constitutional matters. Indeed, one of the first acts of the Wells government was to rescind the approval given by the previous Progressive Conservative government to the Charlottetown Accord that had been designed to bring Quebec on side to the 1982 constitution. That action was a major contributor to the failure of that accord.

The new cabinet included several individuals with backgrounds in education and with intimate knowledge of the denominational system. Several of the ministers were on record as opposing that system. Philip Warren, chair of the 1968 royal commission, became the new minister of education. All this set the stage for a dramatic change of tone towards denominational control of education.

In 1990 a second royal commission was appointed, chaired by Leonard Williams of the Faculty of Education at Memorial University. Like most previous inquiries throughout Canada, the Williams Commission received many submissions centred on the denominational issue, most complaining about perceived waste and duplication. The commission also conducted a poll which found that a large proportion of the population favoured a single public system. It was clear from this that the commission would have to confront this issue directly.

The commission's 1992 report[4] outlined a comprehensive plan of reform, including changes to the denominational structure. Despite the constitutional barriers, the commission concluded that significant structural reform was necessary to achieve the broader end of improving student learning. After examining several options, the commission adopted a model embodied in the following statement: "modifying the existing denominational education system to retain denominational characteristics but including these groups/individuals not presently served in the governance of schools."[5]

The first recommendation of the commission limited the scope of this model by stating that the system should continue to be based on Judeo-Christian principles.[6] However, a second recommendation provided for religious activities and instruction in a student's own religion, where numbers warrant, and proposed that the school system should be responsive to children of all religious groups.[7]

The commission recommended that all existing school boards be dissolved and replaced by new regional boards elected on a non-exclusive and non-denominational basis. It also recommended that a joint body of the denominations and the Department of Education be responsible for advising the government on matters affecting the rights of denominations. It further recommended that the primary role of churches be to develop and deliver religious education programs and pastoral care.

Although the commission did not say so directly, these recommendations amounted to almost a complete abrogation of traditional denominational rights. The commission sought a legal opinion, which concluded that many of the commission's recommendations, however desirable they might be, would not pass a constitutional test. Crucially, it also pointed out that Section 43 of the amending formula could be invoked if necessary.[8]

Following release of the commission report, the government attempted to engage the churches on how to bring about reform. The government's main goal was to persuade the churches voluntarily to accept the commission's model rather than force the issue through constitutional amendment. The government took a second electoral win in May 1993 as a mandate to reform education along the lines of the commission report. The new minister of education, Chris Decker, a former United Church minister and school board chair, was an avowed opponent of the denominational system. Premier Wells, an Anglican and churchman by his own admission, remained somewhat more deferential to church leaders and continued to hold the belief that some type of compromise was possible.

Thus began more than two years of negotiations. Because of their constitutional status, the government accepted the church leaders as equals in the negotiations. A committee of principals was formed, composed of leaders of the seven denominations with recognized rights on one side and government, represented by the premier and a cabinet committee, on the other. Anglican, United Church, and Salvation Army had to be separately represented as they had not abrogated their individual rights after the 1968 integration agreement. Catholics and Pentecostals also had a place, the latter by virtue of the 1987 constitutional amendment. Seventh Day Adventists and Presbyterians were also rights holders, even though the former had only three schools and the latter none.

From the beginning, it was recognized that implementing some of the commission's recommendations would result in violation of one or more of the established denominational rights. The government held to the position that it preferred a negotiated arrangement and was not actively seeking constitutional change.[9] In practice, the government would likely have been satisfied with an expansion of the existing integrated system to include all denominations, appropriate provision for non-adherents to be represented on school boards, and the right of other religions to gain access to schools for religious exercises and observances. In effect, this would have created a system of inter-denominational schools, allowing the churches to retain their constitutional rights but place most of these in abeyance in the interest of creating a fully integrated system. All this implies that the government's position was pragmatic, not ideological. Its position was driven primarily by issues of cost and efficiency rather than by the more fundamental human rights issues embodied in the Charter.

Church representatives initially agreed to reduce the number of school boards but proposed that denominational authorities be established within each board, with responsibility for all the protected areas. A provincial denominational committee structure would also be retained. A joint advisory committee on school construction was proposed, but denominational authority over school construction would have to be maintained.[10]

Government immediately rejected this model as simply transferring the exercise of denominational rights to sub-units within school boards, which would function independently of the full board in many critical areas. The model was also criticized as focusing entirely on denominational rights and not on teaching and learning or on improved efficiency. Given the polling data available, it was also clear that the model would be unlikely to meet public approval.

The government response, entitled *Adjusting the Course: Restructuring the School System for Educational Excellence*[11] was released in November 1993. This model admitted that structural change could not guarantee improved student learning. Nevertheless, it made the case that structural change was a necessary precursor because that was the only way in which resources might be found to support greater attention to teaching and learning. The goal was to shift the emphasis from governance as an end to governance as the means to an end.

The government's model proposed eight to ten school boards each with ten members elected at large plus one representative from each denomination where numbers warrant. Denominational functions within each board would be limited to religious education and pastoral care. All new schools would be interdenominational. However, a few single denomination schools could continue to exist where viable and non-overlapping. Parents would be free to choose schools, subject to proximity and family history with the school.

Release of this model shifted the focus from government accommodation of denominational rights to denominational accommodation of structural change. Church response to this document brought to the fore important differences between the integrated churches, on the one hand, and the Catholics and Pentecostals on the other. The integrated group was prepared to participate in a system where rights were diminished and exercised collectively by all denominations. However, Catholics and Pentecostals continued to assert their right to independently control those areas within their defined rights. The integrated churches were clear that they had no wish to turn their own system into a non-denominational public system if the other two groups were allowed to remain separate.

The issue dragged on for more than another year, all through 1994 and into 1995. From the perspective of the government, it was envisaged that very few denominational schools would remain initially, and all would eventually disappear by the provision that all new schools would be interdenominational. However, Catholic and Pentecostal leaders continued to hold that most schools would have to remain single denominational. Interdenominational schools could only exist by individual agreements among the denominations.

In the end, it became clear that the gap was too wide to bridge. The churches took the position that their rights were absolute and could not be diluted by any considerations of cost or efficiency. The churches were in possession of a legal opinion that reiterated their strong constitutional position. It appears that they also interpreted the earlier statement by the premier that government was not seeking constitutional change as implying that it would never take that action.

While this was going on, the small francophone population of the province launched a claim to have its own school board. Constitutional rights to education in the minority official language had been enshrined in Section 23 of the Charter, subject to a "where numbers warrant" provision. Courts had repeatedly taken the position that even very small numbers would meet that test. The Newfoundland government was thus faced with the dilemma of trying to navigate a constitutional barrier to integrating its denominational schools while under a constitutional requirement to further divide the school system along language lines.

It was clear that any attempt to avoid establishing a francophone school board would face a strong challenge because language rights apply to all provinces and could not be changed through a Section 43 amendment. Rather than face a losing court battle on language rights, the government decided to grant the francophone population its own school board. That decision was not lost on the denominations who could argue, quite accurately, that government was treating one set of constitutional rights as superior to another, while also contradicting its own desire for a more unified system.

As all this was unfolding, a new poll was designed to measure more accurately than before the views of adherents of the individual denominations.[12] The results reinforced those of earlier polls showing that most people wanted to retain some religious presence in education. However, a large majority across all denominations, except for Pentecostal adherents who were divided on the issue, rejected church control over most of the very specifics—control of school boards, student admissions, teacher employment, and school construction, which formed the basis of denominational rights. This raised further questions about the extent to which the church leaders were actually speaking for their adherents.

By mid-1995 it had become clear that no agreement could be reached with the Roman Catholic and Pentecostal representatives. On June 1, 1995, the premier announced to the public that an impasse had been reached and that government intended to invoke Section 43 of the amending formula to implement a revision to Term 17. He also announced that the proposal would be put to the people in a referendum. This set in motion a new chain of events that, from a constitutional perspective, were the most crucial of all. The actions taken over the next three years served as a precedent for parallel action in Quebec. These actions will also almost certainly form the basis for any future changes to sectarian education in other provinces.

The polling results indicated that the preferred route was to allow the denominations to retain responsibility for religious education only. However, having offered the churches the ability to retain some single denominational schools, the government decided not to backtrack from that offer. The result was a fairly complex redraft of Term 17. The core of the proposal was that some denominational schools would remain, based on parent choice, and the denominations would continue to be allowed to elect two-thirds of school board members with a breakdown proportionate to denominational populations.[13]

The referendum date was set for September 5, 1995. The specific referendum question was: "Do you support revising Term 17 in the manner proposed by the government, to enable reform of the denominational education system?" The referendum question did not explicitly explain the government's proposal. That could be found only through reading a separate fairly complex document, circulated to all households, containing the old and new versions of Term 17 and an explanation for the change.

One of the criticisms of the referendum question was that a "No" vote could be triggered by religious conviction without reference to the details, while a "Yes" vote required an understanding of the detailed proposal. In some ways, therefore, the question was biased against the government's position. Indeed, the government took the position that it would not be appropriate for it to mount any election-style campaign to influence the result. On the other hand, the Catholic and Pentecostal denominations mounted a vigorous "No" campaign, hiring professional political strategists, placing advertisements, and engaging in a concerted effort to get out the vote, including bussing large numbers of supporters to polling stations. In the end, despite this effort, the "Yes" side prevailed, with a majority of 55 percent on a turnout of 52 percent of the electorate.

Although this was a clear majority, the result raised the issue of the denominational breakdown of the vote. This was significant because the churches held that their rights could be abrogated only by majority approval within each denomination. That could not be determined from the individual ballots. However, an analysis by electoral district indicated that most districts with large proportions of Catholic and Pentecostal voters gave a majority vote. In districts around St. John's, where Catholics represented a majority or near-majority, the "Yes" vote was substantially larger than for the whole province. Only a few rural districts with large majority Catholic populations showed a majority "No" vote. The status of the Pentecostal vote was difficult to determine because of the scattered nature of that population.

These factors were sufficient to convince the government that the referendum gave it a mandate to seek the Term 17 change. Accordingly, a resolution was introduced in the House of Assembly on October 16, 1995, requesting the federal government to amend Term 17 of the Terms of Union of Newfoundland with Canada, as provided for under Section 43 of the Constitution Act, 1982.

Debate on the resolution was wide-ranging. Issues included fundamental constitutional principles such as protection of minorities, the idea that further negotiations might have led to a settlement, and concerns about the possible fate of individual schools in members' districts under the proposed new regime. On October 31, 1995, in a free vote, the House approved the resolution by a vote of 31–20. The vote was mainly along party lines, with a few dissenters from both main parties.[14] The leaders of both opposition parties voted in favour of the resolution. Indeed, the leader of the Progressive Conservative opposition was on record as believing that the amendment did not go far enough in diminishing denominational rights.

This placed the matter in the hands of the federal government. Despite, or perhaps because of, substantial lobbying on both sides over the next few months, the House of Commons took no immediate action on the issue. It was only after a motion urging the federal government to get on with the matter passed unanimously in the Newfoundland House of Assembly that the resolution was introduced in the House of Commons in May 1996.[15]

The Minister of Justice, Alan Rock, summarized the issues related to the federal role in constitutional amendment. These included the living tree constitutional doctrine, precedents for Section 43 amendments, the uniqueness of the Newfoundland situation, and whether this might establish a precedent for action by other provinces. He also argued that, even though Section 43 was applicable in this case, the federal role extends beyond merely acceding to the province's request but includes an obligation to be satisfied that the province had followed appropriate process leading up to the resolution.

During the debate, Newfoundland found an unlikely ally in the federal official opposition, which at the time happened to be the Bloc Québécois, a Quebec sovereignist party. Bloc members supported the amendment on the grounds that provincial rights in education are paramount. Ever alert to any implications for Quebec, they argued that the referendum result could be seen as precedent for future referendums on Quebec denominational versus language rights or even on Quebec independence.

On the issue of minority rights, Newfoundland argued that the denominations holding Term 17 rights represented 95 percent of the population and hence could not be seen as a minority in need of protection. The counter-argument was that each denomination, taken separately, did constitute a minority. Such an argument could be construed as implying that even the smallest denomination held a veto over change since none was willing to relinquish rights unless all others also did so.

It was not lost on some that Newfoundland was reversing its own previous position, having successfully sought a constitutional amendment as recently as 1987 adding the Pentecostal denomination to the list of constitutionally protected groups. While this fact could not be refuted, a plausible counter-argument was that the proposal at hand was the result of much more extensive consultation, including a royal commission and a referendum. Nevertheless, the fact that seemingly contradictory amendments could be advanced within a short time does appear to conflict with the idea that the constitution should be broad statement of societal values and not something that should be changed at the whim of a particular government. In retrospect, a case could be made that the 1987 amendment had been ill-advised in relation to the Charter because it did not extend rights to all religions.

In the end, the House of Commons approved the original resolution by a free vote of 170–46. That sent the issue to the Senate, where the debate became much more intense. It was clear that a majority in the Senate saw that body as the last guardian of minority rights. The key issue again was whether each denomination should be treated as a minority or whether the rights were held collectively, making the rights holders a large majority of the population. The Senate Committee on Legal and Constitutional Affairs conducted research and public hearings on the issue, calling representatives of the main stakeholders, as well as expert witnesses on the constitutional issues at stake. The testimony of the leader of the opposition in Newfoundland, Loyola Sullivan, was among the most dramatic. He pointed out that he represented a district that was 97 percent Catholic and that he, himself, was a former teacher in the Catholic system. Nevertheless, in the 1996 election campaign he had heard almost nothing from his constituents on the issue. He had concluded from this that, even in such a staunchly Catholic area of the province, there was widespread support for the change, and certainly little grass-roots opposition. In his view, the 1996 election, rather than the 1995 referendum, was the more definitive indicator of widespread support for the constitutional amendment.

There was unanimous agreement among the expert witnesses that Section 43 was the appropriate amending mechanism and that passing the amendment would not likely set precedent affecting minority rights in general. Some spoke to the right of the Senate to accept, reject, or amend the resolution and, more broadly, of its role as protector of provincial rights. However, caution and deference to the primacy of the elected bodies in such matters was urged.

The question of the living tree versus originalist interpretations of the constitution was also raised in the debate. On the one hand was the argument that the constitution must be interpreted, and amended, if necessary, to reflect changing societal conditions. On the other hand, it could be argued that a main function of a constitution is to protect minority rights and to guard against the tyranny of the majority. Even a living tree interpretation of the constitution could not easily be construed as allowing rapid reversal of constitutional provisions, as was the case here.

It is fair to observe that the final report of the Senate committee[16] is one of the most thoroughly documented summaries of the issue. In the end, a majority of the committee concluded that the religions involved would not be oppressed by the amendment and that the amendment would not have a significant impact on other minorities such as Francophones. The majority also supported the living tree doctrine that provisions of the constitution should be flexible and open to change to reflect changing circumstances. The majority recommendation was therefore that the proposed amendment be adopted without change. A minority, comprising the Progressive Conservative members of the committee, issued a dissenting report. That group was more skeptical about the need for constitutional amendment to achieve the desired goal.

The committee report was tabled in the Senate on September 24, 1996.[17] The lengthy debate that followed, extending through October and November, added little of substance to the issue. Parallels were drawn between this case and the federal role in the Manitoba school question, which had caused such great division a century earlier. In the end, almost nobody's mind was changed by the debate. The main motion to adopt the report of the committee, with two minor amendments proposed by the minority on the committee, was approved by a 46–35 vote. This sent the matter back to the House of Commons. The Commons debate on December 2 and 4, 1996, was brief. The Senate amendments were rejected almost unanimously, and the proposal as originally formulated passed on December 4 by a 172–42 margin.

More than a year had passed from the time the proposed amendment was approved by the Newfoundland legislature to its final passage. In the interim, events were unfolding rapidly within the province in a direction that would take the issue on a new and even more radical path. In anticipation of the amendment, legislation to implement the reforms had been prepared. As soon as the Senate committee report was submitted, a revision of two acts, the Education Act and the Schools Act, were introduced at a rare summer session of the Newfoundland legislature in July 1996.

The Education Act[18] outlined the main structural features of the new system. These included a denominational education commission with responsibility for exercising the religious education rights allowed under the Term 17 amendment. The Schools Act[19] was much more comprehensive, addressing students, parents, schools, and school boards. As required by the amendment, some denominational schools were allowed, based on parent registrations. In an almost unprecedented move, both acts were approved unanimously by the House of Assembly on July 25, 1996. However, since the Senate was still working on the matter, no action could be taken to implement the reforms in time for the 1996–1997 school year.

It was expected that some of the parties might mount a court challenge, based on the argument that Section 43 was not applicable because the issue might affect other provinces. When it did come, however, the legal challenge was not on the constitutional issue itself but on the way in which the province chose to implement the student registration process for single denominational schools. Directives issued by the minister of education had established strict limitations on the conditions under which single denominational schools could be established. Specifically, boards were under no obligation to provide single denominational schools should this lead to inefficiencies in use of school facilities or in transportation.

Following some litigation around the closing of individual schools, a more comprehensive challenge was initiated by groups of parents representing the Catholic and Pentecostal faiths. The essence of the complaint was that the act was being interpreted in such a restrictive way as to express a preference for interdenominational schools in violation of the rights given under the new Term 17. The appellants argued that the default option of all new schools being interdenominational amounted to a bias in favour of such schools. Determining that there was a high probability that some sections of the act could be declared unconstitutional under the new Term 17, the court issued an injunction halting the closure of Catholic or Pentecostal schools where such schools were viable.[20]

The decision seemed to leave the government with two choices: either rewrite the impugned sections of the Schools Act or allow the matter to go to trial on the constitutionality of these sections. The first could be done quickly but would change the intent of the act while giving no guarantee against future court challenges. The second could take considerable time, during which the new boards would have limited power to include existing Catholic and Pentecostal schools in their consolidation plans.

Despite the legal setback, government took the view that it was in a strong position, given the unanimous approval of the Schools Act by the House of Assembly, the election result, and clear public sentiment in favour of limiting denominational rights. Even before the 1995 referendum, some had urged the government to reflect this sentiment by rewriting Term 17 in a simple manner, allowing the churches limited right of access to schools for religious education. The main reason this was not done was that Premier Wells was unwilling to backtrack from undertakings his government had given the churches during the original negotiations. The new premier, Brian Tobin, had no such reservations. Polling clearly indicated little support for denominational rights beyond religious education and showed opposition to almost all the original Term 17 powers of the denominations over school boards, schools, and teachers.

Despite the risks inherent in having to make a further appeal to both the people and the federal government, the government decided that its goals for the school system could only be protected from constitutional challenge by yet another amendment to Term 17. A second referendum was called for September 2, 1997, almost exactly two years from the first. This time the issue was much more straightforward. Instead of asking for approval of a complex revision to Term 17, the referendum question was: "Do you support a single school system where all children, regardless of their religious affiliation, attend the same schools, where opportunities for religious education and observances are provided?"

Whether the Catholic and Pentecostal church authorities were by then weary of the protracted conflict or whether they concluded that their cause was now lost, there was no campaign for the "No" side on the scale waged in the first referendum. The momentum was now on the side of the government. The second referendum yielded a much stronger "Yes" majority than the first one, at 73 percent of the vote, on a turnout of 53 percent, about the same as in the 1995 referendum.

On September 4, 1997, the premier called a special session of the House of Assembly to introduce a motion to repeal the version of Term 17, approved just a few months earlier, and replace it with the following:

> 17. (1) In lieu of section ninety-three of the Constitution Act, 1867, this Term shall apply in respect of the Province of Newfoundland and Labrador:
> (2) In and for the Province of Newfoundland and Labrador, the Legislature shall have exclusive authority to make laws in relation to education but shall provide for courses in religion that are not specific to a religious denomination.
> (3) Religious observances shall be permitted in a school where requested by parents.[21]

The first part of this proposition clearly removed any vestige of denominational control of the school system. The second part reinforced the first in that demand for religious observances was placed in the hands of parents rather than church authorities. This proposition also finally addressed, at least indirectly, the issue of accommodating denominations other than those holding Term 17 rights. Any group of parents could, under this proposal, request access for religious observances and the school would be obliged to comply.

On this occasion, even those who opposed the proposition had to concede that the vote was overwhelming, even in districts with strong Catholic or Pentecostal populations. Those who had argued that the previous revision did not go far enough felt vindicated. Leaders of all parties supported the new proposal. Premier Tobin took pains to acknowledge the sincerity of those who took the "No" side and the civility of the public debate, expressing the hope that all could now come to support the final resolution of an issue that had vexed the colony, Dominion, and province for more than one hundred years.[22]

Given the Senate's reaction to the previous revision, the federal government decided this time to appoint a joint committee of the House and Senate to investigate the new request. Whether or not coincidentally, this time the federal government was also faced with a request from Quebec for a change to Section 93 allowing it to restructure its school system along language rather than denominational lines. Federally, the two requests were treated separately but through the same process.

The joint committee heard from many of the same witnesses as the earlier Senate committee. Two expert witnesses argued that there should be some deference to the province when the matter is within provincial jurisdiction. A new note was injected by one expert witness who observed that subsection (3) might be found in conflict with the Charter by allowing religious activities in what would effectively become secular public schools. This time the referendum result was treated as decisive. The overall result, along with a breakdown by district, pointed towards approval by all the affected denominations. The committee majority therefore recommended that Parliament approve the proposed amendment.

The committee report was tabled in the House of Commons on December 8, 1997.[23] This time the debate was led by Stéphane Dion, the minister of intergovernmental affairs, who went to some length to address issues of the possible interaction of this term with the Charter.[24] His position was that, as in other instances of conflict between constitutional terms, one section of the constitution could not be used to override another. He also argued that the right to denominational education could not be seen as fundamental in the same sense as freedom of expression or of religion. This might be interpreted as a critique of the inclusion of Section 29 in the Charter.

Following a federal election, the conservative-leaning Reform Party had become the official opposition, replacing the Bloc Québécois. Its leader, Preston Manning, outlined the position of his party that the amendment should withstand three tests: democratic consent through a referendum, respect for the rule of law, and whether the amendment is in the national interest. Manning's own background as a fundamentalist Christian was evident in his speech: he made several references to doubts as to whether the Pentecostal community had voted to have their rights extinguished, and he introduced a concept of school choice as an alternative to a single secular school system. Nevertheless, despite these reservations, he finally indicated support for the amendment based on the overriding view that this was primarily a matter of provincial jurisdiction. Other members, speaking in opposition to the amendment, tended to introduce their personal convictions about the place of religion in schools. In the end, the amendment was approved on a free vote by a 211–53 margin. Among committee members who had voted on both this and the earlier amendment, very few changed their votes.

After some debate and hearing from further witnesses, the Senate approved the proposed amendment by a 45–28 vote on December 18. Unlike the House of Commons, the most recent proceedings had led some senators to change their minds on the issue.

Not ready to give up, representatives of the Catholic church in Newfoundland sought a further injunction in the Newfoundland Supreme Court to prohibit the governor general from proclaiming the amendment.[25] This time, lawyers for the plaintiffs claimed that Term 17 could not be amended at all and especially should not have been amended under Section 43. The trial judge quickly dismissed these claims on the grounds that the plaintiffs had already accepted the constitutionality of the previous revision when requesting relief from legislative provisions made under that revision. It was therefore contradictory to question the constitutionality of the new term. In any event, the judge concluded that the appropriate amendment procedure had been used and that the constitutionality of the process itself was not open to question. This judgment allowed the amendment to be proclaimed on January 8, 1998.

This did not end the litigation. In June 1998, the same group of Catholic plaintiffs initiated another action, this time directly challenging the validity of using Section 43 in this case and also asking for a further injunction restraining the government from implementing sections of a new schools act. The Newfoundland attorney general countered by requesting an injunction to quash the claim as "frivolous and vexatious or an abuse of process" on the grounds that the constitutionality of the amended Term 17 had already been settled. In his decision, Judge James Adams dismissed both claims, leaving in place the earlier decision.[26]

Undeterred, the same plaintiffs again appealed to the court on a series of new grounds; including the validity of the referendum processes and that their Charter rights had been violated by the absence of funding for the No side in the referendum.[27] The plaintiffs also argued that Term 17 amounted to a perpetual agreement to maintain denominational rights as they existed at the time of confederation and was thus not subject to amendment under the 1982 constitution. Alternatively, if it is subject to amendment, the appropriate process would be given by Section 38, which requires the consent of at least two-thirds of the provinces with at least 50 percent of the population. Finally, they argued that a constitutional convention exists under which the rights of a minority cannot be abrogated without the express consent of that minority.

In this case the judge dismissed all but one of these claims. That allowed the plaintiffs to claim their costs for the referendum campaign. However, a government appeal to the Newfoundland Court of Appeal led to all the appellants' claims, including that for costs, being dismissed.[28]

In a final step, the plaintiffs appealed this decision to the Supreme Court of Canada. On November 9, 2000, that court declined to hear the case.[29] This left the decision of the Newfoundland Court of Appeal as the final legal word on the issue. The amended Term 17 finally gave the province constitutional authority to restructure the school system as it wished. The day after the new Term 17 was proclaimed, the province approved a revised schools act, removing all references to denominational schools and giving school boards the authority to establish school attendance zones on the principle that students should attend the nearest school. A new section was added, conforming to Term 17 (3), allowing parents to request that religious observances be held in a school and also allowing students to be excluded from religious courses or observances on the request of parents.

Hodder,[30] writing from experience as the religious education coordinator at the Department of Education, described the state of religion in schools following the amendment. He observed, first, that because many Newfoundland communities remain almost exclusively Christian, some schools retain a Christian orientation in activities such as Christmas and Easter assemblies. Others judge it better not to conduct any such activities out of concern over their legality. To date, there have been no further court challenges and apparently no significant parent grievances over the state of religious observances. As required by Term 17, a new non-denominational religious education program has been developed. This course is compulsory for elementary students. However, it is one among many options available to secondary students and appears to attract relatively few.

Quebec

After losing in the Supreme Court in its effort to protect the French language by limiting the right of denominational school boards to raise taxes, the Quebec government tried again, introducing in 1988 a new Education Act, known as Bill 107.[31] That act was designed explicitly to divide the school system along linguistic lines. The act dissolved the existing boards for Catholics and boards for Protestants. These boards had no Section 93 protection because they had been originally established as common boards after 1867. Their religious character was a matter of practice and not of law. Although their religious status was confirmed by subsequent legislation, this did not convey the constitutional protection enjoyed by confessional boards in Montréal and Québec City or dissentient boards elsewhere in the province.

Despite its orientation in favour of reform, the government did not engage strongly in the many local debates over governance. Bill 101, for all its radical proposals on language of instruction, was framed to fit (though uneasily) within the denominational structure. However, one consequence was that the focus of opposition to further reform shifted to the Protestant community, less because of any desire for sectarian schools than because the community felt under threat from the language laws and more generally from the independence movement. The Protestant School Board of Greater Montreal chose to become an English school board, effectively allowing it to fight the language battle on its Section 93 rights.

In an effort to head off Section 93 challenges, the government referred the act to the Quebec Court of Appeal for a constitutional ruling. Specifically, the government posed five questions related to sections of the act that might impinge on Section 93 rights. These had to do with (1) the successor status of the French and English language boards, (2) the right to dissent, (3) the right of government to alter the territories of confessional boards and terminate non-functional boards, (4) giving the *Conseil scolaire de l'île de Montréal* the power to borrow funds on behalf of all school boards in the city, and (5) giving the Catholic and Protestant committees of the *Conseil supérieur de l'éducation* the authority to establish rules respecting the confessional nature of the schools, approve the programs of studies or religious education and approve the qualifications of teachers of religion.

The Quebec Court of Appeal ruled that most of the provisions were not in violation of Section 93. The exceptions were those affecting the manner of dissent, the territories of the confessional school boards, and the power of the *Conseil scolaire de l'île de Montréal* to borrow money on behalf of all school boards. In 1990, the National Assembly amended Bill 107 to address these concerns. This did not stop the Protestant and Catholic school boards from appealing the matter to the Supreme Court of Canada. In June 1993, the Supreme Court ruled that the sections of the act in question did not violate Section 93, with the sole exception of the section on changing the territories of confessional school boards.³² The court held that territories could be reduced only if new boards covering any lost territories were established.

After two decades of trying, the province finally appeared to have designed a system to accommodate the conflicting denominational and linguistic dualities. Section 93 rights were confirmed but strictly limited to their 1867 boundaries and to the classes specifically protected. The right of dissent was also protected, though it seemed unlikely that many new dissentient schools would emerge. All other school boards would be linguistically based. The language of instruction for individual students would be determined by Bill 101, whether or not the school or the board was confessional in nature.

With the act now firmly implemented and immune from further court challenges, one would think that the time had come for a new period of stability. However, it could be argued that Bill 107 still left large parts of the province, particularly the two main cities, with four systems based on the twin duality of religion and language. There was also still no explicit accommodation of those with other or no religious affiliation.

Quebec society and politics were continuing to change at such a rapid pace that even the new status quo was destined not to survive for long. The final status of the 1988 legislation had only just been determined by the 1993 Supreme Court decision when the government again changed. The Parti Québécois returned to power with the promise of a second referendum on sovereignty. A year of further turmoil ensued before that referendum ended in a narrow defeat for the sovereignist side in October 1995.

Not content with the apparent new stability in education, the new government immediately decided to establish yet another comprehensive review, known as the Commission for the Estates General on Education.³³ That commission was given a mandate to mount a comprehensive consultation of the public and establish the broadest consensus with a view to action. In its final report, the commission identified ten priority areas for action. Only two of these are relevant to the theme of this chapter:

- Continue moving towards a non-denominational system—transform denominational school boards into linguistic boards; repeal Section 93; encourage the view that the pursuit of religious goals take place outside the school environment.
- Gradually eliminate state support for private schools.³⁴

The Estates General report finally brought to the forefront the dominant public view, long revealed in polls, that schools should become non-denominational and pluralistic while continuing to be separated by language. All previous attempts to accomplish this had either preserved the denominational duality or had run into constitutional obstacles. The Estates General proposed a straightforward, though drastic, solution to the dilemma. The recommendation that Section 93 be repealed finally brought to the attention of government and the public that there was a way around the dilemma of having to write legislation within the constraints of that section.

In retrospect, it is surprising that this had not been considered earlier. Even though the protected rights had been strictly circumscribed by a series of court decisions, it had become clear that the school systems in Montréal and Québec City would continue to be divided along both language and denominational lines unless constitutional action were taken. The action taken by Newfoundland that same year provided a precedent for exactly the type of constitutional change proposed by the Estates General. However, the Newfoundland resolution remained tied up in the courts and the Senate during 1996, so there was no guarantee that a resolution from Quebec on the same issue would easily be accepted.

In any event, on April 15, 1997, the Quebec National Assembly approved unanimously a resolution calling for a constitutional amendment as follows:

1. The Constitution Act, 1867 is amended by adding, immediately following Section 93, the following:
2. "93A. Paragraphs (1) to (4) of Section 93 do not apply to Quebec."[35]

Unlike the Newfoundland resolution, the Quebec resolution left no residual constitutional right to religious education or observances. The resolution also noted that the federal government had already undertaken to proceed rapidly with the amendment.

Anticipation of a positive federal response led the government to introduce amendments to the 1988 Education Act. The confessional school boards in Montréal and Québec City and the dissentient boards in other parts of the province were dissolved and replaced by French and English boards. As a transitional arrangement, Catholic and Protestant confessional councils were established within each school board, intersecting with the existing confessional school boards. The right to dissent on the part of Catholic and Protestant minorities was preserved. However, each dissentient board would have to be either a French or an English board. These arrangements were intended to be temporary, pending approval of the constitutional amendment.[36]

The Section 93 repeal resolution was designed to remove any constitutional constraint on the Quebec government's ability to restructure the system. However, that did not mean that the government intended to remove all vestiges of denominationally based religious education in the schools. On the contrary, provisions remained in the act allowing schools to be designated as either Catholic or Protestant and for student choice or moral and religious education in either the Catholic or Protestant tradition. Indeed, these provisions went beyond the rights protected under Section 93 and were thus open to challenges under either the Quebec or Canadian Charters. To avoid this problem, the notwithstanding sections of both Charters[37] were invoked. Once the Section 93 amendment was approved, the effect of these changes was that any access to Catholic or Protestant religious education was made entirely subject to provincial legislation. The notwithstanding provision of the Canadian Charter, though not the Quebec Charter, requires renewal every five years, thus ensuring that the issue remained on the agenda.

Quebec's Section 93 resolution was introduced in the House of Commons on April 22, 1997, by the minister of intergovernmental affairs, Stéphane Dion.[38] It is likely no coincidence that a francophone minister from Quebec was selected to sponsor this resolution. Meanwhile, a federal election intervened, and the resolution was not again taken up until September. At that time, it was proposed that the matter be referred to a joint committee of the House of Commons and the Senate. While the minister made it clear that he supported the resolution, the government decided that further public consultation was necessary because the Quebec National Assembly had not done so, nor had it resorted to a referendum as in Newfoundland.

This case was slightly different from the Newfoundland one because Section 93 applies to more than one province. It could therefore be argued that Section 43 of the amending formula was not the correct one in this case and that the other provinces with separate systems would also have to approve the change. However, this was countered by the argument that Section 93 was being rescinded only for Quebec and could remain in effect elsewhere. There seems to have been no significant disagreement on this point.

The opposition leader, Preston Manning, reiterated the arguments he had previously made on the Newfoundland amendment. Specifically, the issue was whether the proposed amendment prejudicially affected the educational rights of minorities in other provinces. Manning proposed an amendment asking the joint committee to apply his three tests in their deliberations on the resolution. Debate on this amendment mostly centred on whether the Quebec consensus was sufficient to obviate the need for a referendum. Some noted the irony of Quebec requesting an amendment to the constitution when that province was on record as not having signed the 1982 constitution. The response to that was that the Supreme Court had already ruled that Quebec is bound by the constitution and is thus free to use the amending formula.

The Manning amendment was defeated by a large majority and the main motion to refer the matter to the joint committee was adopted. The joint committee heard from more than 60 witnesses representing various stakeholders in Quebec, as well as from several expert witnesses on the constitution. In its report, the committee made some observations reflecting both the apparent consensus in Quebec and concerns expressed by some witnesses and correspondents. There was agreement that Section 43 was appropriate and that unanimous support of the Quebec legislature, plus the weight of witness testimony, could be taken as consensus within Quebec. On the other hand, concern was expressed about denominational rights being weakened by making these subject to provincial legislation. Concern about insufficient protection for English language education was also expressed but this was considered to be outside the committee's mandate.[39]

In the end, the committee recommended that the resolution be approved. The report generated another two days of debate in the House of Commons. Few new issues emerged. The dissenting committee members' concern that the Quebec population had not been adequately consulted was reiterated. Their view seems to have been that no consensus could be declared if there was opposition from any quarter. Support for and opposition to the amendment came from many of the same individuals as before. The division on the final vote of 204–59 was, in fact, very similar to that in the Newfoundland case. Although the Reform Party as a group appeared to support the right of the Quebec government to manage its education system, most members of that party voted against the amendment.

The issue then moved to the Senate, where, again, the debate was more extensive than in the House of Commons. As they had done with the Newfoundland amendment, some senators took the position that the Senate is the final guardian of minority rights. From that point of view even a consensus is insufficient to justify the removal of minority constitutional rights from those who wish to retain such rights. Specifically, support of a "majority of the minority" should be required. More broadly, it was argued that minority rights that are subject to the will of the majority are, in effect, no rights at all.

Some senators referred to a flood of letters and calls from opponents as evidence that no consensus existed. This obviously conflicts with the view that a referendum should have been conducted, since the history of referenda, particularly in Quebec, is that majority opinion should prevail even if support is far from unanimous. There is a parallel here with the Newfoundland case where some senators were at pains to determine whether a majority of each of the affected denominations had voted for change.

One of the more interesting points raised in the Senate was why Quebec decided to pursue the constitutional amendment when its 1988 Education Act creating linguistic school boards had already been declared constitutional by the Supreme Court. The denominational issue could therefore not be considered a major deterrent to implementing a linguistically based system. The response to this argument seemed to be that the issue is about provincial control of the entire system rather than leaving some large outlier boards in Montréal and Québec City, which then would have to be further divided along linguistic lines. There was an undercurrent of concern by some senators that the Parti Québécois government may have been using the amendment to advance its broader sovereignist goal.

Use of the notwithstanding clause to protect some elements of religious rights following the constitutional amendment generated some debate. In principle, it might be seen as contradictory to expunge rights through constitutional action and then restore these same rights through legislation. The question in the Senate was whether the Quebec government had any intention of renewing the notwithstanding clause once its five-year term had expired. This concern was evident in a submission to the government by the Catholic Committee of the Superior Education Council, which viewed the use of the notwithstanding clause as a time bomb that could explode at any point if the government declined to renew the clause.[40] At the same time, the Catholic Bishops of Quebec had indicated that their support of the move to linguistic school boards was contingent on a continuing guarantee for denominational rights. In retrospect, these concerns were justified as the notwithstanding provision expired and was never renewed. However, there seems to have been no significant fallout from that decision.

Senate debate on the Quebec resolution overlapped with that on Newfoundland's second attempt to amend Term 17. This provided opportunity for comparison of the two resolutions. Several differences emerged in the discussion. First, it was argued that Term 17 was unique to Newfoundland and that changing that term would therefore be less likely to cause ripple effects in other provinces than attempting to change Section 93. Second, the Newfoundland resolution was accompanied by a strong majority vote in a referendum, something that many senators argued should also have been done in Quebec. Third, the Newfoundland resolution did preserve some religious rights that were lacking in the Quebec constitutional resolution.

On December 15, 1997, the Quebec resolution was approved by the Senate by a 51–17 vote. Three days later, the second Newfoundland resolution passed by a 45–26 vote. All senators who voted against the Quebec amendment also voted against the Newfoundland one.

Lessons from Newfoundland and Quebec

What lessons can be learned from these two cases? First, and most obvious, the legal path to constitutional amendment in this area is now clearly established and is not at all complex. Formally, the only requirement is approval of the appropriate resolutions by both the provincial legislature and the Parliament of Canada. There is no need to hold a referendum or any other form of consultation, though that would be desirable. Other provinces do not have to be consulted. Indeed, the precedent has now clearly been set. Should any other province decide to follow the lead of Newfoundland and Quebec, it is highly unlikely that either the House of Commons or the Senate would reject a provincial resolution.

The second lesson is that the political process will certainly be more complex and controversial than implied by the constitutional precedent. Those with a vested interest in Catholic separate schools are well placed to make their opposition to change heard. Indeed, low-level campaigns along these lines are a conspicuous feature of Catholic agencies who may, with justification, perceive their rights to be under threat. Governments have historically been wary of confronting the major religions out of concern with their electoral impact. In the two cases at hand, the issue came to a head because of some overriding issue: language in Quebec and financial constraints in Newfoundland. In neither case was the issue of religious discrimination under the Charter the overriding concern. Certainly, in Newfoundland, had the churches agreed to some form of integration to facilitate school consolidation, there would have been no constitutional amendment. Even in Quebec, had the government agreed to allow separate dualities for language and denomination in Montréal and Québec City, as was done in Ontario, this may have obviated the need for the amendment.

Nevertheless, once the issue is joined, the case for common schools is not particularly difficult to make. This point will be examined in more detail later. Suffice it to say that governments, if so inclined, have powerful means at their disposal to make a case for policy change. In Newfoundland, the Williams Royal Commission and subsequent work drew attention to the inefficiencies inherent in maintaining four separate school systems for a small and scattered population. In the end, a large majority of the population supported the idea that religion has some place in schooling but concluded that this did not require that churches control student admissions, teacher employment, school board elections, school construction, or bus routes. In Newfoundland, the economic case was initially more compelling than the discrimination argument. However, once the issue was out in the open, the discrimination inherent in excluding even small segments of the population from educational governance became more apparent.

If the views of Catholics in Ontario, Alberta, or Saskatchewan are at all similar to those of their compatriots in Newfoundland, a properly framed argument might persuade many to support a system in which there is no need for the church to control school boards or use religious criteria in hiring teachers or selecting students. An argument that these rights are fundamentally discriminatory might be expected to carry considerable weight among people who, whatever their own religious beliefs, are accepting of the beliefs of others and who fundamentally believe in equal treatment of all religions in matters of public policy or public services. If some accommodation could be made for all religions, such as allowing access to schools for religious teaching, that could be even more persuasive.

The impact of the demographic and financial arguments should also not be underestimated. In Newfoundland, though perhaps less so in other provinces, half-empty schools in close proximity, long-distance bussing to keep separate schools in operation, and new schools being attached to church buildings as a way of consolidating control were all highly visible elements of the system. On the other hand, the public seemed not to be as concerned with these matters as was government. There is only a tenuous connection between governance and budget, especially in the more centralized financial regime now in place in most provinces. The debate is mainly about the distribution of funds rather than the total budget. Indeed, in Newfoundland expenditures increased substantially following the reforms. However, that had much more to do with the province's new-found oil wealth than with the reform of governance. Had that wealth come earlier, as it had in Alberta, the main issue driving the constitutional amendment may not have been as pressing.

A further lesson from Newfoundland has to do with whether the issue can, or should, be settled by referendum. The well-known arguments for and against such exercises in direct democracy have been well aired in recent cases, including the Scottish independence referendum in 2014 and the 2016 Brexit referendum. A more recent referendum in the Catalan region of Spain, not to mention the earlier Quebec exercises, brought to the fore the potential divisiveness of such exercises. Especially on issues of minority rights, an argument can be made that existing rights, especially those granted as a condition of nationhood, should not be abrogated without the consent of the affected minority. Nevertheless, it can be said that the two Newfoundland referenda were conducted in a climate of vigorous debate, under clear rules, and largely without rancour. There was no violence or even any significant street protests or other actions often associated with referendum campaigns. There is certainly room for debate over whether a referendum is appropriate. However, in the Canadian context, and on a narrow and well-defined issue, there is little doubt that a referendum can be conducted in a spirit of reasoned debate. In the Newfoundland case, the decisive result in the second referendum carried particular weight because it could legitimately be argued that the minorities themselves had agreed to give up their rights in favour of the larger public interest.

The Quebec situation was quite different from that of Newfoundland. As far as can be seen, the economics of education was never a major issue in the Quebec debate. The Quiet Revolution's rejection of the Catholic church as a primary political influence, accompanied by renewed emphasis on the French language, illustrates how cultural shift can trigger a demand for change in institutions. The confluence of secularism and language created the overriding conditions necessary for Quebec society to accept that denominational education was no longer compatible with the new societal ethos. The inclusion of minority official language rights in the Charter exemplifies an evolutionary approach to constitutional change. By the 1980s, most of the country was prepared to embrace the language duality that had previously been a source of much controversy. That was likely also true for denominational education had the framers of the Charter been prepared to take the risk.

The Quebec case shows that considerations of cost and efficiency need not be the main driving forces for change. Under the right circumstance, more fundamental principles can come into play. Nevertheless, it is important to recognize that the issue in Quebec was not religious discrimination or parent rights nor was it the contradiction within the Charter. Indeed, the Quebec government had made several attempts to achieve its desired language goal without resorting to abolition of denominational rights. Furthermore, even after the constitutional amendment had been achieved, Quebec used the notwithstanding section of the Charter to keep its denominational schools in place for a time. Although that may seem contradictory, and even deceptive, it may have avoided short-term political turmoil and allowed the system time to adjust. This may be an important lesson from the Quebec experience.

In both Newfoundland and Quebec, the actual rights holders, specifically members of the classes of persons identified in the constitutional provisions, proved to be at odds with their church leaders on many of the core elements of denominational rights such as control of school boards and selection of students and teachers. As chapter 8 will show, there are indications that this also may be the case in Ontario, where division among Catholic agencies has become evident in the sex education controversy. More generally, some would argue that the Catholic church has lost any moral authority to operate schools because of its record of abuse and its stand against broadly supported public policies in areas such as sex education. While provinces might be wise to avoid a divide-and-conquer strategy in taking advantage of such divisions, there is reason to argue that the wishes of the actual rights holders should take precedence over those who purport to represent these classes.

A final important lesson is that, in both provinces, the furor soon died down, and the issue faded from public discourse as soon as the amendments were approved. The issue of reasonable accommodation remains an active source of debate in Quebec. The most recent example is the ongoing controversy over the legislation prohibiting many public servants, including teachers, from wearing religious symbols on the job. Indeed, that legislation would almost certainly be declared unconstitutional except for use of the notwithstanding clause. However, this seems to be unrelated to the earlier conflicts over denominational rights in schools. Both Quebec and Newfoundland quickly moved beyond this issue once the matter was constitutionally settled.

There is no evidence of any movement to restore denominational rights in either province or to extend these in any provinces where they have not previously existed. Other provinces might be reassured that, no matter how controversial while active, once settled the issue of separate schools would soon fall from the political agenda. This would clear the way for the more important debate over the extent to which religious differences and other forms of diversity should be accommodated in public or private schools.

CHAPTER 5

Catholic Schools in Canada

Historically, the presence of Catholic schools in Canada had two origins: the French presence in Quebec, and prejudice against Catholics (and Francophones) elsewhere in Canada. In Quebec, education was largely synonymous with the Catholic church. Elsewhere, much of the English establishment was anti-Catholic. However, many local Catholic communities existed, initially mainly French but later of broader origin. Common schools, though open to all, were effectively Catholic in Quebec and Protestant elsewhere. As Canadian society became more diverse, Protestant schools, though having the same constitutional protections as Catholic schools, largely evolved into non-sectarian public schools, though many retained vestiges of Protestant influence in prayers and other religious activities. This raises the question of why Catholic schools have managed to retain their distinctive character. This is especially true in the Charter era, as almost all other vestiges of religious influence in public institutions have disappeared. If the constitution has not served to protect distinctively Protestant schools, why has it served so well to protect Catholic schools?

Outside Quebec, there is plenty of evidence of widespread prejudice against Catholics, and especially against francophone Catholics, in the early years of the development of education. In some cases, this prejudice was embodied in legislation supporting religious and language discrimination. Entrenchment of Catholic rights may be seen as a response to discrimination. However, it is difficult to argue that anti-Catholic sentiment remains a significant reason for the continued existence of separate Catholic schools. While prejudice has certainly not disappeared in Canada, the advent of the Charter and of human rights legislation offer safeguards against discriminatory behaviour. In today's political climate, prejudice against much smaller minority religious groups, notably Muslims and Jews, is certainly more prevalent than that against Catholics. Again, this raises the question of why Catholic religious schools remain while others have not been allowed the same protection.

Further explanation may lie in the legal and political efforts exerted by the Catholic church leadership and its agencies over the years. These groups have been quick to lobby and litigate to preserve and expand their rights. This is illustrated by the long-running campaign in Ontario to expand Catholic schooling to the secondary level and in Alberta by the effort to allow separate school boards to determine local assessment rates. While the courts have been careful not to broaden Section 93 rights, they have also on many occasions struck down provincial legislation seen as limiting these rights. Courts have also been clear that provinces are free to expand the scope of separate schooling, even though such expansion does not convey any new constitutional rights. In the face of all this effort, and the potential political fallout, it is not surprising that provincial political leaders have been reluctant to confront the issue unless driven by overriding circumstances, as in Newfoundland and Quebec.

The Catholic Perspective

This brings us to a more fundamental issue: specifically, a Catholic world view under which Catholicism must pervade the lives of its adherents. This view derives from the ultramontane doctrine as discussed earlier. While ultramontanism seems no longer to be as overtly expressed as it was a century ago, its precepts certainly pervade Catholic views on such matters as contraception and abortion. State laws in these areas are quite simply not accepted as valid by the Catholic leadership. While Canadian Catholics today appear not to adhere very strictly to church doctrine in these matters, loyalty to separate schools, if not to the details of control of these schools, remains strong.

In Catholic schools, church doctrine declares itself explicitly in "permeation," the concept that Catholicism must pervade all aspects of schooling. To Catholics, or at least to the Catholic leadership, education is fundamentally sectarian and confessional. Moral and spiritual goals are as important as academic goals. There is no way that this Catholic world view can be accommodated within a secular school system. Allowing time for prayer, religious activities, or religious observances is considered insufficient, as these activities are not consistent with the goal of permeation.

The idea of permeation is found in the mission statements of Catholic provincial school authorities and school boards. A typical example is the following statement from the Calgary Catholic School District:

> The Calgary Catholic School District adheres to the principle that the element of faith is integrated into every program and every aspect of school life: this is called permeation. The concept of permeation recognizes that Catholic identity finds expression in every dimension of a Catholic school. Even though there is continuous pressure in society to separate the secular and the religious (Church and State), as Catholics we are called by Baptism to live our faith every moment of every day.[1]

A consultation conducted in 2007 by the Ontario Catholic School Trustees Association reinforced this concept and, in fact, went further in outlining some distinctive characteristics of Catholic schools as expressed by a wide sampling of participants. Five main characteristics were identified:

- a place to exercise freedom to practise the Catholic faith tradition;
- reinforce the teaching of our Catholic values;
- students to learn about social justice and service to the community;
- respect for the dignity of all people; and
- promote the strong home-school-parish relationship.[2]

Respondents identified a distinct Catholic culture, the teaching of values, morals, discipline, and Catholic traditions as valued features. Catholic schools were also identified as countercultural, which, in the context, appears to mean resistant to the increasing secularism of society. Threats to the continued existence of Catholic schools, inadequate parish involvement in schools, apathy and indifference, inadequate commitment to the Catholic faith, and the negative impact of ministry of education priorities were identified as the key issues facing Catholic schools today. Communication, self-promotion, and political action were given as strategies for dealing with these issues.

With these imperatives at the forefront, it is not surprising that Catholics would be expected to rally to the cause of separate schools and go to some length to ensure their survival. On the other hand, it is by no means clear that many Canadian Catholics conform to church teaching in matters spiritual and moral or to the structures, such as schools, designed to perpetuate church influence in the broader society. The complete break with the Catholic church in Quebec was obviously not forced by government on the population. Similarly, in Newfoundland, once the specifics of church control of schools became a matter of public debate, it became clear that Catholics were more concerned with leaving room for religion in schools than with church control of school governance and administration.

Indeed, there are indications of a shift in thinking about the purpose of Catholic schools, even among those responsible for running the system. For example, towards the end of the Newfoundland negotiations, Catholic representatives argued that Catholic schools should be preserved for those who want them, implying that other Catholic parents should be free to choose public schooling. This seems to imply that only the devout are welcome in Catholic schools. This shift appears to reflect a broader loss of authority on the part of the leadership, which may now be content to exercise control over those still inclined to adhere strictly to church doctrine.

The Decline of Religiosity and Church Influence

Surveys have shown a decline in religiosity among Canadians extending over several decades. According to the Pew Research Center, the percentage of Canadians professing no religion grew from four percent to 24 percent from 1971 to 2011.[3] The proportion identifying as Catholic has declined from 47 percent to 39 percent while those professing to be Protestant has dropped from 41 percent to 27 percent. Those claiming some religion other than those two has increased from 4 percent to 11 percent over the same time. The proportion attending religious services has also declined, dropping from 43 percent to 27 percent from 1986 to 2012. However, that decline has been almost exclusively confined to native-born Canadians. There has been no comparable decline among those born outside the country. Younger people are much less religious than their elders. There are regional differences as well. British Columbia residents are much less religious, and those in Quebec more religious than those in other regions. Nevertheless, the Pew survey identified a precipitous drop, from 48 percent to 17 percent in religious attendance in Quebec.

The results for Quebec are especially interesting. Even though Quebec has arguably moved further than other regions in the direction of a secular state, most residents of that province still identify as Catholic. This suggests a greater drop in religious attendance among Catholics than among the general population. Using data from the General Social Survey, David Eagle[4] attributed about half of the overall decline in religious attendance to a drop in attendance at Catholic Mass. It is possible that claiming a Catholic identity is as much a matter of ethnicity or family ties as of attitude towards religion itself.

The surveys also indicate that immigrants tend to be more religious than native-born Canadians. More immigrants identify themselves as Catholic than any other religion, though almost as many immigrants identify themselves as of no religion. Also, taken together, more immigrants identify themselves as Muslim, Hindu, or Sikh than Catholic. The latter groups are also the fastest growing. All this is consistent with the relatively slow trend towards the country becoming less Christian.

The last half of the twentieth century saw a proliferation of scandals, in Canada and worldwide, involving the sexual abuse of children by Catholic priests and members of religious orders. As time went on, it also became clear that this extended to the church leadership, bishops and archbishops, either through direct involvement in abuse or through efforts to cover up the abuse. These scandals have been well documented and need not be addressed in detail here. Most of the abuse seems to have occurred in settings in which clergy have had direct power over their victims, especially over children. In many cases, this has involved schools. The most notorious example in Canada is that of the residential schools for Indigenous students, an issue taken up in a later chapter. The Mount Cashel Orphanage scandal in Newfoundland, which some believe first broke the secrecy around abuse by Catholic clergy, was also an example of children schooled in a residential setting. While abuse in residential schools was by no means unique to those run by Catholic agencies, the Catholic church has been the most reluctant to issue apologies to victims, and debates continue over the liability of the church as a whole for the abuse. The tendency of senior Catholic officials to cover up abuse is arguably another manifestation of the ultramontaine doctrine. The official church position was clearly that these matters should be handled internally by canon law rather than state law.

Enrolments in Catholic Schools

The scandals, along with the more general decline in religiosity, raise questions about the moral authority of the Catholic church to control schools. This, in turn, might be expected to have had a significant impact on enrolments in Catholic schools. However, this seems not to have been the case. In Ontario, total enrolments declined approximately 5 percent over the decade from 2006 to 2016. However, the proportion attending Catholic schools has stayed the same at just under 32 percent. This closely mirrors the proportion of the population that identifies as Catholic.[5] Interestingly, the number of schools in both systems has stayed about the same. Schools are thus becoming a bit smaller.

Alberta breaks down its enrolments differently from Ontario, as the enrolment figures include charter schools, First Nations, and other types. Looking only at public versus separate schools, the latter constitutes about 26 percent of the total. This has remained stable over the past few years.[6] Again, separate school enrolment closely mirrors the 24 percent of the overall population identifying as Catholic.

Figures for Saskatchewan are more difficult to determine as official sources do not give the breakdown between public and separate schools. Statistics Canada reports a total of approximately 180,000 students in public, including separate, schools in 2017.[7] A 2017 statement by the Saskatchewan premier, in reference to the *Theodore* case described in chapter 3, placed the number of students in Catholic schools at about 40,000, or 22 percent of the total.

These figures suggest that church scandals and the general decline in religiosity have not had much of an impact on Catholic school enrolment. It is possible of course, that enrolment is driven by factors other than religious conviction. This is illustrated on a very small scale by the *Theodore* case, where non-Catholic students appear to have enrolled in the Catholic school for convenience of transportation. The Catholic school board welcomed these students as they brought added revenue, leading to the court challenge by the public school board. With enrolment declining, especially in rural areas, conditions similar to the Theodore school may be expected to become more prevalent. The final judgment in that case has confirmed the constitutionality of this practice, at least for Saskatchewan.

It is difficult to find reliable data on this issue. However, a recent investigation by the *Globe and Mail* has drawn attention to the situation in Ontario. Driven by a desire to maintain per-student funding in the face of declining enrolments, both public and separate school boards have been engaging in campaigns to recruit students.[8] Part of this involves relaxing religiously based admission requirements in separate schools. Data compiled by the newspaper show an increase, from 7.3 percent in 2013–2014 to 8.3 percent in 2016–2017 in the proportion of non-Catholic students in Catholic schools. While these proportions remain small, there is a clear trend. This has led the *Globe and Mail* to editorialize that it is quite possible for Ontario to follow the lead of Newfoundland and Quebec in amending the constitution and that, even if this is not done, to restrict funding for Catholic schools to Catholic students.[9] The latter is precisely the argument raised by the *Theodore* case. However, it is not clear if the decision in that case would apply to Ontario, where the protected rights are somewhat different. The *Globe and Mail*'s work on this issue has led others, in op-ed articles and letters, again to argue for abolition.

From a provincial funding point of view, competition among school boards is a zero-sum game; what one board loses another gains. The total funding level need not change. However, the question of whether competition is leading to a one-way flow of students from public to Catholic schools has not been answered, nor has the broader question of whether such competition, regardless of its religious basis, might lead to improved schools for all. The interesting political question is whether this type of development can function as a trigger for change.

It is possible that governments and school boards are rather sensitive about publishing such data. Admission policies between public and separate schools are not symmetrical. Public schools are required to accept all, including Catholic, students with no question asked about religion. However, Catholic schools are free to ask the religion question, to exclude anyone who does not profess Catholicism or to establish policies on acceptance of non-Catholics.

A few examples suffice to illustrate how this is addressed by school boards. The website of the Calgary Catholic School District states that "The Alberta Education Act requires us to prioritize the enrollment of Catholic students who live inside a school's attendance area, but we are pleased to enroll non-Catholic students and students who live outside a school's attendance area when we have sufficient resources and facilities to do so."[10] The Regina Catholic School District refers to the need for parents to direct school tax to the Catholic district on registration of a student in that district but states that registration is the responsibility of the school. However, school websites refer directly back to the district site for inquiries about admission.[11] The Ottawa Catholic School Board mentions that its programs are based on Catholic traditions but welcomes students of all faiths. The registration form for that board requires a Catholic baptism certificate but indicates that this is not required if the student is admitted under the board's space allocation policy.[12] The Hamilton-Wentworth Catholic School District mission and vision statements are explicit about its Catholic mandate. Admission requires a birth and baptismal certificate and there is no reference to admission of students of other faiths.[13]

The general impression gathered from websites and related sources is that separate school districts in all three provinces do use religious criteria for admission. This policy is legal and appropriate given the status of these schools. However, policy may be applied with varying degrees of stringency depending on the availability of space. Parents may well decide based on factors such as school proximity rather than religion. Since most school funding is based on a per-student formula, schools have a strong incentive to attract as many students as possible. This is especially true if excess space is available. While there are few economies of scale in education, marginal efficiencies are possible. For example, school funding can be enhanced if a slight increase in enrolment can be accommodated without adding teachers or classroom space.

The underlying issue, of course, is whether the entire *raison d'être* for Catholic schools might be undermined by selection of non-Catholic students. Certainly, the desired characteristics of Catholic schools reflected in the Ontario consultation described above could be weakened by the presence of a substantial number of non-Catholic students. The issue was at the core of a recent human rights case in Ontario in which a student in a Catholic school claimed exemption from religious classes. The school accommodated the request, but the student claimed that this let to reprisals in the form of restrictions on other courses. To settle the case, the school board and other Catholic boards in the province agreed to amend their policies on exemptions to ensure that no reason need be given for the request.[14] A notable point made during the presentations in the case is that about half the students in the school in question are non-Catholic. While this does not appear to be the provincial norm, it does illustrate the difficulty in maintaining a pervasive Catholic atmosphere in schools that may become increasingly diverse.

Are Catholic Schools Superior to Public Schools?

The issue of superiority has been the subject of much debate. Even a casual search on the question yields a massive amount of material, much of which is partisan in nature and little of which includes much hard evidence. Superiority can mean different things to different people. However, most of the debate has to do with academic achievement. This is not the place for a full review of research comparing Catholic and public schools. However, some important points need to be made so as to separate what is known from what people believe, advocate, and promote.

Studies in the United States, dating from the work of Coleman and colleagues in the 1980s, have been widely cited as showing that average academic achievement is higher in Catholic than in public schools. Coleman had gained earlier fame for his report on inequality of educational opportunity, which concluded that the educational and economic attainment of the parents, rather than quality of schooling, was the main factor contributing to academic success. Coleman's 1982 study of Catholic and public schools concluded that Catholic school students scored higher than public school students on standardized tests.[15] No doubt because of Coleman's high profile, that study attracted widespread attention. It has been followed by studies that show varying results, most marginally favouring Catholic schools.

These studies have been widely criticized because they either compare raw scores on standardized tests or use rankings. The better designed studies attempt to control for what is known as selection bias. Examples of such bias is the tendency for schools to select students on their past performance or the tendency for parents who are most concerned with their children's academic achievement to select schools based on reputation, which, in turn, is likely related to selectivity. This tends to create a self-fulfilling prophecy. Schools that are reputed to be better fulfill that expectation by attracting more academically adept students. Studies often use statistical techniques to control for selection bias, but the usual method used (multiple regression analysis) is considered by many to be inadequate to control for the many factors, other than type of school, known to influence achievement.

A recent study in the United States, using more robust methods, has called into question the Catholic school effect.[16] After accounting for differences in background factors, that study concluded that the Catholic school effect is largely illusory. Indeed, the effect on mathematics achievement was reported to be universally negative. That was also the case for behavioural and non-cognitive outcomes.

For our purposes, a more salient criticism is that American results are unlikely to be generalizable to Canada. Catholic schools in the United States are private whereas most Catholic schools in Canada are part of the public system. Catholic schools in Canada may select by religion but they are unable to select on student ability or socioeconomic status. Catholic and public schools in Canada mostly follow provincial curriculum, have similarly qualified teachers and receive similar levels of funding. However, this does not mean that they are free from bias related to parent self-selection or other factors.

Both Alberta and Ontario have well-established standardized testing programs that could lend themselves to studies of differences between public and separate schools. However, relatively little of the accompanying data shed much light on selection factors or other school characteristics that may differentiate public and separate schools. At the same time, it is not difficult to find raw score differences being used for comparison purposes. In particular, the school ranking reports produced by the Fraser Institute[17] are often used to support the argument that Catholic schools (and private schools) show higher performance. Indeed, these studies are often cited as useful in helping parents choose schools. Ranking studies are widely criticized for emphasizing very small differences as well as for their lack of control of selection factors. However, this does not prevent their widespread use to compare schools. A huge volume of Internet traffic on this issue illustrates that research of this sort can have a significant impact, regardless of its design flaws. While parents might be forgiven for using inferior quality information if that is the only information available, there is certainly a risk that parents will place undue credence on weak evidence, mistake opinion for evidence, or rely on evidence that supports some predisposition towards schooling.

The debate over school quality is often framed as one of parent choice. In practice, the ability to choose schools in Canada is relatively limited. In most provinces, the choice is between public school or a limited selection of private schools. In the three with separate schools, the choice extends to these schools but only to the extent that Catholic schools are willing to accept students of other faiths. Factors such as school proximity also play a large part. If most parents prefer neighbourhood or community schools, choice can occur only if more than one school exists within reasonable distance from the home. In cities where separate and public schools are often found in proximity, choice can be exercised, but only at the discretion of the separate school authority. That becomes less true in smaller communities. Some families no doubt go as far as to choose where to live based on their perception of school quality. However, that is not feasible for most.

Despite some evidence that Catholic schools are beginning to recruit non-Catholic students, the student body in most Catholic schools remains largely Catholic. This suggests that religion is a greater driving force than other factors in choice of school. It is also possible that parents give little thought to choice, perhaps taking for granted that Catholics attend Catholic schools or basing their decision on family history, school proximity, or other non-ideological reasons. Unfortunately, despite the proliferation of opinion, there is virtually no evidence on the reasons used by parents to select schools. Any government contemplating the future of separate schools or, more generally, of school choice as a policy, would need to consider how to fill this gap. This point is again considered in the last chapter.

CHAPTER 6

Religion and Private Schools

Private schools have always been part of the educational landscape in Canada. In the early colonial period, all schools were essentially private, mainly run by churches or their affiliates. Even when the state became involved, its initial actions were to provide grants in aid to existing schools. From these origins may be traced a pattern of local control through school boards that persists in some measure today. In many communities, local control was largely synonymous with church control. From this grew the concept of separation of schools by religion and eventually the constitutional protections that have sustained separate schools.

Although not all contemporary private schools are religious in orientation, religion appears to play a significant part in parents' decisions to use private schools. In some provinces, these serve as an alternative to separate publicly funded religious schools and perhaps as an outlet for some religious groups who might otherwise become stronger advocates for a greater religious focus in public schools. Some provinces provide partial funding to private schools while others do not. This chapter gives some data on the extent of private schooling and examines major reviews and significant court cases that have helped clarify the scope and limitations of religious practice in private schools.

The Ontario Commission on Private Schools

As far as can be determined, the most comprehensive study of private schools in Canada and the place of religion in these schools is the 1985 Shapiro Commission in Ontario.[1] The report of that commission addressed the underlying arguments for and against private schools and provided a model that might be considered a template for public support of private schools in several provinces.

At the time, Ontario legislation permitted private schools and home schooling but provided no provincial support. The province placed relatively few restrictions on private school programs. According to Shapiro, in 1983 there were 535 such schools in Ontario, enrolling more than 85,000 students or about 5 percent of the total. A majority were religious in orientation, with most of these being Catholic secondary schools. The latter group was soon to be absorbed into the Catholic separate school system.

The Shapiro Commission reiterated that private schools historically predated state-supported schools. By the mid-twentieth century, private schools had largely been displaced by fully state-supported public and Catholic separate systems. The commission noted, however, that private schooling had enjoyed somewhat of a resurgence in Ontario in the late twentieth century as more parents took the view that neither the public nor the Catholic systems fitted their religious, academic, or social values.

The commission addressed comprehensively the philosophical, legal, and constitutional underpinnings of private schools including parent versus state rights, the place of religion, societal diversity, school choice, and voucher systems. Most submissions to the commission opposed public funding, a position supported by polling conducted at the time by external agencies. However, strongly favourable views were also found. This raised the philosophical and political question of whether the majority view should prevail or whether the wishes of minorities should be accommodated. The commission noted that the existence of private schools was not strongly in question. The main issue was whether, and to what extent, public funding should be used to support such schools. A subsidiary issue was what form such schools should take and how much independence they should enjoy should public funding be made available.

The commission gave three arguments in support of private schools:

(a) the prior right of parents—in the name of either natural law or the importance of maintaining sub-cultural identities in a multicultural society—to select, free from financial considerations, the kind of education they believe to be appropriate to their child(ren);
(b) the perceived discrimination in the province providing to the Roman Catholic community an educational option not offered to other communities—at least other religious communities;
(c) the alleged inequity arising from the "double taxation" of parents who must pay both private school tuition fees and their share of the education taxes raised in support of the publicly funded schools.[2]

Three main arguments against such funding were also identified:

(a) whatever one's views about the funding of private schools in principle, the present constraint on resources in the public schools in relationship to the breadth of their mandate make any programme designed to extend public funding to other schools inappropriate at this time;
(b) in a heterogeneous society such as Ontario, the role of the public schools in providing a common acculturation experience for young citizens and thereby building the social cohesion, tolerance and understanding necessary to our common future should be reinforced rather than set aside;
(c) only in a context in which almost all young people attend the common public schools can these schools even potentially act so as to provide equality of educational opportunity for those of the young who do not bring to schooling particular advantages of background and experience.[3]

In the end, the commission had to admit that no consensus could be found and that none of the arguments for or against could be taken as definitive. Any recommendations that could be made would obviously fail to satisfy some interest groups. The commission took it as its task to find a balance between the demand for diversity and greater parental choice and the integrity of the public school system, while ameliorating the discrimination inherent in constitutionally protected support for one religious group but not others.

Nevertheless, the commission finally concluded that the arguments in favour of private schools were stronger than those opposed, that there is more than one way to meet the goals of public education and there is reason to encourage diversity in approaches. This led to key recommendations that private schools should continue to exist, be recognized in legislation, and receive public funding. The commission also recommended that they be renamed "independent schools." These recommendations were subject to conditions related to quality of instruction and employment of qualified teachers, intended to ensure that private schools met basic standards. Access to public funding should be subject to schools meeting specific goals of public education while allowing for religious and cultural diversity. In particular, the commission was of the view that, to the extent possible, arrangements be negotiated between school boards and independent schools. Those reaching such agreements would be defined as "associated schools."

The commission took the position that associated schools should receive most of the operational funding available to public schools, that such schools not charge tuition fees, and that boards receive funding for transportation and learning materials for associated school students. For non-associated schools, the commission recommended that funding take the form of direct grants to schools rather than vouchers or tuition fee tax deductions. Such schools would also be free to raise funds for capital projects and special programs but not to support tuition.

Shortly after the Shapiro report was issued, the Ontario government changed, and no direct action was taken on that report. Rather than creating an opening for other religions, as Shapiro recommended, the new government decided to move ahead with extending the Catholic separate system through the end of secondary school. Although Ontario has never acted, some other provinces have embraced many concepts in the Shapiro report and have provided some funding for independent schools.

Scope and Characteristics of Private Schools

It is helpful to distinguish between two distinct classes of private schooling in Canada. The first encompasses schools that are not under provincial or territorial control and receive no public funding. The second is schools run by independent boards of governors but receive partial provincial funding and adhere to most provincial program requirements. These are often called independent schools, following the model of the Shapiro report. Almost all private schools are governed by not-for-profit community or parent boards. Only a few fall into the for-profit category. Some may consider charter schools as a third class because they have a greater degree of autonomy under local governing councils than regular public schools. However, in Canada, Charter schools are unique to Alberta and, even there, make up only an extremely small proportion of schools. Also, charter schools are prohibited from being denominational in character.

In 2016, the Fraser Institute completed the first-ever survey of the scope of private schools in Canada.[4] Tables 6.1 and 6.2 show some of the characteristics of interest here. The number of private schools and the proportion of total enrolment in these schools vary widely across provinces. Quebec and British Columbia have a substantially larger proportion of private schools and higher enrolments in these schools than any of the other provinces. Both these provinces also provide some funding for private schools. The smallest proportions are found in the Atlantic provinces and Saskatchewan. Ontario, Alberta, and Saskatchewan have the lowest proportion enrolled in Catholic private schools. This is expected as these are the provinces with publicly funded Catholic systems. According to an earlier Fraser Institute study, private school enrolment is increasing at a slow but constant pace.[5]

Table 6.1. Private and independent schools by province

Province	Number of Schools	Total Enrolment (2013-2014)	Total Provincial Enrolment	% of Total Provincial Enrolment
Newfoundland	6	957	67,923	1.41
Nova Scotia	31	3,488	121,029	2.88
Prince Edward Island	2	209	20,133	1.04
New Brunswick	20	1,032	99,921	1.03
Quebec	285	123,161	869,898	14.16
Ontario	954	116,824	2,015,385	5.80
Manitoba	97	15,260	179,109	8.52
Saskatchewan	55	4,308	170,866	2.52
Alberta	145	28,076	611,874	4.59
British Columbia	340	75,402	527,460	14.30
Canada	1,935	368,717	4,683,598	7.87

Source: Schools and enrolment data adapted with permission from Table 1 in D. J. Allison, S. Hasan, and D. Van Pelt, *A Diverse Landscape: Independent Schools in Canada* (Vancouver: Fraser Institute, 2016). Total provincial enrolment adapted from Statistics Canada CANSIM Table 477-0035.

Table 6.2 shows that close to half of all private schools have religious affiliation. Contrary to what may be expected, the largest proportion is not Catholic but other Christian. That is also explained by the existence of separate Catholic schools in three provinces. A more detailed look at a sample of the other Christian schools reveals that most have what is generally thought of as an evangelical Christian orientation. A few long-established schools are identifiable with mainstream Protestant denominations, particularly the Anglican church.

Table 6.2. Religious affiliation of private and independent schools

	Catholic	Other Christian	Islamic	Jewish	Other	Total Religious	Percentage of Total that Are Religious
Newfoundland	2	1	0	0	0	3	50.00
Nova Scotia	1	10	1	0	0	12	38.71
Prince Edward Island	0	2	0	0	0	2	100.00
New Brunswick	2	13	0	0	0	15	75.00
Quebec	40	10	11	33	0	94	32.98
Ontario	15	325	69	44	4	457	47.90
Manitoba	17	40	2	2	1	62	63.92
Saskatchewan	3	30	3	0	0	36	65.45
Alberta	4	58	4	3	2	71	48.97
British Columbia	79	94	5	6	4	188	55.29
Total	163	583	95	88	11	940	48.58
Percent of Total	8.42	30.13	4.91	4.55	0.57	48.58	
Percent of Total Population	38.99	28.28	1.00	3.21			

Source: Adapted with permission from Table 4 in Allison, Hasan, and Van Pelt. *A Diverse Landscape*.

Comparing the last two rows of table 6.2 gives a rough estimate of how religions are represented in private schools relative to their population proportions.[6] This indicates that Catholics are underrepresented in private schools. Again, this reflects the existence of Catholic separate schools. The Jewish population, though only a small proportion of the total, is over-represented in private schools, as is the Muslim population by a smaller margin. Interestingly, the major South Asian religions, specifically Hindus and Sikhs, who together make up about 3 percent of the population, seem not to have been active in establishing private religious schools.

Despite the widely held view that private schools are becoming ever more popular and widespread, the above table shows that the enrolment proportion for Ontario is only slightly higher than that reported by Shapiro in 1983. However, the number of private schools has almost doubled. This implies that private schools, on average, have become much smaller. This is likely related to the absorption of former Catholic private secondary schools into the separate school system. Data for a similar time spread are not available for other provinces. Statistics for the past ten years for Alberta show a stable proportion of just over 4 percent of total enrolment attending private schools. The most recent Statistics Canada figures, based on data from the provinces, show a five-year increase in private school enrolment, from 6.8 percent to 7.2 percent.[7] Most of the growth is found in Quebec and British Columbia, both of which also have the greatest overall proportions attending private schools.

Private School Legislation

Legislation governing private schools varies significantly by province. Some have separate acts governing such schools while others have sections or regulations on the topic within their school acts. At a minimum, provinces regulate matters such as building safety and enforce compulsory attendance. Most require ministerial permission in the form of certificates or licences. Some require conformity to provincial programs and inspections if the school wishes to issue provincial graduation certificates. Although religion is not a primary theme in legislation, it is a significant motivating factor in establishing private schools and in parent decisions to use such schools.

A few legislative provisions do refer to the place of religion in private schools. For example, the Nova Scotia legislation explicitly states that "A private school may offer a religious-based curriculum."[8] British Columbia legislation refers to religion only in the negative, prohibiting "religious intolerance or persecution"[9] in private schools. Saskatchewan defines a religiously based independent school as one that "(i) is owned or operated by a non-profit corporation; and (ii) has, as its principal object, the advancement of education from a religiously-based philosophical perspective."[10]

The main distinction in legislation is between those provinces that provide some form of provincial assistance and those that do not. Table 6.3 shows the levels of funding available in each province. In all cases, funding is provided only to schools that meet certain criteria, typically conformity to provincial programs and assessment standards and hiring certified teachers. The religious affiliation of the school appears to have no bearing on funding.

Table 6.3. Provincial Private School Funding Provisions

Province	Funding
Newfoundland	None
Nova Scotia	None
Prince Edward Island	None
New Brunswick	None
Quebec	
French	50%
English (secondary schools only)	50%
Ontario	None
Manitoba	50%
Saskatchewan	50%
Alberta	
Independent	60%
Charter	100%
British Columbia	
Group 1	50%
Group 2	35%

Source: Provincial education ministry websites.

In addition to the direct provincial funding shown, income tax regulations allow a tax deduction for that proportion of a private school program that is explicitly religious in nature.[11] The school must be a registered charity and must either teach religion exclusively or operate in a dual capacity providing both religious and secular education. In the latter case, the religious component must be distinguishable from the academic component.

Private schools in Canada are well promoted. Many have elaborate websites and employ advertising and other recruitment strategies to attract students. Several more general websites extolling the benefits of private schooling may also be found.[12] Long-established schools have extensive alumni networks that serve both recruitment and fundraising purposes. Some such schools have an elite reputation stemming from their long history, perception of quality, distinguished alumni, and other factors. Private schools also tend to attract students from more affluent families, which contributes to their reputation for elitism. However, according to the Fraser Institute study cited earlier, the elite prep school is not the most common type of private school. Most are either religiously oriented, specialized in some way such as in the arts, science, or sports, or are intended to serve students with disabilities.

A review of the websites of some Christian, Jewish, and Muslim schools indicates that religion is a key part of their programs. Students and/or parents are often required to sign a statement that the student will adhere to the religious identity of the school. References to the religious atmosphere of these schools suggest an orientation similar to what Catholic schools refer to as permeation—a pervasive atmosphere that reflects religious values. Given these characteristics, it seems clear that, even if open admission is available, few parents would send their children to these schools unless they were adherents or supporters of the particular religion identified with the school. A similar point may be made about teacher employment. References can be found to policies implying that these schools seek teachers of appropriate background. Even though supported schools are required to hire certified teachers, the religious orientation of these teachers would likely be a condition of employment.

Supreme Court Decisions on Private Schools

Several of the Charter cases discussed in chapter 3 have a direct bearing on the scope and limitations set by the courts on private schools. In the *Jones* case[13] in Alberta, the Supreme Court held that the right of parents to educate their children as they see fit is not infringed by the existence of compulsory state standards, even though those are the very standards to which some parents object. In Ontario, the *Adler* case drew attention to the privileged place of the Catholic church and raised the question of the possible role of private schools in serving other religions.[14] The Supreme Court made it clear that the non-discrimination provisions of the Charter cannot be used to override Section 93 and that constitutional amendment is the only means of removing the privilege accorded to Catholic schools under Section 93. Private religious schools may exist and may be provincially funded, but they enjoy no constitutional protection.

In the *Loyola High School* case the court attempted to strike a balance between the provincial interest in school programming and the right of a private school in matters of religion.[15] The ruling required the school to teach the mandatory provincial religious education course but allowed it to supplement this course with material taught from a Catholic perspective. Although widely seen as a victory for private schools, the implication of the decision seems to be that freedom of religion cannot be exercised in a school in a way that is discriminatory towards other religions.

Student Performance in Private Schools

Many parents send their children to private schools in the belief that they are somehow better than public schools. This raises the same issue examined for Catholic schools in the previous chapter. While that belief may be grounded in religion, there are many other possible reasons for such decisions. These include performance, discipline, selectivity, programming, competition, family history, parent rights, or the elitist reputation of some private schools. Any combination of such factors may be at play in any individual decision.

While there is no shortage of opinion, there is little hard evidence on the overall merits of private schools or specifically on the part played by religion in these schools. The research on private schools shows similar results to that on Catholic schools and also suffers from many of the same design limitations. However, some private school research is based on more comprehensive data bases and incorporates some design improvements. In general, private schools achieve better results than public schools on provincial, national, and international achievement measures. Most of the difference is attributable to student background and socio-economic status or, more specifically, to selectivity. For example, a recent Statistics Canada study of long-term outcomes (e.g., test scores, high school graduation, post-secondary attendance) for students in public and private schools indicates that most of the variation in these outcomes is due to student background factors such as parent education rather than type of school.[16] A more comprehensive international study, based on data from the OECD Programme for International Student Assessment, reached the same conclusion.[17] That study also indicated that countries having a large proportion of private schools do not perform better on average than those with small proportions. Unfortunately, other than those that focus specifically on Catholic schools in the United States, the studies shed no light on the performance of religious schools relative to other private schools.

The Policy Issue

The critical policy question is whether there is any need for private schools in a country where comprehensive public education is available to all. More specifically, should such schools receive public funding, even on a partial scale? Some argue that the existence of private schools helps meet the fundamental obligation of states to honour the prior right of parents to educate their children as they see fit. Others hold that private schools provide an element of competition, thus helping hold the public system to higher standards. Related to both these points is the concept that choice in schooling is inherently a good thing and that greater choice promotes harmony in society. The latter is especially appealing to those whose religious beliefs and practices are seen to be compromised in a secular public system.

All these arguments support the conclusion reached by the Shapiro Commission that private schooling should be publicly funded at the same level as public schooling. The double taxation issue that was the subject of so much controversy and litigation in the early years of public schooling remains as valid today as before. If, for religious or other reasons, parents wish to exercise a right to an alternative form of education, why should they pay for both that education and for public schools? That argument is strengthened by the fact that one religion remains privileged in having access to full public funding. Despite these arguments the courts have consistently ruled against those claiming relief from double taxation.

The issue of inherent parent rights versus the obligation of the state to provide common public education is addressed in more detail in the final chapter. Suffice it to say that, in the end, this is a political matter, involving difficult trade-offs. The arguments for and against private schools presented by the Shapiro Commission remain the same today as when that report was written. Nevertheless, it is clear that a large majority of the population supports non-sectarian public schooling. Whether the majority will continue to accept the existence of private or separate schools in the interest of accommodating dissenting minorities, or whether the majority will eventually force governments to address the issue more fully, is by no means clear. For our purposes, the issue of private schools based on religion should be separated from their existence for other reasons. Indeed, other than the issue of discrimination against non-Catholics, no constitutional question arises over provincial legislation governing private schools. While there is no constitutional barrier to provinces establishing and funding private schools, an issue would likely arise if they attempted to do this for some additional religious groups while excluding others.

CHAPTER 7

The Churches, the Federal Government, and Indigenous Education

The full story of the treatment of Indigenous Peoples by churches and governments is beyond the scope of this book. Nevertheless, the issue is relevant because this is the only aspect of education that is constitutionally the responsibility of the federal government. As in other areas, it is fair to say that the churches were there from the beginning, with missionaries accompanying the earliest settlers. Neglect by colonial governments and by the federal government following confederation led to a dominant role for the churches. For more than a century, Indigenous education was effectively contracted out to the various Christian denominations. The collaboration of the churches in the federal government's assimilation policy following confederation is one of the most ignominious chapters in Canadian education.

This chapter focuses mainly on the role of church and state in the rise and fall of the residential school system. Some reference is also made to day schools. The chapter draws extensively from the work of the Truth and Reconciliation Commission of Canada. The report's volume on history is by far the most comprehensive account of the intersection of religious and government policy, effectively subsuming almost all else that has been written on the subject. That document is readily available to readers desiring more detail on the issue.[1]

The Colonial Era

The Truth and Reconciliation Commission began with the assertion that the relationship between European and Indigenous people is the consequence of an imperialist culture based on the "doctrine of discovery," the belief that God had given the Christian nations the right to colonize the lands they discovered as long as they converted the Indigenous populations, and the conviction that Europeans were bringing the benefits of civilization to the heathen.[2]

The doctrine of discovery fitted well with the doctrine of the Catholic church, which saw the values of the church as universal truths to be promulgated to the entire world. Other Christian sects adopted much the same view. All the European colonizing nations took the view that the lands being claimed were *terra nullius*, that the native populations merely occupied but did not own the land, and that these populations needed to be civilized and Christianized.

The explorers and settlers of New France were accompanied by members of Roman Catholic religious orders whose main mission was to spread the gospel. Although these early efforts are often considered as assimilative, Magnuson[3] has argued that this was not the case and that the Jesuits did not see it as their mission to turn the native tribes into Europeans, despite their efforts at religious conversion. In addition to carrying out their self-appointed mission of conversion, the missionaries also taught practical skills such as agriculture and carpentry, skills thought necessary to function in the colonial society.

Catholic missionaries were clear in their mandate to convert the world to the one true universal religion. Protestant sects were united mainly in their antipathy to Catholicism. Anglicans tended to see no distinction between their desire to convert and their service to the Empire. Other denominations saw their mission in pragmatic as well as evangelical terms, sometimes even taking the position that their mission was to save the Indigenous people from the ravages brought by the white men.

Residential schools had their origins in the belief that Indigenous people needed to be taught agricultural and mechanical skills. One of the earliest examples was the Mohawk Institute, a residential school for boys, operated by the Anglican Church from 1828 to 1885. Even by the 1840s, however, it was becoming apparent that the civilization policy was failing. In 1846, the Conference of the Narrows was convened in Orillia, at which leaders of the Indian Affairs Department met with

Indigenous leaders to promote a more radical version of the policy, based explicitly on the removal of children from their families. One of the main goals was that graduates of the schools would be able to return to teach and make the schools self-sufficient. Although there was some disagreement among the Indigenous leaders, in the end they agreed to support the proposal.

Egerton Ryerson, the superintendent of schools for Upper Canada, was asked to prepare a report on how this should be implemented. Ryerson's proposal for industrial schools was to form the basis for the residential school movement. Two schools were established the next year at Alderville and Munceytown, operated by the Wesleyan Methodist Society. Descriptions of life in these schools given by the Truth and Reconciliation Commission attest to the harsh conditions faced by the children and the problems of recruitment and attendance caused by the separation of children from their families. As a result of these conditions the schools had a short life, with both closing by the early 1860s.

The relatively large French and Métis population of Western Canada gave a much stronger Catholic presence in the West than in Ontario. In the early 1840s, Bishop Provencher arranged to have nuns from the Sisters of Charity of Montréal (the Grey Nuns) and members of the Oblate Order, both of which had become established in Quebec, move to Red River to found schools. One of the first two Oblates to come to the territory was none other than Alexandre Taché, who eventually became Archbishop of St. Boniface and a fierce defender of separate schools in the West. The Oblates were more assiduous than others in establishing residential schools. By 1870, fourteen such schools were operating in the North-West. Even though these schools were able to attract only a small proportion of all the Indigenous children in the area, they were considered by the federal government as successful enough to warrant a subsidy and a policy to expand these schools throughout the territory.

Confederation and the Indian Act

Subsection 91 (24) of the British North America Act assigned responsibility for "Indians and lands reserved for Indians" to the federal government. Education was one of the many areas implicitly covered by the subsection. Its effect was to separate Indigenous education policies from those applying to the settler population. This divergence was to have lasting effects on the Indigenous population.

The constitutional protections granted to Catholics and Protestants in provincial systems did not apply to the federal government. Although education was critical to the policy of assimilation, the federal government appeared to take no direct interest in providing education services. This left the churches with a virtual monopoly on education. If conversion and civilization were to be the goals and separation of children from their parents and culture the means, then residential schools seemed to be the only institutions through which this could be accomplished. Despite the earlier failures, the period from 1867 to 1900 saw a dramatic expansion of the residential school movement throughout the provinces and the Northwest Territories.

In 1876, all previous legislation pertaining to Indigenous populations was consolidated into "an Act to amend and consolidate the laws respecting Indians," commonly known as the Indian Act.[4] By then, most of the earlier provisions designed to treat Indigenous Peoples as independent nations had been abandoned. The ultimate goal of the Indian Act was enfranchisement, though this was interpreted in terms of assimilation. That act remains in existence to this day though it has undergone many amendments and revisions.

The sole reference to education in the original version of the Indian Act was to the responsibility of chiefs to make rules and regulations for the "construction and repair of school houses, council houses and other Indian public buildings."[5] However, an 1880 revision added the following:

> 74 (1). [The Chief may make rules and regulations] ... as to what religious denomination the teacher of the school established on the reserve shall belong to; provided always, that he shall be of the same denomination as the majority of the band; and provided that the Catholic or Protestant minority may likewise have a separate school with the approval of and under regulations to be made by the Governor in Council.[6]

This amendment established the exclusively denominational nature of schools established under the Indian Act. No direct provision was made for common schools or for any form of non-Christian Indigenous religion or spirituality. It is unclear if Protestant schools were intended to be generically Protestant, as in most provinces, or exclusive to one denomination. However, the missionary legacy created a situation in which most schools were operated by a single denomination.

Anglicans, Methodists (later United Church), Presbyterians, and other denominations were all active in operating residential schools, though on a smaller scale than the Catholic orders.

Residential Schools

Most of the early Indian schools were day schools. Nevertheless, from 1870 onward, several of the church-run schools had begun to take on children from other communities as boarders. The Truth and Reconciliation Commission reports that Prime Minister John A. MacDonald, who was responsible for Indian affairs, wrote in 1882 that "although the day schools in the North-West were suffering from poor attendance, due to the indifference of the parents and from incompetent teachers, as a result of the remoteness of the schools, the residential industrial schools of eastern Canada had 'improved greatly during the last four or five years.'"[7]

This seems to have been the beginning of federal government policy favouring residential schools over community day schools. The 1879 Davin report specifically called for the erection of four more residential schools in the North-West. Davin recommended that one of these should be operated by each of the mainstream denominations: Anglican, Catholic, Methodist, and Presbyterian.[8] The churches appeared more than willing to accept this responsibility, no doubt to the relief of the government.

Indian day schools were community-based and were usually established at the initiative of missionaries and community members. Residential schools, on the other hand were established largely through government initiative, received more government funding and were more explicitly designed to serve the government goal of assimilation. Nevertheless, the churches had an obvious vested interest in these schools. Indeed, according to the commission, a government attempt to wind down the system in the early 1900s was blocked by the churches who saw these schools as a primary tool in their competition for converts.[9]

The number of residential schools increased rapidly over the next few years; by 1886, about fifty such schools were in operation. The Catholic orders were more active than others in establishing these schools, operating about three-quarters of them at that time. Broad policies for such schools were intended to support the government goal of assimilation. However, day-to-day running of these schools remained in the hands of the churches, whose own policies were almost entirely in accord with those of the federal government.

It is impossible here to do justice to the description of the harsh conditions in the residential schools. That has been amply documented by the Truth and Reconciliation Commission. Suffice it to say that from the beginning there was evidence of appallingly poor conditions and mistreatment of children. Issues ranged from the state of the buildings, access to water, the need for manual labour superseding the educational purpose, the effects of infectious diseases, restrictions on native languages and cultural practices, and instances of physical and sexual abuse.

The government seemed to be reluctant to challenge the control of the churches. Indian Affairs officials prepared many reports and proposed many policy directions, most of which seem to have been ignored. A couple of these reports touched on the issue of church control. For example, an 1886 report by J. A. Macrae, the school inspector for Manitoba recommended "that Indian Affairs, rather than the churches, should have 'control of the schools in all essential points.' This would include approval of the hiring of staff, the description of the duties of teachers, teacher salaries, and the school regulations."[10] Hayter Reed, the Indian commissioner for the North-West Territories and Manitoba, also reported that "no hope need be entertained of the various denominations relinquishing the hold they already have upon the rising generation through such schools." Nevertheless, he recommended that "in the future, any residential schools that were to be supported solely by the government should be non-sectarian."[11] The Macrae and Reed proposals went nowhere. The government appeared to believe that the churches represented a source of cost-savings because their staff would work for lower salaries than others and that the schools could become self-supporting through child labour.

The growth of residential schools is illustrated by statistics given by the Truth and Reconciliation Commission. In 1895–1896, approximately 1,300 children were enrolled in each of the boarding and residential schools and about 7,000 in day schools. At its peak in the late 1930s, about 9,000 children were enrolled in 79 residential schools and 9,300 in 288 day schools. By 1968–1969 there were still about 8,000 students living in residences, which by then was only a small minority of all the First Nations children in school. The others had either been integrated into provincial schools or were enrolled in schools controlled by

First Nations bands. After that, the residential schools were reclassified as residences and no further enrolment statistics were kept.

Despite the recommendation that future schools be non-sectarian, the various churches competed to establish new schools, sometimes opening the school first and then lobbying for government funding. Catholics were most successful at expansion, having more than half of all residential schools by the 1920s. Government efforts to reduce competition were largely unsuccessful. Any government attempt to achieve efficiency was offset by church claims to equal rights among the competing denominations.

One area on which the churches and government appeared to differ was that of religious education. Turning Indigenous children into good Christians, of the appropriate denomination, was the primary goal of the churches. In the residential school setting, the jurisdiction of the school authorities extended over the full lives of the students, making it easy to enforce compulsory participation in religious activities. On the other hand, the Indian Act said nothing about religious education. While government policy aligned with that of the churches in almost all respects, some Indian Affairs officials felt that too much attention was being paid to religious education at the expense of other aspects of the program. In the Catholic schools, in particular, religion was often taught in the native languages, a practice contrary to the government position that the emphasis should be on English.

Day Schools

Before continuing the story of residential schools, it is useful to examine briefly what we know about the state of day schools at the time and the role of the churches in their operation. Unfortunately, there seems to be no comprehensive history of such schools comparable to that for residential schools. However, available documentation gives a picture of government and church policy similar to that for residential schools. A couple of examples serve to illustrate the point.

Coates examined the relationship between church, state, and the Native Peoples in the Yukon from 1840 to 1973.[12] For the churches, there seems to have been little distinction between missionary work and education. The goals were the same: the clergy doubled as teachers and the churches were able to use the meagre state support available for education to support their missionary work. Coates documents the close collaboration between church and state, quoting one missionary's comment that "both are aiming to prevent crime and evil. One has the law while the other has the Gospel."[13] However, he also makes a case that the reality on the ground seldom matched the ideology. Indeed, he argues that "local conditions including high costs, a pessimistic forecast of the region's potential for development, difficulty securing suitable personnel, native mobility, and the activities of non-natives who seldom shared the idealists' objectives, prevented the quick achievement of the idealists' objectives."[14]

A 1995 article by Susan Gray paints a picture of Methodist schools in Northern Manitoba at the end of the nineteenth century and the first quarter of the twentieth.[15] That account tells of a request by the Methodists to Indian Affairs for funding for a day school at Nelson House. Part of their case was based on the fact that the Anglicans and Catholics already had several schools in the area. When officials countered that that these schools should suffice, the Methodists went ahead and set up a school without a grant, presumably hoping that once the school was in operation the grant would follow.

Gray also reports that members of this and other communities were dissatisfied with the day schools, preferring boarding schools, perhaps so that the children could continue their education while the adults were away in the bush. This suggests that community support did exist for residential schools, albeit with an entirely different motive from that of the churches and government. There is no way of knowing the extent to which the position of the communities was influenced by officialdom. Written requests from chiefs may well have been prepared by church or government officials. There is certainly nothing to suggest that conditions in the day schools were any better than those at residential schools or that the community had much influence on what went on in these schools.

Doubts about the Residential School System

As early as 1907, Dr. Peter Bryce, the chief medical officer of the Department of Indian Affairs, reported on conditions in the Indian schools of Manitoba and the Northwest Territories.[16] Bryce drew attention to the poor health and sanitary conditions of these schools, the high incidence of tuberculosis, and the high death rates of children in these schools. Apparently that report was never published, but it was leaked to the press, leading to demands for reform. After what appears to be his forced retirement, Bryce wrote a short pamphlet appealing for justice for the Indians of Canada which was highly critical of his superiors in Indian Affairs for their neglect of the Indian population.[17]

By the late 1930s, the federal government was becoming more convinced that the residential school policy was failing. A 1938 Indian Affairs report indicated that these schools accounted for about half the total enrolment of Indian students but more than three-fourths of the total education budget.[18] The main recommendation was that residential schools be replaced by on-reserve day schools providing a combination of academic and vocational training. This proposal was opposed by all the churches involved. Though acknowledging that the residential model had largely failed, the church reaction was that it should be intensified rather than abandoned. Blame for the failure rested not with the churches but with Indigenous families and leadership for not fully buying into the system. This led to a deadlock between government and churches that lasted another generation.

In 1946, a joint Senate and House of Commons committee was formed to conduct a broad review of Indian policies. While it appeared that the preponderance of Indigenous opinion favoured day schools over residential schools, the latter had some defenders. The strongest defence came from the Catholics, who compared these schools to the private boarding schools attended by the country's elite. The Anglican church also expressed its continued support, stressing that Canada had been founded as a Christian state and that secular education was inadequate to allow Native Canadians to become full citizens. Nevertheless, the Anglicans were of the view that some residential schools could be transformed into hostels where children could board while attending public schools.

The United Church took a more nuanced position, arguing that it was time to abandon the policy of segregating Indigenous people on the reserves. It particularly opposed any move to extend the residential school program to include secondary education, a position directly at odds with that of the Catholic church. The United Church was also the only denomination to argue that Indigenous education should be reorganized on a non-sectarian basis, with appropriate provision for religious education.

The joint committee issued its report in 1948. At the same time Indian Affairs produced a draft of a new Indian act. The draft authorized the minister to enter into agreements with provincial and territorial governments, school boards, religious bodies, and charities to arrange for the education of children with status under the Indian

Act. It also provided bands with the opportunity to determine if day schools on reserves would be denominational or non-denominational. This represented the first sign of a breach in the long-standing federal government compact with the churches. These provisions were strongly opposed by the Catholic church. Any movement of students to provincial systems, particularly to public schools, would obviously undermine church control.

These changes to the Indian Act resulted in a rapid increase in the number of students attending provincial and on-reserve day schools. Despite the manifest failure of residential schools as a tool for assimilation, the churches held to the view that any limitations of these schools were due to insufficient insulation of children from their culture. The Truth and Reconciliation Commission captured this view in the following quotation from a 1958 article by a senior Oblate, André Renaud: "[day schools were inferior to residential schools] because when the day school students went back to their homes at the end of the school day and for the weekend, the pupils are re-exposed to their native culture, however diluted, from which the school is trying to separate them." A residential school, on the other hand, "could surround its pupils almost twenty-four hours a day with non-Indian Canadian culture through radio, television, public-address system, movies, books, newspapers, group activities, etc."[19]

Around the same time the deputy minister of Indian Affairs was quoted as characterizing the funding regime as "a system of making outright donations to the religious denominations."[20] Indeed, over the 1946–1951 period, the level of funding for residential schools more than doubled even though enrolment had not changed. Further increases were accompanied by greater federal control of major expenditures such as teachers' salaries, which the government started to pay directly in 1954. Catholic religious orders were paid an aggregate sum with no individual member being assigned a salary. This allowed the orders to retain funds that were beyond government control. Under a funding formula introduced in 1957, the government entered into new contracts with the main church bodies. The Catholic contract was with the Oblates. Contracts with the other churches were with their national missionary organizations.

The slow pace at which the system was transformed is accounted for largely by the absence of suitable alternatives to residential schools. Also significant was the continuing intense competition between the Anglican and Catholic churches. In principle both the Anglican and

United churches supported integration. However, Anglican actions were more in keeping with the rivalry with Catholics than with the principle. The Truth and Reconciliation Commission cites a 1947 Anglican report,[21] which made numerous references to the need to keep schools open to counter the Catholic presence. The rivalry was supported by a policy that no Protestant child be assigned to a Catholic school and no Catholic child to a Protestant school.

The expansionist position of the Catholic church was a source of intense tension between the church and the federal government. The church not only opposed in principle the emerging policy of integrating children into provincial schools, it was also eager to expand residential school programs to the secondary level. Indian Affairs opposed this initiative for many reasons, including inconsistency with the integration policy, its cost, and the difficulty in finding qualified teachers. Senior Catholic officials were relentless in pressing their case, often to the point of ignoring Indian Affairs directives against expanding schools. Though largely indifferent to the wishes of Indigenous parents and leaders in other areas, it did not hesitate to solicit their support in disputes with the government. As a result, Catholic residential schools continued to expand in contravention of government policy.

The End of the Residential School System

The whole matter came to a head in the late 1960s. The Canadian Labour Relations Board ruled that teaching staff in residential schools were effectively public employees, which left the government and the churches two options: bypass the ruling by placing the schools back under full control of the churches or, accept the ruling, forcing the government to take over the schools. The government favoured the second option, despite its added cost, because a takeover would allow it to finally wind down the residential school system. The major denominations were divided on the matter, with the Anglican and United churches indicating their willingness to get out of residential schooling and the Catholic church insisting on the right to run its own schools.

Another issue soon emerged in the form of increased activism among Indigenous groups. The main trigger for this activism was a white paper on Indigenous affairs issued by the government of Prime Minister Pierre Trudeau.[22] That paper proposed a more radical version of the integration policy, intended to erase any distinction between Indigenous and other citizens. That precipitated a strong reaction against the proposal to phase out these schools. The Truth and Reconciliation Commission seems to have captured the mood in this quote attributed to an Indigenous leader: "You got us into the residences kicking and screaming; you will now have to drag us out kicking and screaming."[23] The battle that ensued had less to do with residential schools than with the emerging desire of Indigenous people to control their own education.

In July 1970, a group of First Nations people began a sit-in at the Blue Quills school near the Saddle Lake reserve in Alberta, in protest of a federal plan to turn the school into a hostel and send its students to a provincial school. The minister, Jean Chrétien, no doubt by then resigned to the fact that his white paper was a failure, finally agreed to turn over administration of the school to the council. In turn, the council agreed to use the Alberta provincial curriculum with modifications to include Native culture.

After this and several less prominent disputes, there was no turning back from bringing schools under Indian control. A 1972 policy paper entitled *Indian Control of Indian Education*, prepared by the National Indian Brotherhood made a case for Indian control based on principles of parental and local control. *Indian Control of Indian Education* specifically argued that transfer of control can only be from the federal government to Indian bands.[24] The document proposed that, even while handing over control, the federal government continue to provide full and enhanced funding. Agreements with provincial authorities would have to be with individual bands. Indian representation would be required on provincial school boards serving Indian children.

The document made only one reference to any denominational presence in schools. "As in all other areas of education, the parents have the right to determine the religious status of the local school. In as far as possible, there should be an attempt to satisfy the preference of everyone."[25] That statement seems to affirm the principle of denominational education, though it did not explicitly state a requirement for separate schools or give any other detail on how this might work if parents differed in their denominational affiliations. What is clear is that any decision on the matter was to be in the hands of the community and not the church leadership.

After that, the numbers in residence continually declined. However, the need to accommodate orphans and children in care made it impossible to abandon residence life entirely. Although the last residential school, Grollier Hall in Inuvik, did not close until 1997, church control of these institutions effectively ended in 1969. The Oblates were by then experiencing a decline in recruits, and the Catholic church was suffering from a series of scandals. Even had there been no change in policy, the days of control of schools by clergy and religious orders would likely soon have ended.

However, this is far from the end of the story. The Truth and Reconciliation Commission documents in excruciating detail the long history of neglect, mistreatment, and abuse of children at the hands of staff and administrators of residential schools. Even before that, the 1996 Royal Commission on Indigenous Peoples was prominent in drawing attention to abuse.[26] Citing a Methodist church report of 1911, the commission summed up the attitude of both government and churches at the time in these words:

> Politician, civil servant and, perhaps most critically, priest and parson all felt that in developing the residential school system they were responding not only to a constitutional but to a Christian obligation to our Indian brethren that could be discharged only through the medium of the children and therefore education must be given the foremost place.[27]

The royal commission was direct in observing that opposition to closure of residential schools came almost exclusively from the Catholic church. Although the stated motive was altruistic, the commission also noted that this was related to the fact that Indigenous students in Manitoba and British Columbia would have no access to Catholic schools if they were transferred to the provincial system.

Apologies, Litigation, and Resolution

By the 1990s, the mainstream denominations had begun to reflect on their role and redirect their efforts towards support of Indigenous aspirations. In 1991, the Oblate Conference of Canada became the first group to apologize to the Native Peoples of Canada for their part in the abuse in residential schools. In it, they acknowledged that their actions originated in a belief in the superiority of Christian European culture and the ethnic, religious, and linguistic imperialism that followed from this belief.[28] Apologies from the Anglican Church,[29] the Presbyterian Church,[30] and the United Church followed.[31] It is notable that all these other churches adopted the position that responsibility lay with the church itself. However, for many years afterwards the Canadian Conference of Catholic Bishops held that it could not issue an apology in the name of the Catholic church because each diocese and religious order is independent and not responsible to the conference.[32] This long-held position finally changed after the discovery in 2021 of hundreds of unmarked graves at several residential school sites. The universal revulsion at these revelations meant that the issue could no longer be ignored. The long-awaited apology by the bishops was issued on September 24, 2021. In carefully chosen words, the bishops acknowledged the abuse by "some members of the Catholic community" and by those "Catholic entities" involved. This apology led to renewed emphasis on the Truth and Reconciliation Commission's calls for an apology from the Church as a whole; an act that could only be carried out by the Pope himself. In a swift series of events, arrangements were made for delegations from First Nations, Métis and Inuit communities to meet the Pope at the Vatican. This occurred during the last week of March 2022, during which the Pontiff issued apologies to each group.[33] The Pope also agreed to the demand of these groups that he visit Canada. At the time of writing, that visit has been scheduled for July 2022 (following a joking comment from the Pope that he would not visit in winter). Despite these actions, the issue remains controversial because no commitment was made on compensation. Many Indigenous groups are also concerned with the proposed restriction of the visit to three locations, while church officials plead that this is because of the Pope's age and physical disabilities.

Beginning in the late 1980s, a flood of civil litigation was unleashed. These cases raised many questions over the balance of responsibility across organizations, individual versus institutional responsibility, and the links between institutional abuse and the dysfunctionality of families and communities. The federal government and the churches mounted vigorous defenses, denying or attempting to shift responsibility to smaller groups or individuals. Nevertheless, the Truth and Reconciliation Commission recounts cases in which vicarious responsibility was assigned on a proportional basis to both churches and the federal government.[34] With respect to the Catholic church, the courts tended to uphold the claim that the church effectively does not exist as a national body and that only specific entities such as the Oblates could be sued.

It was apparent that many of the implicated entities would be unable to pay even if found liable. Many Catholic orders were in decline and some dioceses were close to bankruptcy from the abuse cases. The federal government thus decided to pursue negotiations towards an out-of-court settlement. Early negotiations with the churches failed, leading the federal government to unilaterally declare that it would fund 70 percent of any claims that could be validated by an alternative dispute resolution (ADR) process. The churches would be liable for the remainder. On that basis, an agreement was reached with the Anglican and Presbyterian churches. The United church objected to the government's decision to exclude compensation for cultural, language, and spiritual loss. However, it did agree to contribute 25 percent to 30 percent of individual awards in individual cases. No agreement was reached at the time with the Catholic entities.

It soon became clear that the process did not have the support of the Assembly of First Nations (AFN). In a highly critical report, the assembly complained that survivors of the Catholic schools would still have to sue specific Catholic entities such as the Oblates for the remainder. Two cases, known as *Cloud* and *Baxter* after the named claimants, were the most prominent of many attempts to launch class action suits. The claims against the churches were eventually dropped, leaving the federal government as the sole defendant. This, in turn, led the government to file a claim against the churches.

The *Cloud* case was originally heard in the Ontario Superior Court.[35] The trial judge declined to certify the case as a class action. That decision was overturned by the Ontario Court of Appeal[36] and the Supreme Court of Canada declined to hear the case.[37] However, by then it had become apparent that even class actions would be complex, costly, and time-consuming. This finally led the government, the churches, and Indigenous organizations to begin negotiations towards a settlement.

By the end of May 2005, the government and the Assembly of First Nations released the framework for a settlement. A draft agreement made no reference to the role of the churches. However, it seemed to be understood that the previous cost-sharing agreements with the churches would be part of the settlement. The final agreement, known as the Indian Residential Schools Settlement Agreement (IRSSA), was signed on May 23, 2006.[38] That agreement provided for common payments to all residential school survivors based on length of attendance, with additional payments to those who had suffered physical or sexual abuse or neglect. Crucially, the agreement also provided for the establishment of a Truth and Reconciliation Commission.

The final step in the saga was taken when Prime Minister Stephen Harper formally apologized to all former students of residential schools for the abuse, suffering, and generational and cultural dislocation that occurred in these schools.[39] All other parties in the House of Commons supported and gave their own version of that apology. For the most part, Indigenous leaders spoke with approval and optimism that this would end the long history of attempts at assimilation and lead to a new era of reconciliation.

Despite its broad scope, the agreement excluded several classes of persons who had been exposed to the schools. These included Métis students, those who had attended residential schools not primarily intended for Indigenous students, and those attending day schools but living in private boarding homes. Persons in Newfoundland and Labrador were also excluded because these were under provincial jurisdiction under the Terms of Union. Finally, day-school students in schools run by the churches were excluded. However, a settlement has also recently been reached in a class action lawsuit involving these schools.[40] This settlement appears to involve the federal government only and makes no direct reference to the role of churches in operating day schools.

The number of First Nations schools has continued to grow over the past few decades. For 2012, just over 500 such schools were in operation across Canada. These schools enrolled approximately 70,000 of the total of 109,000 First Nations students living on reserves.[41] However, fewer than half of all First Nations people live on reserves. Also, Métis and Inuit people are not part of the reserve system. This means that a large majority of Indigenous children now attend provincial or territorial schools.

In 2010, the Assembly of First Nations updated the 1972 document *Indian Control of Indian Education*, under the revised title *First Nations Control of First Nations Education*.[42] The revised document asserts that treaty rights and the rights of Aboriginal people under Section 35 of the constitution and Section 25 of the Charter must be respected, and reiterated the vision of local control of education. The document argues that the federal government has not lived up to its agreement to honour the spirit of that policy and has failed to provide adequate support for First Nations schooling. The federal government has responded by bringing forward a new collaborative framework and funding formula.[43] However, it is not yet clear if this will lead to significant change.

As for religion, the *First Nations Control* document retains the statement in the original that "As in all other areas of education, the parents have the right to determine the religious status of the local school. In as far as possible, there should be an attempt to satisfy the preference of everyone."[44] The document makes no further reference to religion, though its emphasis on preserving and enhancing Indigenous culture might be interpreted as including Indigenous spirituality.

It is difficult to find information on the extent to which the current situation on the ground is in accord with this statement. It is not difficult to imagine a scenario in which the majority denomination in a community might wish the school to reflect its teachings while people of other denominations might find this objectionable. In the extreme, this takes us back to the issue of separate schools. A search of available websites for some schools and of associations representing these schools yielded no direct reference to denominational character or to religion. A strong influence of Indigenous culture is evident, but it remains unclear if this includes denominational affiliation or Indigenous spirituality.

A recent British Columbia case illustrates the dilemma of how to address Indigenous spirituality in provincial schools.[45] In that case, a parent objected to a smudging ceremony held in a school. Candice Servatius, an evangelical Christian, held that the Bible is the sole authority for religious life and that the smudging ceremony, accompanied by a prayer offered by an Indigenous elder, violated her Charter right to be free from exposure to other religions. The school board countered that about one-third of the students in the school were Indigenous and that the activity was part of its effort to expose students to Indigenous culture. School personnel and the daughter of the plaintiff gave contradictory accounts of whether the daughter was offered an opportunity to leave the classroom during the ceremony.

The line of reasoning used in the case is complex and will not be recounted here. The case was dismissed on the grounds that exposure to alternative cultures and religions does not interfere with freedom of religion. What might interfere would be a requirement that children participate directly in such activities: for example, by requiring them to expose themselves directly to smoke or recite the prayer. The judge cited several of the cases, reviewed in chapter 3, in which the Supreme Court of Canada has held that exposure to a variety of religions in school does not infringe on freedom of religion.

Similarities and Differences in Indigenous and non-Indigenous Policies

Despite the dramatic difference in the development of Indigenous education compared to that for the settler population, some common elements exist in the role of churches. In both cases, the churches had established a presence before any significant state involvement. The churches shared a common belief that instilling Christian values was critical to the education of young people, whether Indigenous or settlers. Each church held the firm belief that its own brand of Christianity was the right one and that its role was to ensure that its own children were educated separately from the others. Even though the mainstream Protestant denominations moved away from that position in provincial education systems, they maintained it in their work in Indigenous schools. The Catholic church, persistent in its belief in the supremacy of church over state, has never willingly acceded to a common form of schooling.

Two main points of contrast stand out. The first is that the abuse found in Indigenous schools seems to have been less prevalent in non-Indigenous schools operated by religious groups. Discipline may have been harsh by contemporary standards. However, that did not usually deteriorate into systemic abuse in provincial denominational schools. The difference likely lies in the residential school model, where the churches were able to exert full control over the lives of the children. Indeed, the Mount Cashel scandal in Newfoundland, perhaps the most notorious case of abuse outside the Indigenous schools, occurred in a residential setting.

The second difference is the relative indifference of the federal government to its education obligations and its willingness to contract out the work to the churches long after that had been largely abandoned in provincial education systems. This was particularly incongruous because the federal government, unlike the provinces, had no constitutional obligation to protect any religious group. Even if the churches were willing supporters of the federal assimilation policy, there was no constitutional requirement that they become the main agents in implementing that policy.

In some ways, the position of the churches is more understandable than that of the federal government. Religious organizations, by definition, are driven by a firm belief in the righteousness of their cause. Conversion to Christianity was inherent in their mission worldwide. Education was seen as the primary means of serving that mission. Absent the motive for Christianization, there would have been no point in the churches becoming involved in Indigenous education. The churches could have pursued their mission without being complicit in the policy of assimilation. However, that would likely have deprived them of state support for their core mission.

It is likely, of course, that many of the federal politicians and officials responsible for Indigenous affairs were as firm as the churches in their belief in the virtues of the Christian religion. Nevertheless, it is interesting that the federal government seems to have learned no lesson from the controversy over its earlier interventions in the New Brunswick and Manitoba school issues. It is difficult to avoid the conclusion that the federal government saw its collaboration with the churches as key to implementing the assimilation policy and that this, in turn, contributed to the perpetuation of church influence in Indigenous education.

CHAPTER 8

The Contemporary Debate

Controversy over separate schools seems to have largely dissipated in jurisdictions where such schools no longer exist. Even in Newfoundland and Quebec, which arguably had the most entrenched systems, the debate effectively ended once the constitutional amendments came into effect. There is little evidence of any impetus anywhere to restore separate schools once they are dissolved. On the other hand, there seems to be no immediate existential threat to separate schools in Alberta, Ontario, or Saskatchewan. In the latter province, the final judgment in the recent *Theodore* case has reinforced separate school funding rights. Although the issue remains controversial in all three provinces, neither the governing nor opposition parties have made this issue an active part of their agendas. The notable exception was the Ontario Progressive Conservative Party's proposal in the 2007 election to extend public funding to schools of other religions—a proposal that arguably led to its defeat in that election.

The contemporary debate extends well beyond the Protestant / Catholic duality from which separation of schools originated. Increased religious diversity, the rise of secularism, parental rights versus state responsibility, accommodation of small religious minorities, religion as an issue of individual conscience, and the primacy of individual versus group rights as embodied in the Charter all serve to broaden the debate. This has led to flash points that have attracted public attention. This chapter gives some examples of such issues, reviews public opinion polling, and examines some judicial decisions that bear on freedom of religion, parent versus state rights, and accommodation of diversity.

What are the fault lines underlying the contemporary debate? Although the most obvious issue is the constitution, the Newfoundland and Quebec cases demonstrate that this can no longer be treated as either an absolute guarantee of denominational rights or a barrier to change. Much contemporary debate has shifted away from the traditional issues of control of school boards, taxation, teacher employment and the like, and towards social and moral issues. Much of this is driven by evangelical Christian denominations as well as some non-Christian religions. Catholic sentiment has shifted from demands to expand separate school systems to defence of the status quo. The Catholic position also seems to have evolved from an absolutist insistence that the church is the primary determiner of education to one that places greater emphasis on parent rights. In the Newfoundland case, for example, the Catholic church modified its position that all Catholic children should be educated in church-controlled schools in favour of an argument that Catholic schools are primarily for those who desire a Catholic education.

Current controversies are mainly about the reach of the public school system into areas of morality and particularly the intersection between the secularism of public schools and the religious beliefs of some individuals. Although the fundamental issue of parent rights and religious freedom versus state responsibility for education is sometimes lost in the noise, it is not difficult to trace much of the controversy to this duality. Politically, other considerations, such as cost, efficiency and language, not to mention political ideology, identity and wedge politics, also help drive the debate.

Sex and Health Education

No area seems to bring to the fore the issue of parent rights versus state responsibility more than that of sex and health education. A variety of conservative religious individuals and groups appear to have made common cause with the Catholic church in opposing recent moves in some provinces to expand and liberalize the school curriculum in this area. Much of the controversy is found in Ontario and Alberta, where the Catholic church can claim some right to dissent from provincial mandates in areas integral to church teaching. It is not clear if this has encouraged other like-minded people to protest curriculum changes viewed as impinging on religious freedom. However, this issue now seems to overshadow the more traditional debate over separate schools and bring into sharper focus the question of the scope and limits of religious freedom. Some examples of recent events illustrate the point.

In 2012, the Ontario legislature approved Bill 13, amending the Education Act to address the issue of bullying in schools. That bill included references to acceptance of all persons including those of any sexual orientation, gender identity, and gender expression.[1] The bill also required school boards to support students who wish to establish organizations to promote safe and inclusive schools. This specifically includes "activities or organizations that promote the awareness and understanding of, and respect for, people of all sexual orientations and gender identities, including organizations with the name gay-straight alliance or another name."[2] The bill went further in stating: "For greater certainty, neither the board nor the principal shall refuse to allow a pupil to use the name gay-straight alliance or a similar name for an organization described in clause (1) (d)."[3] In effect, this provision explicitly identifies sexual orientation as a potential point of contention on the way to schools becoming safer and more inclusive.

Responses to the bill by Catholic organizations show a division of views. The initial response from the Assembly of Catholic Bishops of Ontario raised concerns that the bill identified specific groups based on sexuality as requiring special attention. Nevertheless, the general tone of the response was positive. At the end, the assembly issued the following statement:

> Recognizing that the Accepting Schools Act is now the law, Catholic partners will seek, as we have always done, in a way that is in accord with our faith, to foster safe and welcoming school communities. Bullying, in any form, is unacceptable. At the core of our Catholic Christian beliefs is the command to welcome every person with love and respect.[4]

Just before Bill 13 was passed, the Ontario Catholic School Trustees Association issued its own document on bullying, entitled *Respecting Differences*.[5] While affirming the association's support for anti-bullying initiatives, the document makes it clear, in very carefully worded language, that all school programs and activities must conform to Catholic teaching. Specifically, the document recommends that the organizations be named "respecting differences" and not gay-straight alliances. It also specifically states that peer counselling and other forms of activism, protest, or advocacy not in accord with Catholic teaching are inappropriate activities for these organizations. In practice, although students cannot be prevented from forming clubs with the name gay-straight alliance, neither are they required to use that name. The desire seems to be to encourage students to use other names, avoiding confrontation over the issue.

Not all Catholics support these moderate positions. Parent protests led some Catholic school boards to consider defying the legislation. The Toronto Catholic School Board in 2013 heard presentations from parents on the issue before debating and rejecting a motion to ban gay-straight alliances in its schools.[6] The chair of that board, when pressed by a CBC reporter, declined to use the term gay-straight alliance in reference to student clubs in the board's schools.[7] The position seems to be that the board will comply with the law and allow the term to be used on student request but will encourage using other terminology. In an assertion of church rights over the judgment of school trustees, Parents as First Educators, a lobby group for Catholic parents, reported that it had obtained a legal opinion stating that Catholic school trustees are obliged to refuse to implement legislation that undermines the Catholic character of their schools.[8]

On the opposite side, the Ontario English Catholic Teachers' Association came out in support of gay-straight alliances. Its president was quoted in the *National Post* as saying that "Catholic bishops need reflect on whether a club like a gay-straight alliance is really going to be about advocating for a lifestyle. And the answer they should arrive at is no. These clubs are about building dialogue and safer classrooms and that's a good thing."[9] What is most striking about this statement is the fact that a prominent Catholic group has challenged the position of the church leadership. This, along with the fact that the official church took a more moderate position than usual on such matters, may reflect a shift in the church's position away from absolutism on issues of government policy that impinge on church doctrine. Possible reasons for this may be found in the recent Supreme Court cases on the limits of parents' rights to refuse on religious grounds participation in provincially mandated programs.

The controversy over gay-straight alliances might be seen as merely a skirmish compared to the furor over Ontario's introduction of a new health and physical education curriculum. Although sexual issues occupy only a small part of that program, that part is notable for taking a more explicit approach to the topic than before and especially for emphasizing consent over abstinence and for direct discussion of homosexuality, gender identity, and same sex marriage and parenting. These topics outraged not only some Catholic organizations but also conservative parents and organizations of various stripes. This led to street protests, petitions, a storm of social media activity, and threats to remove children from school.

The official Catholic position seems to be that Catholic schools are obliged to teach the program but must interpret it from a Catholic standpoint. The Association of Ontario Catholic Bishops responded to the curriculum by issuing its own document entitled *The Human Person, Love and Sexuality*.[10] That document recommends that educators avoid such terms as gay, lesbian, transgender, or cisgender because such terms fail to acknowledge the possibility of episodic or transient same-sex feelings or gender confusion, but they can cause a student to be labelled by one exclusive characteristic. The document also holds to the doctrine that acting on same-sex attractions is never acceptable.

Even before this document was issued, Catholic school boards were forced by parent protests to take a stand on the curriculum. In June 2015, the Toronto Catholic District School Board narrowly defeated a motion to write the minister of education requesting a delay in implementing the program.[11] At around the same time, the Halton Catholic District School Board also debated a motion to delay its implementation for one year. Part of that resolution cited the exclusive constitutional mandate of Catholic trustees to adapt Ministry of Education programs to ensure that they do not contradict Catholic teaching.[12] That motion was also defeated. In both cases, as with the motions on gay-straight alliances, majority of board members appear to be of the view that defying the legislation might be counterproductive, drawing unwanted attention to the continued existence of separate schools.

Protest over the health and physical education program is not confined to Catholic parents and organizations. Many conservative religious groups condemned the program and mounted protests. On April 14, 2015, the *Globe and Mail* reported that thousands of people gathered at Queen's Park to protest the program and that many ethnicities and religions were represented, including "Sikhs, Chinese, Muslims, Arabs, Caucasians and Eastern Europeans."[13] In response, Premier Kathleen Wynne reiterated the government's intention to go ahead with the program, reminding parents that they have a right to ask that their children be exempted from classes they believe conflict with their moral or religious beliefs.

The street protests were reinforced by websites and social media threads, many of which generated extreme reactions. Conspiracy theories abounded, many stemming from the premise that an openly gay premier and a former deputy minister of education who had been convicted of child pornography represent the leading edge of a conspiracy to corrupt the morals of children. Several parent groups advocated that children be kept home from school during the week of May 4–11, 2015. However, it appears that few followed that advice. Despite the protests, the program took effect in September 2015.

The involvement in this issue of religious and ethnic groups other than Catholics again brings to the fore the fundamental difference between the rights of Catholics and those of other religions in the Ontario school system. Having their own schools allows Catholics to adhere to the letter of the law while developing alternative approaches to the curriculum. In the absence of complaints from within the Catholic system, it is unlikely that such alternative approaches will be challenged. Other religions have no such opportunity.

This issue continues to simmer in Ontario. It again came to the fore in 2018 through a candidate for the leadership of the Ontario Progressive Conservative Party, who ran mainly on opposition to the sex-education curriculum. Doug Ford, the eventual winner of that contest, also supported this position. One of the first acts of the Ford government was to rescind the new program and direct schools and teachers to use an interim program based on an earlier version dating from the 1990s. This, of course, precipitated protests from the other side, including a court challenge led by the Elementary Teachers Federation of Ontario and the Canadian Civil Liberties Association. That challenge was based on the freedom and discrimination sections of the Charter and on the minister's authority to change the curriculum. The judges dismissed the case, arguing that the case raised no Charter issues and that the change was within the authority of the minister.[14] While the plaintiffs indicated their intention to appeal, the matter appears to have been resolved with the introduction of a revised program that, according to most reports, closely resembles the one that had been repealed. This suggests that the government's initial proclamations on the issue were more a matter of political ideology and electoral politics than of school programming.

The subject of gay-straight alliances has been a political issue in Alberta as well. In March 2015, facing an election, the Progressive Conservative government reversed its historical position and allowed these clubs to be formed in schools at the request of students.[15] Like the Ontario bill, that amendment specifically allows the use of that name or any other chosen by students, with no right of veto by the school principal or board. That government was defeated soon after. One of the early acts of the New Democratic Party government was to pass further amendments to the Human Rights Act, adding gender identity and gender expression to various sections of the act as categories for non-discrimination.[16]

Both these bills generated similar reactions to those in Ontario. Some Catholic reaction seems to have been moderate. For example, the Alberta Catholic School Trustees Association issued a statement saying that "Catholic Schools will be able to work with the legislation."[17] In January 2016, the Edmonton Catholic School Board decided to send a letter from Bishop Henry of Calgary about "totalitarianism" in Alberta schools to all parents in its district. However, the chair of the board, who was absent from the meeting where this was approved, distanced herself from that action and apologized to anyone who might have been offended by the letter. Again, this is indicative of a division within the Catholic establishment, with some individuals in influential positions acting in ways contrary to the wishes of the bishops.

The legislation generated significant media debate. Conventional media have been almost universally supportive. A *Calgary Sun* editorial on March 11, 2015, argued that Alberta had finally made the right move with its legislation on gay-straight alliances. In an op-ed article in the *Edmonton Journal* on January 16, 2016, David King, a former minister of education, took issue with the bishop of Calgary's assertion that separate schools are an instrument of the Catholic church.[18] King went as far as to remind the bishop that Catholic schools are effectively public schools with some rights to teach Catholic religion. King questioned whether the continued existence of separate schools is the best way to protect minority rights and noted that it is quite possible for Alberta to follow the lead of Newfoundland and Quebec in changing the constitution. King also launched a petition asking for a provincial referendum on the issue.[19]

The web and social media show a pattern of active vocal opposition to the legislation. This seems to be driven by parents and parent organizations who have framed the issue as one of parent choice, something that has always been significant theme in Alberta educational debates. The most public demonstration to date took place on May 14, 2016, when a group called Parents for Choice in Education attracted large numbers to protest rallies in Edmonton and Calgary. That same group also organized petitions calling for repeal of the legislation.[20] In a blog post, the former bishop of Calgary held that sex is determined at conception genetically, anatomically, and chromosomally and cannot be determined by self-identification.[21] Religion is clearly an underlying driving force in all these actions. Diverse groups, and not just Catholics, are represented in the protest movement.

The gay-straight alliance controversy was kept active by a 2017 Alberta government bill amending the School Act in a manner that prohibited schools from informing parents that their children are members of such clubs.[22] The newly formed United Conservative Party opposed the bill, invoking the argument that parents have a right to know what their children are doing in school. However, its leader, Jason Kenney, was careful to avoid the accusation that the party favours outing LGBT kids.[23] The Alberta Catholic School Trustees Association also voiced concern over the bill's erosion of school board autonomy and its effect on parent-school relations.[24] Despite these and many other objections, the bill was passed in November 2017.

The issue again came to the fore when the United Conservatives defeated the NDP government in 2019. The new government decided to proclaim an education act that had languished since the previous Progressive Conservative government was defeated four years earlier. The new act explicitly allows the use of gay-straight alliance and similar names for student organizations but no longer prohibits school staff from informing parents about membership in such organizations.[25]

One might gather from the high-profile activity around the sex education issue that a large part of the Canadian public opposes the liberalization of policies and programs in this area. Certainly, most of the controversy is being generated by those opposed to change. The activist opponents are obviously most seized with the issue, while much of the population is not particularly engaged. Nevertheless, one does not have to search far to find a significant amount of low-level advocacy in favour of a fully secular system. Many examples of this can be found in newspaper articles, columns, and editorials. Indeed, while many news reports focus on the active protests, most editorials and op-ed commentaries in the mainstream media tend to favour liberalization. Many activists certainly question the continued existence of separate schools. There is no way to judge trends in broader opinion from these competing narratives.

Reasonable Accommodation and Quebec Bill 21

The controversy over health and sex education is part of a broader debate over what should be included in or excluded from the school program. A significant aspect of this debate involves the accommodation of religious and cultural diversity in Canadian schools. This has found its most explicit expression in Quebec, where the concept of *reasonable accommodation* has been a significant topic of debate since the early 2000s. In Quebec, this is seen as fundamental to the need to reconcile the increased pluralism of Quebec society with the desire to protect French language and culture. It also reflects Quebec's adoption of the French concept of *laïcité* or strict secularity in public institutions.

The 2008 Bouchard-Taylor Commission report urged a shift in thinking from multiculturalism (tolerance or acceptance of cultural differences) to interculturalism (integration of cultures). However, far from settling the issue, that report set off a further decade of debate over how the province should accommodate diverse cultures. In 2018, that debate culminated in provincial legislation (entitled in English) *An Act Respecting the Laicity of the State,* commonly known as Bill 21.[26] Section 6 of that act explicitly prohibits a long list of public service personnel from wearing religious symbols in the exercise of their functions. That list includes "principals, vice principals and teachers of educational institutions under the jurisdiction of a school board established under the Education Act [. . .]".[27]

Bill 21 has provoked considerable controversy in Quebec and beyond. Although not specifically directed at any particular religion, human rights agencies and religious groups have argued that the law discriminates against groups for whom clothing and other symbols of religion are essential elements of their faith. The most specific criticism has been that the law discriminates against Muslim women for whom wearing the traditional *hijab* is a conspicuous symbol of that faith. The main argument seems to centre around whether wearing the hijab is a matter of choice (or perhaps simply a fashion statement) or is emblematic of the unequal status of women in Muslim societies.

Although Bill 21 is not explicitly about religion in schools, teachers and other education personnel are one of the largest groups affected. The impact on teachers has come to the fore in a high-profile case in which a Muslim teacher was removed from her position for wearing the hijab. The action has been widely condemned by human rights and women's groups and has led to a series of protests against the law.[28] Some studies have reported that a majority of current and former education students who wear religious symbols are considering leaving the province.

Many human rights groups and legal scholars have taken the position that the law violates the non-discrimination sections of the Charter. To shield it from constitutional challenges, the Quebec government has invoked the notwithstanding provision of the Charter. This, in itself, has become a point of contention, out of concern that frequent use of that provision can undermine fundamental Charter rights and freedoms.

Use of the notwithstanding clause has not stopped some groups from initiating legal action, including attempts to find ways around the notwithstanding clause. Perhaps the most significant case as it applies to education is one brought by a number of individuals and religious groups, together with the English Montreal School Board.[29] In that case, the Quebec Superior Court judge was critical of the law but upheld it in the main because of the notwithstanding clause. However, the ruling held that the law does not apply to English school boards because it violates the right to education in English. A Quebec government appeal led to that ruling being overturned by the Quebec Court of Appeal. Bill 21 is now in full effect, though its long-term fate remains unclear. It will almost certainly be appealed to the Supreme Court of Canada. It will be interesting to see if ways can be found to obviate the notwithstanding provision. In any event, that provision must be renewed at five-year intervals. An earlier Quebec precedent for allowing its expiry can be found in its use to preserve denominational schools after the 1997 constitutional amendment. In that case, the clause was used to reassure the Catholic establishment but was quietly dropped on expiry, with no significant consequences.

The long-term consequences of Bill 21 are unknown. However, it is clear that the issue will remain controversial for some time in Quebec. Elsewhere, the important implication for this discussion is that, while the end of separate schooling addresses a significant constitutional contradiction, it does not resolve all the issues surrounding the place of religion in schools. Some form of accommodation for religious minorities will continue to be required even in secular school systems. The lesson from Quebec Bill 21 is that imposition of an extreme form of secularism, no matter what the justification, is likely to prolong rather than resolve the controversy. Replacing one Charter conflict with another is not a long-term solution.

Public Opinion Surveys

Well designed public opinion surveys are better than activist opinion in determining how the public thinks about the issues at hand. It is therefore worth looking briefly at some of the polling information available.

The longest-running ongoing poll on education in Ontario is that conducted by the Ontario Institute for Studies in Education (OISE). That survey has tracked trends in Ontario education biannually for more than 30 years. The most recent iteration, in 2018, gives the trend of opinion on public and separate schools since 1984.[30] In the 1984 survey, a slight majority (51 percent) supported the current public-separate system. That dropped to 40 percent two years later and has not changed much since. The 2018 poll showed support for the current public and Catholic system at 37 percent. Support for a public-only system has increased since the 1980s from the mid-20 percent to 42 percent in 2018. Support for a system that includes all religious and / or all private schools was around 30 percent around the turn of the century but declined to 15 percent in 2018.

In the 2018 poll, a large majority of Catholics supported the existing system. However, only 46 percent of the total support from the system came from Catholics, indicating that the status quo draws considerable support from non-Catholics. Most Catholics supported extending funding to all religious groups. However, that percentage was much lower for respondents of all other religions and for those of no religion. A large majority of non-Catholics favoured no funding for any religious group.

One of the more notable shifts in the 2018 survey was on the narrow question: "If it were a choice between funding schools for all religious groups or not funding schools for any religious groups, what would you choose?" In 2000, respondents were almost evenly divided on this question. However, in 2018, the percentage supporting not funding any schools for religious groups increased to 62 percent.

Overall, the results indicate a gradual shift away from support for the status quo and towards a single public system. However, the authors conclude that the results continue to show that no consensus yet exists on the issue. This points to a distinction between the rule of electoral politics that even the smallest majority is sufficient to govern and the view that changes to minority rights requires a much more substantial consensus.

A 2015 poll conducted by Forum Research, also in Ontario, showed that about one-half of Ontario residents approved of the new sex education curriculum while one-third did not.[31] About three-fourths of the population believed that sex education should be taught both at home and in school. Disapproval of the program was reported as higher among evangelical Christians (69 percent) (with less accuracy because of small sample size) than among either Catholics (44 percent) or Protestants (40 percent). Disapproval of the program was lowest among non-Christians (23 percent) and those with no religion (20 percent). There was little difference in opinion among supporters of public versus separate schools, suggesting that the sex education issue is viewed as largely independent of the separate school issue.

Another poll conducted by that same firm in 2016[32] revealed that 38 percent of Ontario residents believed that funding for Catholic schools should continue while 52 percent were opposed to such funding. These results were virtually unchanged since the same question was asked in 2015, despite the ongoing controversy over programs. These results are somewhat different from those of the OISE poll, perhaps because the Forum question was more specifically about funding. More people appear to support the existence of a separate system than support its funding.

A poll conducted in Alberta by Mainstreet Research in April 2016, showed that about 60 percent of respondents opposed public funding of private schools, 27 percent were in favour, and 12 percent had no opinion.[33] When the question was narrowed specifically to charter schools, 47 percent were opposed, 31 percent were in favour, and 21 percent had no opinion. No direct question was asked about the existing separate schools.

The only time the issue of denominational rights was put directly to the full electorate was in the two Newfoundland referenda in the 1990s. It is significant that 55 percent of those voting approved the first proposition, which allowed some denominational schools to be retained, while more than 70 percent approved the second, which effectively eliminated all denominational rights. Polls leading up to these two referenda showed that a large majority disapproved of specific denominational powers such as control of school boards, school locations, teacher employment, and student selection. These are the very rights that Catholic leaders have fought so hard to retain.

As already noted, the most recent occasion on which the issue directly became a matter of electoral politics was in the 2007 Ontario provincial election. In that election, the Progressive Conservative Party promised that, if elected, it would extend public funding to faith-based schools. That proposal became a defining issue in the election. As the campaign progressed, opposition became so strong that the party was forced to withdraw the proposal. Many reports at the time took the position that, despite the withdrawal, that proposal was a major factor in the defeat of the party.

Overall, the polls reveal a division in the population on both the existence of separate schools and the narrower issue of mandated programs in controversial areas such as sex education. On balance, opinion seems to be more in favour of a common public system than of separation by religion. However, except for the second Newfoundland referendum, a clear binary choice has not been given in the polling questions. As for sex education, the current flashpoint, a majority, at least in Ontario, approve of the new program being used.

Unfortunately, public opinion polls and, as some would argue, even referenda, cannot settle the issue of minority rights or such matters as the right to opt out of programs. Public opinion, no matter how expressed, cannot override constitutional protections for individual rights and freedoms or for currently protected denominational rights. Only legislatures can do that, using the appropriate constitutional amendment processes. On the other hand, these rights and freedoms must be ones on which some consensus exists in society. The problem is that consensus reached in earlier years will not necessarily hold into the future. The living tree approach to constitutional interpretation is intended to accommodate long-term shifts in the consensus.

To advance the discussion, it is necessary to assume that the Charter itself now represents a consensus on individual rights and freedoms. With a few exceptions, these individual rights override the collective views of specific groups within society. The problem here is that the Charter itself is internally contradictory. It is by no means obvious that the inclusion of Section 29 reflects the public consensus on denominational rights. More likely, this was included to avoid distraction from the main objective of constitutional patriation. There is some irony in the idea that it was necessary to create an internal contradiction within the Charter to ensure that the Charter as a whole could be adopted.

Other Opinion Sources

In the past, news reports, editorials, columns, and articles constituted a significant source of public opinion and were influential in shaping opinion. With the proliferation of new media, the debate can now encompass many more people. However, this also makes it much more difficult to find any pattern among the noise. There is no doubt that both the constitutional issue of separate schools and the broader issue of parent choice and control remain significant topics of discussion. It is almost impossible to present the full range of views that can be found in both traditional and new media. However, the discussion would not be complete without giving just a few examples of how the debate is playing out in the media.

Not everyone accepts that the contradiction between Section 93 protected rights and the Charter sections on freedom of religion and non-discrimination should remain. It is even likely that most Canadians are unaware of the contradiction. Nevertheless, as noted earlier, there is considerable low-level activity in the direction of removing the Section 93 protections.

A further example is an initiative by a group calling itself One Public Education Now (OPEN) to mount yet another legal challenge to separate schools in Ontario.[34] The test case is a family whose children must be bussed a long distance to a French public school when a French Catholic school is nearby. The specific point on which the case is based is the 1987 reference on Ontario Bill 30, which extended Catholic school rights to the secondary level. More broadly, the group argues that the original basis for Section 93, namely Ontario Catholics' demand for rights comparable to those for Protestants in Quebec, is no longer valid because Quebec itself has abandoned that protection.

The same group has also taken up the cause of a Hamilton teacher who claimed discrimination under the Charter because, as a non-Catholic, she is ineligible to apply for positions at Catholic school boards. The group has launched a website and seeks donations to the cause.[35] While it is not clear if this group is getting any traction, its activities have attracted some attention in major newspapers.[36] Not all commentators agree that a lawsuit is the best way to settle the issue, noting that this has already been tried unsuccessfully. However, it is also worth noting that much of the litigation reported throughout this book started through test cases of this sort and that the argument now being made is clearly different from that in earlier cases.

These are but a few examples of the broad range of discourse on separate schools and related issues. Any keyword search related to these issues turns up material from a vast array of advocacy groups, complete with articles, blogs, exhortations to join their cause, and invitations to join in legal actions. Much of this has been triggered by recent legislation, especially in Ontario and Alberta, around sex education and anti-bullying initiatives. It is likely no coincidence that most of the controversy over these issues has occurred in the provinces that still have separate schools and thus have organized means of opposition to such initiatives. While opposition is by no means limited to Catholic organizations, these are at the forefront of much of the activity because Catholic school boards and related agencies have a constituency to which they must respond and have well-established means of ensuring that their views are known.

To some degree, the controversy over the continued existence of separate schools is a distraction from more fundamental debates over parental versus state rights and the place of religion in education. A case can be made that settling the Catholic separate school issue is prerequisite to a more comprehensive discussion of the scope and limits of parental rights, the place of religion in education, and whether some accommodation of religious groups should be part of public schooling.

The Economic Argument

In principle, cost should not be a major consideration in determining whether basic constitutional rights should be upheld. On a pragmatic level, however, the issue of economic efficiency and appropriate use of public funds is relevant to the debate. Cash-strapped provincial governments are always in search of ways to save money or redirect funds to high priority areas. As a large-scale example, the changing age distribution of the population has led to greatly increased pressure on the health care system but decreased pressure on education. Education's share of provincial budgets has been declining for some time, while that for health care has been increasing. Some may argue that there are many unmet needs in education and that any money saved from declining enrolment should be used to provide better services within education. However, the reality is that both education and health care costs are driven largely by demographics, and governments must respond to changing demographic realities.

A 2012 study by a group called the Federation of Urban Neighbourhoods of Ontario claimed that, by eliminating separate schools, Ontario could save between $1.3 and $1.6 billion per year, or about 5 percent of the total provincial budget for elementary and secondary schools.[37] Unfortunately, that report gives little information on the methods used. It also makes some broad assumptions about the effect of school board mergers, better utilization of school facilities, transportation, and economies of scale. The report has been criticized for these shortcomings and for naïveté in projecting that any significant economies of scale can be achieved. Nevertheless, the author's experience in making similar estimates for Newfoundland in the 1990s suggests that 5 percent saving is not an unrealistic expectation. School consolidation, transportation, and administration are examples of areas that might be targeted for savings.

Even if the projected savings are exaggerated, it is rather surprising that the economic argument has not featured more prominently in Ontario, especially with the election of a government that seems determined to bring about a significant reduction in provincial expenditures. If realistic, the estimated savings would be greater than those proposed by the Ford government through class size increases and other smaller measures that have been the source of significant controversy.

Where money is spent is a matter of provincial priority. If accommodation of religion or providing greater choice of schools are high priorities, then the cost of these accommodations needs to be met, even at the expense of other areas of funding. This principle has been well established in the case of minority official language education and education of special needs children, where courts have ruled that the non-discrimination provisions of the Charter override any consideration of the additional cost of providing the services. The same argument can be applied to separate schools. As long as the constitutional mandate is in place, separate schools must be funded on a non-discriminatory basis, even if this does not yield optimal cost efficiency.

In any event, there are other means of cost control. Provinces are free to set the total education budget at any desired level or to raise taxes or incur debt to meet the demand. Although constitutionally mandated programs must be funded, there is no constitutional requirement that the total budget be increased for this purpose.

For these reasons, the economic issue is not considered primary to this discussion. If religious accommodation or parent choice, in whatever forms these may take, are overriding principles, then the cost of these actions becomes largely irrelevant. The overriding principles become the top priorities for funding within whatever overall budget the province can allocate. Nevertheless, the issue cannot be disregarded. Priorities may be reconsidered if their costs are seen as excessive. The cost of duplication of services was the main driving force behind reforms to denominational education in Newfoundland. In the end, this was sufficient to drive a decision to override long-standing constitutional protections. The economic argument can obviously become politically important even if not a critical issue of principle. Indeed, should governments be so inclined, it would not be especially difficult to produce reasonably accurate cost estimates for a range of system options, including those to be discussed in chapter 9.

CHAPTER 9

The Way Forward

The major Christian denominations, historically, have played a significant role in state institutions in Canada, including schools, hospitals, and child welfare agencies and were certainly influential in provincial and federal politics. The fact that the missionaries were there first, filling a void that existed because of weak state institutions, gave the churches a foothold in education long before concerns with economic and democratic development led to state intervention in education. From modest support for church-run schools, state involvement extended throughout the nineteenth and twentieth centuries to a situation of almost full state control of schools.

The doctrine of separation of church and state, explicitly recognized in the constitutions of France and the United States was not a foundational principle of the Canadian confederation. At the time, the political influence of the Christian churches was strong. Outside Quebec, the dominant influence was Protestant, and strong anti-Catholic sentiment was prevalent. After the British conquest, Quebec remained mainly French and Catholic. However, the smaller English population was politically dominant, allowing Protestant institutions to flourish. Patterns of settlement led to a high degree of separation of communities by both religion and language, allowing the dominant denomination in a community to establish schools reflecting that dominance. Where the denominations intersected, rivalries led to the establishment of separate Protestant and Catholic schools.

By the time of confederation, the reality on the ground in Ontario and Quebec had become so entrenched, and church political influence so strong, that it required the founders to strike a bargain allowing Catholics and Protestants to continue to operate their own schools. This bargain was expressed in Section 93 of the Constitution. Nova Scotia and New Brunswick, with smaller Catholic populations, along with strong anti-Catholic and anti-French sentiment, required no similar bargain. As other provinces joined the union, their own religious and educational histories came into play, with variations to Section 93 applying in some provinces but not in others. Over time, Protestant schools tended to become more secular, partly because, as the majority in most communities, these were effectively the common schools, open to all students. Being more exclusive, and no doubt also because of strong advocacy, Catholic schools were able to retain a much more pervasive religious identity.

The question of exactly what rights were conveyed by Section 93 was the subject of a significant amount of litigation from 1867 onward. Early points of contention involved the status of French Catholic schools in New Brunswick and Ontario, whether separate schools even existed in Manitoba before confederation, distribution of local tax assessments to school boards, the status of Jews and other religions, and the responsibility of the federal government to intervene should a province enact legislation in violation of Section 93. Between the 1950s and the 1980s, the right to Catholic secondary schools in Ontario, efforts by Quebec to promote the French language, and the status of the Pentecostal church in Newfoundland were prominent issues.

All this led to clarification of the scope and limitations of Section 93 rights. There was plenty of evidence of judicial dissent and numerous reversals of lower court decisions, reflecting the controversial nature of the issue. However, the highest courts were consistent in preventing provinces from infringing on rights held by denominations at the time of confederation, while also holding that there was no obligation to expand these rights. Since there was no constitutional impediment to provinces using legislation to expand rights, a pattern of incremental expansion became apparent over the years, notable in secondary education in Ontario and in greater equality in funding between public and separate school boards.

The landscape changed dramatically, in principle though not immediately in practice, with patriation and adoption of the Charter of Rights and Freedoms in 1982. Although the Charter makes no explicit statement on the separation of church and state, the sections on freedom of religion and non-discrimination on religious grounds clearly embrace that principle. The Charter embodies the Enlightenment concept that religion is a matter of individual conscience. Freedom of religion means, among other things, that persons may engage individually or collectively in private forms of religious expression. However, such expression cannot be officially sanctioned in public institutions, nor can public funding be allocated in a manner that discriminates by religion.

Section 93 and its variants, now reinforced by Section 29 of the Charter, offer the sole exception to these provisions. Because of Section 29, Charter challenges demanding equal status for other religions have been unsuccessful. It was not the Charter, but the amending formula in the 1982 constitution that gave rise to change in the status quo for religious schools. Specifically, provinces are now able to use Section 43 of the amending formula to alter the established denominational rights. Section 43 amendments in Newfoundland and Quebec in the 1990s make it clear that this section can be used to negate the intended impact of Section 29 of the Charter.

The courts have responded to Charter issues by upholding Section 93 rights in separate schools, while restricting residual religious activities in public schools. Courts have also not responded favourably to the few attempts by parents to claim an absolute right on religious grounds to educate their children as they see fit or to religious groups demanding equal rights to those held by Catholics. A consequence of this is that the very activities prohibited by the Charter in public schools can be mandated in separate schools. In no other area can the Charter be interpreted as leading to such conflicting application across provinces or institutions.

Status Quo versus Change

Major commissions on education in several provinces prior to the 1990s found that the denominational issue generated intense interest and occupied much of their agenda. However, all took the position that their hands were tied by the constitution. As far as can be determined, none of the remaining three provinces with separate schools have initiated comprehensive reviews on the scale of the Williams Commission or the Estates General since the 1980s. However, there have been many other commissions on various issues of school governance, finance, and programming. The most recent review in Ontario, the Commission on the Reform of Ontario's Public Services (the Drummond Commission) was silent on the separate school issue, despite its broad mandate to find ways to reduce provincial expenditures.[1] A 2016 review of educational governance in Saskatchewan (the Perrin Report) made several recommendations on possible consolidation of school divisions but had no comment on the principle of separate schools.[2] The most recent large-scale review of education in Alberta dates from 2003.[3] That commission focused on teaching and learning and was also silent on the separate school issue.

It is difficult to know why none of these studies addressed the issue of separate schools, especially considering the precedents from Newfoundland and Quebec. The Drummond Commission in Ontario had a mandate to find cost savings. School consolidation is one area in which at least some savings might plausibly have been found. Consolidation would almost certainly be facilitated by integration of public and separate systems. As far as can be determined, none of these commissions were given an explicit mandate to either address or avoid the issue. Commissioners must have been aware that the pre-1982 constraint on constitutional amendment no longer applied. It is not clear if the commissions believed that the issue remained intractable. However, their silence appears to have been a lost opportunity.

At least three arguments may be advanced for preserving the status quo in Alberta, Ontario, and Saskatchewan. First, an originalist interpretation of the constitution holds that the 1867 compromise preserving pre-confederation rights is absolute. Indeed, the main argument for the status quo is that the unity of the country might be jeopardized by change in the denominational structure of schools. Even if discriminatory by today's standards, separate schooling might be considered part of the socio/cultural fabric of Canada, to be preserved in the interest of national unity. This argument was reinforced in 1982 by including Section 29 in the Charter.

Second, a human rights case can be made for offering some choice in education. Catholic advocacy groups have often made this point in their own defence. Some non-Catholics actually exercise this choice by enrolling in separate schools. However, such access is at the discretion of Catholic school boards and is not based on any general policy of promoting choice. The existence of separate schools for Catholics and Protestants could be seen as appropriate when that duality was a defining characteristic of society. Indeed, the situation at confederation might have been used as a precursor to extending rights to other religions as they became established in the population, had governments thought in such terms. This was the case in Newfoundland as newer Protestant denominations were able to establish separate schools on the same basis as Catholics and Anglicans. Elsewhere in Canada courts have rebuffed all efforts made by religious groups in that direction. The proposal along these lines in the 2007 Ontario election also went nowhere in the face of public opposition. All these points indicate that choice is not the primary driving force for separation by denomination.

The 1867 compromise may also be construed as an effort to accommodate oppressed minority religious (and language) groups. Certainly, anti-Catholic and anti-French sentiment played a part in the establishment of separate schools. As argued earlier, accommodation of minorities may be seen as a mark of maturity in a democratic society, and as a step away from the religious, ethnic, or cultural discrimination that plague many other societies.

Part of what sustains the status quo is that there is no large-scale public pressure for radical change in the form of either extending or limiting minority rights. There is perhaps a widespread perception that any effort to bring about change, especially if directed against Catholic schools, would imperil any government wishing to go down that road. Although there is considerable activity among advocates on both sides of the issue, it is not obvious that the larger population is much engaged.

The main arguments for change are essentially the opposite to the above points. In almost all Charter cases, the courts have promulgated a living tree interpretation of the constitution. On religion in schools, Charter cases have resulted in restriction rather than expansion of religious activities in public schools. The Supreme Court of Canada has almost always adhered to an expansionary interpretation of rights and freedoms, favouring individual rights over those of collectives, including governments. Some may feel that this amounts to judicial overreach and, in a few instances, governments have used the notwithstanding clause of the Charter to override or head off judicial decisions. Nevertheless, there seems to be no widespread backlash over the direction taken by the courts.

As for the perception of lack of public consensus, the Newfoundland and Quebec cases show that achieving a consensus is not as difficult as it might appear once the public becomes engaged in the issue. Both approaches—negotiation followed by referenda in

Newfoundland and direct legislative action by Quebec—yielded the same result. While highly controversial at the time because of the intensive efforts by denominational authorities to preserve the status quo, a clear consensus emerged once the public became sufficiently engaged.

In Alberta, Ontario, and Saskatchewan, the status quo holds if provincial governments do nothing. Politically, this has the advantage of stability, at least in the short-term. Unlike in the past, governments are unlikely to rise or fall by supporting separate schools or simply being indifferent to the issue. However, they may rise or fall on any proposal for more radical action in either direction. Although this did not happen in Newfoundland or Quebec, governments may be wary of the political turmoil that this issue engendered in these two provinces or may feel that this is not high on their political agenda.

While the status quo may be politically expedient for now, it is difficult to see how this can be sustained in the longer term. The most important reason is that the current situation perpetuates the fundamental contradiction within the Charter and is incompatible with the diversity of modern Canadian society. Politically, other religions are becoming more aware of this contradiction and are also, in some constituencies, politically active enough to advocate for change. As events in both Ontario and Alberta illustrate, what many would regard as relatively minor program changes can bring the issue of religious schools to the fore for groups other than Catholics. Also, Catholics are no longer a monolithic group obedient to the strictures of church leadership. At some point, a trigger event may be expected that will force governments to deal directly with the continued existence of separate schools. The core argument here is that a more rational debate is possible if provinces were to decide to act on principle now rather than await a crisis.

In Newfoundland and Quebec, constitutional amendment was seen as a last resort way to achieve specific provincial policy objectives. These cases have shown that there is no legal obstacle to constitutional amendment. It seems extremely unlikely that either the House of Commons or Senate would deny a request from Ontario, Alberta, or Saskatchewan for the type of amendment already granted to two other provinces.

A Framework for Change

The position taken here is that the arguments for change outweigh those for the status quo. For those who take the opposite view, a case can be made that the exclusive nature of existing religious rights is an anomaly in modern Canadian society that needs to be addressed, regardless of one's stand on the place of religion in schools. The broader issue of religion in schools can be separated from that of separate schools. While the separate school issue applies only to three provinces and the territories, the question of where religion fits into the school system remains an issue in all jurisdictions. Other provinces have not yet found a way to accommodate religious beliefs in the face of the strict secularism in public schools imposed by court decisions.

The case for change rests on three pillars. First, any reforms need to be consistent with the religious freedom and non-discrimination provisions of the Charter. This requires that the constitutional contradiction inherent in Section 29 be resolved. Second, a clear position is required on whether religious belief, as opposed to religion as a subject of study, has any place in schooling and, if so, how this can be accommodated in a non-discriminatory manner. Third, the extent and limits of parent rights need to be established. This, in turn, relates to how much choice in schooling should be made available.

The most fundamental, foundational principles—specifically, equality of citizens under the law, freedom of religion, and non-discrimination by religion—have been largely established in Canadian constitutional law. Furthermore, although strict separation of church and state is not explicitly prescribed by the Charter, it is clearly implied and has been reinforced by court decisions restricting religious activities in public schools. Absent Section 93 and Section 29, there is little doubt that school separation by religion, as currently structured, would be declared unconstitutional.

Legally, Section 29 is as much a part of the Charter as any other section. Courts can interpret constitutional terms and use these to uphold or strike down laws but they but cannot change the constitution or dictate what should be done politically. However, that does not mean that the contradiction should remain forever unresolved. It is up to governments, not courts, to seek solutions that will help minimize conflict even if this, occasionally, requires constitutional amendment.

Court rulings in the Charter era offer three guidelines on the place of religion in public (non-separate) schools. First, individual religious displays and observances are allowed (except in Quebec where the constitutional status of legislation prohibiting the display of religious symbols by those in positions of public authority has not been settled). Second, institutionally sanctioned activities such as prayers or bible readings are prohibited. Third, religion is appropriate as a subject of study if it is approached in a non-doctrinaire manner. As for separate schools, the courts appear to have had little to say about religion in such schools. While these schools must teach the provincial program, there seems to be nothing to preclude their use of various forms of religious expression or observance.

All this applies to the system as now structured. However, the main argument here is that the existence of separate schools is not now in broad compliance with the Charter. They are saved only by Section 29. Ensuring that the system is compatible with the Charter requires that all religions be treated in the same manner. The question is how to accomplish that goal. Only two options are fully compatible with the Charter sections on freedom of religion and non-discrimination: removing religion entirely from schools or accommodating all religions. Various ways to accomplish this, and the merits and drawbacks of each, are discussed in the next section.

The issue of parent rights and parent choice of schooling extends well beyond religion. Parents may desire any number of specialized forms of education for their children. Not all these will be compatible with the state's responsibility for programs and standards applicable to all. A case can be made that unified secular school system serves to promote unity in an inherently diverse population and particularly facilitates teaching common values that benefit the whole society. On the other hand, Canadian society is built on respect for, even celebration of, diversity, and some would argue that this requires diverse institutions. This discussion must be limited to the issue of religious choice. However, any decisions based on the principle of choice might also accommodate other forms of choice. Choice based on religion takes us directly back to the principle of accommodating all religions, with all that entails.

All provinces, not just those with separate schools, need to consider appropriate ways to respect religious freedom and accommodate religious differences within schools. The underlying questions are clear. Should religion play any part in schooling? If so, how can this be done so as to respect and accommodate all those who desire some role for religion? To what extent, in a society that is increasingly both more secular and more diverse, should individuals or minority groups based on religion (or, for that matter, ethnicity, culture or other characteristics) be accommodated in their desire for variation from the common educational experience embodied in public schools? What is the appropriate balance between the state and parents in their responsibility for the education of children?

In summary, a framework for change would be expected to encompass the following elements:

- A restructured system to be fully compatible with Sections 2 and 15 of the Charter.
- Action in three provinces (and possibly the territories) to resolve the discrimination inherent in existing denominational rights. This will require either an agreement with the Catholic church to place rights in abeyance or repeal of Section 93 and its variants.
- A clear position on the place of religion in schools, consistent with religious freedom and with the concept of religion as an individual rather than a collective set of beliefs.
- A clear position on the extent of parent choice, particularly religious choice, and its place in designing a school system.
- Mechanisms to accommodate religious differences within the school system.

Models of Change

This section outlines some specific routes to change and examines their advantages and drawbacks. These are offered in the hope that a principled discussion leading to change is preferable to change based on crisis, financial constraints, advocacy, or electoral politics.

The country models given in chapter 1 present several scenarios, ranging from full separation of church and state (France and the United States) to full accommodation through public support of schools of any religion (the Netherlands). Intermediate models include partial support for private religious schools (Australia) to full support of separate schools for established religions (parts of the United Kingdom). Where full separation is the norm, provisions for private schools allow individuals or groups to opt out of the public system.

For the three provinces with separate schools, the immediate question is what to do about the discrimination inherent in that system. Any further restructuring to accommodate religious beliefs must first address this issue. We now know that the Charter contradiction posed by Section 29 can be resolved through a Section 43 constitutional amendment but likely not by any other means.

In principle, the rights now held by Catholics in the three provinces can be extended to other religions by provincial legislation. Doing the same in the territories would require federal action, in concert with the territorial governments. Court rulings suggest that there is no constitutional impediment to funding other separate schools, though it is difficult to predict the outcome of any new litigation that this might engender. Such a system could exist in parallel to the public system in a manner similar to that in Australia or in England and Wales. Although this arrangement would have no constitutional protection, it would be a substantial step in the direction of removing the discrimination that now exists. In reality, it is unlikely that a large demand would exist for these schools. Some fundamentalist Christian groups and perhaps small numbers of Jewish and Muslim families might take advantage of this opening. However, a dramatic expansion of sectarian schools is not to be expected.

Such a system is best thought of, not as many separate denominational systems, but as a single public system with some differentiation by religion. Most schools would almost certainly remain secular and open to all. There would probably be no need for separate school boards. Schools could be differentiated by parent choice, with the individual school the focus of choice. This would look much like an extension of the charter school model, in which religious schools could exist side by side with other forms of specialized schools. A more highly differentiated version would require vouchers or some other form of individually targeted funding.

The main obstacles to such a move in Canada are political and not constitutional. The proposal advanced by the Progressive Conservative Party in the 2007 Ontario election was an example of an effort to establish this type of system. However, that proposal seems not to have been accompanied by any detailed plan on how that might be operationalized. The fact that the proposal was quickly withdrawn in the face of public opposition illustrates the political obstacle but may also illustrate that the model was not well thought out or presented. This does not mean that it should not be considered in a discussion of principle.

However, a more fully developed model would have to be presented to overcome what would likely be initial adverse reaction.

Unfortunately, this option is fraught with other difficulties, in both principle and practice. The main issue here is how to determine what constitutes a religion. The legal definition of religion based on individual conviction rather than adherence to the doctrine of any recognizable faith group opens the door to significantly greater religious fragmentation. It also allows the possibility of individuals claiming a religious basis to demand separate schooling and finding sufficient followers to establish a case for a separate school. While individual action of this sort is discouraged by other court decisions, such as *Jones* in Alberta and *Benitto* in Nova Scotia, opening the system to any religion increases the risk of such extreme claims. In practice, such occurrences may not happen with any frequency. However, it is often the extreme cases that define the scope and limits of what is possible.

It would be a perilous exercise indeed for a province to keep a list of which religions should receive support and which not. This has become a significant issue in Australia, where some states allow religious denominations access to schools for special religious instruction. Inability to determine what constitutes a legitimate religious group has led some schools to ban such access and Australian states to reconsider the provision. All the major religions have many offshoots that adherents may claim make them different. While a "numbers-warrant" limitation may be imposed, this would lead to a need to enumerate people by religion and to make perhaps very nuanced distinctions among groups.

This leads us to the opposite extreme, that of abolishing existing denominational rights and imposing a strict version of separation of church and state on public schools. Private schools aside, this is now the situation in most provinces. Constitutionally, the means of accomplishing this are clear. Given the Newfoundland and Quebec precedents, it is extremely unlikely that the federal government or the Parliament of Canada would raise any objection to any provincial proposal for a Section 43 amendment to abolish separate schools.

One possible scenario would be for all three provinces to act together on this issue. For the territories, change to federal legislation would be required. However, it would be appropriate for any proposal for change to be initiated by the territorial governments and not the federal government. While this would be difficult to coordinate, the Newfoundland and Quebec cases illustrate the value of such an approach. Although the two cases proceeded separately within each province, they happened to reach the federal level at about the same time. This allowed the two cases effectively to feed upon each other. For example, the official opposition at the time, the Bloc Québécois, supported the Newfoundland resolution because of their belief in the primacy of provincial jurisdiction. This helped avoid a situation in which the amendment might be approved for one province but not the other.

Having three provinces acting in concert would have the advantage of allowing Section 93 and its Alberta and Saskatchewan variants to be repealed entirely, something that could not be done on petition from one province. This would make Section 29 of the Charter redundant. Indeed, an argument can be made that repeal of Section 93 is a necessary precursor to any further reform, whatever direction that reform might take. Even though this may raise the spectre of a broader opening of the constitution, this issue is a relatively narrow one that would not require other changes.

A less extreme version would be for the protected denominations to voluntarily either relinquish their rights or place these in abeyance. As a practical matter, this would achieve the same end as constitutional change without having to invoke the amending formula. While it may sound far-fetched to think that the Catholic church would agree to any such proposition, this approach was, in fact, tried in Newfoundland before that province resorted to constitutional change. It was clear from polling that Catholics in the province did not necessarily share the church's official position that its rights were inviolable. While supporting religious activity in schools, many Catholics did not see a need for church control of school boards, school construction, teacher employment and the like to accomplish that end.

The attempt at voluntary integration failed in Newfoundland, not due to lack of public support, but because of the all-or-nothing position taken by the Catholic and Pentecostal church leadership. In the 1990s, the new amending formula had not been fully tested and the churches appeared to hold the view that any effort at constitutional amendment would fail. Now that the constitutional pathway is clear, voluntary integration might be viewed as more palatable than constitutional amendment. Catholics might look more favourably on that route if some alternative form of religious accommodation were on offer.

One small step in the direction of voluntary integration seems already to be occurring. Driven by declining enrolments, there are indications that Catholic systems are beginning to accept, even recruit, non-Catholic students. For some, separate schools are now seen not for their religious value but as a vehicle for parent choice. Moreover, recent human rights rulings in Ontario have reinforced the right of non-Catholic students to opt out of religious activities in Catholic schools. Should this become widespread, it is difficult to see how separate Catholic schools could maintain the pervasive religious character embodied in the concept of permeation. Indeed, it is by no means clear if this is the case even now, despite the official position of the church. Recent divisions among Catholic groups on sex education and related issues call into question the actual extent of permeation of Catholic teachings in schools. This issue begs further study as part of any proposal for change.

Voluntary suspension of rights would not address the underlying constitutional principle. This is illustrated by the experience in integration of the major Protestant denominations in Newfoundland. Though operating their schools as a single system for 30 years, the constitutional rights of the individual churches were not relinquished and were asserted independently during the negotiations leading up to the constitutional amendments. Nevertheless, the attractiveness of this option is that it would represent an act of altruism and a gesture of acceptance of Canada's religious diversity and even of a diversity of views within the Catholic community. Politically, this might also be an easier proposition to place before the electorate than a proposal for constitutional amendment. It would be difficult for the Catholic leadership to reject such a proposition if it could be demonstrated to have support among its own adherents.

Given the obstacles to extending denominational rights to all religions, and assuming no agreement to relinquish rights, constitutional amendment appears to be the only viable route to a school system based on the principles given here. Before considering other alternatives, the question of constitutional amendment must be addressed directly. For this purpose, it is worth recalling the lessons from Newfoundland and Quebec. In both these cases, a series of royal commissions and other studies, extending from the 1960s to the 1990s, almost universally reported that the issue was high on the minds of those consulted. However, most of these studies concluded that, no matter how desirable, rights could not be challenged without constitutional amendment. They also concluded that the obstacles to taking that route were simply too great.

Once it became clear that a path to amendment might be available, events moved quickly. In Quebec, the issue was first addressed directly by the 1996 report of the Commission for the Estates General on Education. In Newfoundland, a similar path was taken by the 1992 Williams Royal Commission. The Newfoundland case is most instructive because it involved an intense period of negotiation with the churches, based initially on the possibility that the rights holders might be persuaded to come together to allow a full integration of schools without relinquishing rights. The two Newfoundland referenda showed that much greater support existed for a proposition to abolish all denominational rights than for one involving accommodation of some of these rights.

There is no indication that Quebec followed the Newfoundland path of negotiation, polling, and referendum. Instead, Quebec took the path of a unanimous resolution of the National Assembly, perhaps because the government was secure in public support for replacing religious division by division by language. That process caused Quebec some difficulty at the federal level because it was less obvious, especially to the Senate, that a consensus for change existed in Quebec.

If Section 93 were repealed and no further action taken, the result would be a fully secular school system. In the absence of any accommodation of religion, the courts would certainly prohibit any form of officially sanctioned religious activity in schools. Politically, it would be desirable to accompany any proposition to repeal with some statement about a place for religion. Three main ways of accommodation seem to present themselves: allowing representatives of religious groups access to schools in some form, enhancing the status of private religious schools, or providing for specialized religious schools whether within public school boards or as charter schools. Several possible variations of each of these are possible.

Two questions would need to be addressed in any proposal along these lines: Who constitutes a religious group? And what level of access would be appropriate? In keeping with the Supreme Court definition of religion in its *Amselem* decision, a religious group would have to be identified by application or petition from like-minded parents and not by religious authorities. This would preclude any specific denomination from claiming to represent parents and would avoid the problem of having the state determine what constitutes a religion. It would not preclude a religious group from organizing an application or from having its staff provide the desired religious services. However, the onus would shift from religious leaders to parents.

Some might argue that allowing access to schools to any group claiming to be religious might encourage activities that would violate laws or fundamental freedoms or might, themselves, be discriminatory. Some religious adherents certainly possess beliefs that are not in accord with the Charter. Nevertheless, school boards or governments might find themselves on tricky ground in attempting to adjudicate what constitutes legitimate religious beliefs or activities or who might constitute a legitimate religious group. This has been occurring in Australia, to the point where many are beginning to question the existence of religious schools.

Nevertheless, it would make sense not to interfere in religious activities conducted in schools outside the official school program any more than is done outside of schools. Any activities that might violate laws on discrimination, for example, could be referred to human rights tribunals or the courts, which have proved adept at adjudicating such issues. Any accommodation for religion could hardly be condemned as discriminatory if similar accommodations apply equally to all. This would free religious groups to place their own interpretations on matters of spirituality and morality, just as they can do at home, without interfering with school programs that touch on such areas. The school facility would simply be a convenient venue for such activities without their having to be sanctioned by school authorities. Indeed, this would be an example of public facilities being used to accommodate community activities, something that is already the case in many schools.

While numbers might be an issue in some cases, access arrangements would be capable of accommodating very small groups. For example, there is no compelling reason for a group to be confined to children in a single school. It would not be particularly difficult for school boards to designate a site for a group drawn from several schools. Those desiring such activities would pay for religious staff and programming and might qualify for charitable tax deductions for the purpose. Some schools cite issues such as maintenance costs and insurance as reasons not to allow external access to schools, while others encourage such access. However, it is difficult to make a strong argument against public use of facilities that are mainly idle outside regular school hours. There might even be a case for charging a nominal fee for use of school facilities. Solutions to such practical matters should not be difficult to find. Indeed, the level of demand for religious access is unlikely to be great enough to present significant logistical difficulties.

This brings us to the question of what level of access is appropriate. The assumption here is that access would occur outside of regular school hours and that developing and delivering religious programs would be the responsibility of the petitioning group. Other than space, neither the school, the school board, nor the province would determine program content or provide staff, transportation, or other resources. The extent of access would have to be governed by provincial legislation. In practice, afternoons following regular school hours or weekend time could be used. The "Saturday schools" or "Sunday schools" operated by some religious (and cultural) groups could fit directly into this scheme.

Early legislation in some provinces allowed for just such accommodation. Such legislation remains in place in Manitoba and Newfoundland. In Manitoba, this is governed by Section 84(8) of the Public Schools Act, which states:

> If a petition asking for religious exercises, signed by the parents or guardians of 75 percent of the pupils in the case of a school having fewer than 80 pupils or by the parents or guardians of at least 60 pupils in the case of a school having an enrolment of 80 or more pupils, is presented to the school board, religious exercises shall be conducted for the children of those parents or guardians in that school year.[4]

Other parts of Section 84, specifying the forms religious exercises were to take, were struck down by a Manitoba court in 1992, and the matter was not further appealed. The fact that Section 84(8) was allowed to stand indicates that this type of arrangement might pass constitutional muster.

The Manitoba provision is close to that given in the revised version of Newfoundland Term 17. The difference is that Term 17, as a constitutional provision, is not open to court challenge. The relevant parts of that term are:

> (17) (2) In and for the Province of Newfoundland and Labrador, the Legislature shall have exclusive authority to make laws in relation to education but shall provide for courses in religion that are not specific to a religious denomination.
>
> (3) Religious observances shall be permitted in a school where requested by parents.[5]

Subsection 2 mandates the province to establish a denominationally neutral religious education program. Subsection (3) is close to the above Manitoba provision. There is nothing to prevent other provinces from enacting such a constitutional provision in lieu of Section 93. However, there is probably no need for this. A legislative provision such as that in Manitoba would suffice. What might be open to legal challenge in either case would be any attempt to prescribe the form or content of the religious activity or to specify eligible religions.

This model has much to recommend it. It provides an element of parent choice in an area that seems to matter most to those who oppose having to send their children to secular schools. It would allow religious interpretations to be presented in areas of controversy without directly affecting the mandated school program. Some issue might arise if religious teachings are contradictory to school program content or violate existing laws. However, dissenting opinion on any such matter is an inherent part of religious freedom. In practice, the most likely result is that relatively few parents would opt in to such a program while it would provide an outlet for those who feel most strongly about the issue.

Would such a system be consistent with the Charter? While there is no way to prejudge how the courts might act, there seems to be no religious discrimination inherent in the proposition as long as provinces have no authority to deny a properly constructed application from any parent group. Care would have to be taken to avoid legislation that might bias a request based on numbers, different levels of access, or qualifications of personnel providing the religious services. Indeed, provinces and school boards should have no authority to approve the content of religious programs as these would be outside the school program. The only exceptions might be those that advocate violence or behaviour that violates existing laws. An example would be activities that promote discrimination against women or argues that church law supersedes state law. Such instances would likely be rare and could almost certainly be dealt with under the relevant laws. Supreme Court rulings that have limited religious activities in schools or other public places would likely not act as precedents to prohibit what amounts to private religious activities that happen to take place on school property.

The main disadvantage of such a system, especially from the point of view of Catholics, is that the Catholic concept of permeation would be lost. Again, however, the privilege of providing this atmosphere is not available to others and would not be possible under any other scenario short of separate schools for all religions. No compelling argument can be made for continuing to allow the privilege of permeation for Catholics and not for others. Indeed, permeation is more likely a construct of the Catholic leadership than an expression of the views of the Catholic population.

This brings us to the next option, that of providing some level of public support for independent schools. The main advantage of this option is that it would allow greater scope for those who feel strongly about religion and, more specifically, would allow all religions equal access to their own schools if they so desire. This option is not limited to provinces now subject to Section 93. Provincial legislation and funding formulas now in place in Quebec and British Columbia could provide models. Alberta and Saskatchewan also provide partial funding for private schools. However, this is less widely used in the latter two provinces, likely because of the existence of Catholic separate schools.

Under this proposal, Catholic schools in Alberta and Saskatchewan will have to convert to private status if they wish to maintain the right to a religious orientation. Should the current partial funding models remain in place in these provinces, the result would be a transfer of some public funding from public to private schools, though at a lower level. Ontario and some other provinces would have to go further as no funding for private schools is now in place. Even if partial funding were provided, some cost savings might be achieved in Ontario if significant numbers of Catholic schools were to go private. It is interesting to note that after failure of the registration proposal in Newfoundland, no public funding was offered to schools choosing to go private following the constitutional amendment. Only a couple of Catholic schools and no Pentecostal schools did so.

Public support should be set at a sufficient level to forestall outcry over double taxation but at a somewhat lower level than for public schools. This could be justified on the grounds that the public system is a public good available to everyone. Anyone wishing to opt out of that system should have to pay something for the privilege. Also, some restriction is needed to avoid the proliferation of schools that might emerge if there were no cost for departing the public system. Though some may argue that this is discriminatory, the Supreme Court has already ruled in the *Adler* case that the state has no obligation to fund schools for religious groups beyond those protected by Section 93.

Private schools opting for public funding would be under the same obligation as existing independent schools to offer provincial programs, hire certified teachers, and meet provincial performance standards. However, they would be allowed greater scope to maintain a religious atmosphere and teach religious beliefs. The Supreme Court's *Loyola* decision suggests that such a system could pass constitutional muster.

Supporters of more choice in schooling, not only for religious reasons, would almost certainly welcome such a development. However, there are some disadvantages to this option. This would certainly make the system more complex. As an example, governments would have to decide whether to allow public school boards to approve or monitor such schools and determine the level of funding to be offered. Discrimination in teacher employment and student selection would also have to be addressed. Because of numbers, the availability of the option would also be largely limited to cities or to religiously homogeneous rural areas. The presence in any small community of even a few dissenters would have to be considered, leading us back to the original basis for school separation. Finally, any significant expansion of independent schools could undermine the desire to promote religious tolerance and diversity and other broader goals inherent in a public system.

An alternative to the private school model would be to allow specialized schools with a religious focus to be established within the public school system. That approach was embodied in the first version of the Newfoundland constitutional amendment. That version provided for single-denominational schools within public non-denominational school boards. The intent was that the initiative for such schools would have to come from parents, through a registration process, and not from denominational authorities. That proposal failed, not for any constitutional reason, but because the churches mounted successful legal challenges to the registration process itself. Rather than attempting to fix the registration process with even more complex rules, the Newfoundland government decided to take the more drastic step of a second constitutional amendment removing all denominational rights and influences on the schools.

Some might see the idea of specialized schools as resembling the charter school model. As usually conceived, charter schools are public schools established at the initiative of a group or organization desiring some variation from the typical public school. While charter schools have become widespread in the United States, in Canada only Alberta makes any provision for such schools. In that province, charter schools are explicitly intended to broaden school choice. Charter schools are established through application to the ministry and are governed by boards independent of the public or separate boards. The rules for establishing these schools are highly restrictive, with the latest figures indicating that only 28 such schools exist in the province.[6]

Of most direct relevance to this discussion is that charter schools in Alberta cannot be affiliated with a religious faith or denomination. This precludes their use as a means of religious accommodation. In principle, this could be changed, either under the existing model of independent boards or under a model of religious specialization within public boards. However, the Newfoundland experience suggests that this would require complex regulations that might well become an issue for litigation.

On balance, the advantages of the access option appear to outweigh those of either the private or the specialized public school options. Such a system would be non-discriminatory, support the principle of religious choice and place the onus to act on those who believe this to be important. It would be simple to implement and have little or no cost. Finally, though there is no clear indication of the extent to which this option is used in Manitoba and Newfoundland, it seems likely that only small numbers would take advantage of the provision.

The option of accommodating religion by allowing access to schools applies in equal measure to all provinces. Provinces need only establish legislation similar to that found in Manitoba and Newfoundland. Where provinces may differ is in the number of parents likely to take advantage of such a provision. Assuming that this is a small number in most provinces, the impact on the whole system is likely to be minimal.

The option of partial support for private schools (whether or not religious) is also available to the five provinces where such support does not now exist. Any such proposal would likely draw more attention than the access option in provinces with no history of such support. The relative merits and drawbacks of the partial funding versus the access model for any province would be an appropriate issue for any consultation about religions accommodation. No violence is done to the underlying principles in any case.

There remains the question of whether some small distinct religious groups, such as those living in communal settings, should continue to be treated as exceptions, with different forms of accommodation for these groups. Indigenous schooling also needs to be considered for the same reason.

On the first, it is difficult to make a principled case for treating some small religious minorities differently from any others. Under the principles advanced here, there is no reason to treat, say, Hutterite communities differently from Sikh, Muslim, or other religious minority communities. The only discernable difference may be the communal living arrangements of such religious groups, something that may also apply to small numbers of Orthodox Jews or Muslims. That results in effective separation of these groups from others, much as might have been the case with French Catholic communities in the past. In a completely religiously homogeneous community, there is no need to accommodate dissenters and hence, at one level, no need for much state intervention in the religious orientation of a school.

Publicly supported schools in such communities are required to teach provincial programs, hire certified teachers, and in other ways conform to state requirements. All this suggests that the religious function in these schools could be separated from their academic function. Given that, there seems to be no compelling reason the access model should not apply to these schools. The main difference is that religious activity might be of broader scope and intensity. That, however, would be for parents and their religious leaders to determine and implement. Under these conditions, schools in strongly religious communities would be no different from other public schools in their mandate and operations. Religious activities would be separate and conducted outside the main school program at whatever level desired by the community. What would be inappropriate under the access model would be to allow school program modification for some groups and not others. That would take us back in the direction of school separation.

As for Indigenous schooling, a full analysis of future directions for religion in this area is beyond the scope of this book. Indigenous schooling is a particularly sensitive matter because of the failure of past federal and church policies and practices. Also, the rights of Indigenous groups, like minority official language communities, fall under constitutional sections that are not amenable to Section 43 amendment. First Nations leaders have long advocated for control of schools on reserves, based on treaty rights. What it important is that, after a long and inglorious history, official churches no longer have any direct role in Indigenous education.

As already noted, a recent update of the 1972 document *Indian Control of Indian Schools* (now titled *First Nations Control of First Nations Schools*) leaves in place the statement that the denominational nature of the school is a matter of local choice and that efforts should be made to accommodate all preferences. It remains unclear how this is being implemented in practice, though it seems that most Indigenous people remain Christian despite the residential school legacy. A brief overview of websites of some First Nations schools reveals nothing to indicate that denominational orientation is a prominent feature of these schools. However, a strong emphasis on Indigenous culture is evident, and it is possible that this now includes spirituality in some form in keeping with community traditions.

If the Indigenous rights sections of the constitution are to be strictly interpreted, and are not subject to Section 43 amendment, there is little that either the federal or provincial governments can or should do about the denominational orientation of First Nations schools. However, as already noted, First Nations schools are found only on reservations. Most Indigenous children, in fact, attend provincial or territorial schools.

The AFN policy on local decision on the denominational character of schools illustrates the dilemma being faced in addressing Indigenous rights and culture. The reference to denominations is indicative of a continuing Christian presence in First Nations communities. The desire to satisfy everyone is reminiscent of the origin of separate schools. It is not difficult to imagine a scenario in which not everyone can be satisfied, leading to pressure for separate schools within a community. It is not known if any such situation has arisen or how it would be addressed.

As for provincial schools, the *Servatius* case discussed earlier reinforces the value of teaching about Indigenous culture in all schools, and especially in schools with large numbers of Indigenous students. However, it precludes any requirement that students participate in Indigenous religious ceremonies any more than in any other form of religious activities.

All this points to a need to consider that Indigenous students in provincial schools should have the same level of access as others to provincial schools for their own religious activities. Such activities might, in fact, go beyond what is conventionally thought of as religion, and extend into broader aspects of culture. Again, the onus would be on parent groups to request access and perhaps on the Indigenous leadership to prepare suitable material and provide staff.

Concluding Comments: Process and Implementation

In summary, a compelling case can be made for repealing Section 93 and related constitutional terms. These are clearly discriminatory and out of step with Canadian diversity. This discrimination would almost certainly be prohibited under the Charter were it not for the doctrine that one constitutional provision cannot be used to override another.

The mechanism for repeal of Section 93 is well established by the Newfoundland and Quebec precedents. What is lacking is direction on pathways that might be taken in the aftermath. Quebec's position on strict secularism of schools is the default alternative. However, this has led to legislation prohibiting forms of individual religious expression, such as style of dress, which have been ruled constitutional in other instances. The Quebec position is likely to result in even further litigation. The only other precedent is that given by Newfoundland and Manitoba legislation, both of which provide for access to schools for religious activities, outside the school program, on parental request.

This chapter has laid out a range of other alternatives that might be considered, not only in the three Section 93 provinces but also in other jurisdictions. All these have their merits and drawbacks. On balance, however, the only alternatives that seem to have a chance of both constitutional backing and political support are access to schools for religious activities or partial support of religious private schools. These are not mutually exclusive, though, in practice, it might make sense to avoid complexity by focusing on one. Newfoundland and Manitoba provide templates for the first, while British Columbia, Alberta, Quebec, and Saskatchewan offer variations on the second. Ontario is the outlier among provinces with separate schools, offering no support for private schools. The three Maritime provinces also have no provisions for either of the proposed alternatives. However, since these provinces have no separate schools, the main point of contention is avoided.

Judging from the current positions of political leaders in the affected provinces, it seems unlikely that any major political party would currently include in its electoral platform an explicit proposal for unilateral action to nullify Section 93. Taken alone, such action might trigger a backlash that no party would wish to face, especially at election time. That does not imply, however, that nothing can or should be done. The fact that the issue remains controversial in the three affected provinces, though not elsewhere, suggests that governments may eventually have to take some action. The ongoing debate, though not particularly high profile at present, continues to be driven by advocacy groups rather than by broad public engagement. All the alternatives examined here warrant public debate. The emphasis on principle promoted in this book offers a pathway to this debate that is free from the crisis atmosphere that drove the Newfoundland and Quebec actions and that could allow governments to pursue the issue in a more thoughtful and principled manner.

The most obvious starting point would be for a political party or an incumbent provincial government to declare its intention to initiate a public consultation on the scope and limitations of parent rights, school choice, and the place of religious and moral values in schooling. While it would be appropriate to identify the issue of separate schools and the special status of Catholics, there would be no need to take any initial position on constitutional change. The more immediate focus might be on specific issues such as sex education, religious studies, the right to opt in or opt out of programs, the place of separate and private schools, and discrimination. The broader issue would be the appropriate scope and limits of parent choice. The stated goal would be to determine if any consensus exists or if there is substantial majority support for change.

There is little doubt that all this would be controversial in the three most affected provinces. Some would likely in this see a hidden agenda to precipitate constitutional change. An honest response to this would be that some way must be found to resolve the discrimination inherent in the current system and that the goal is to engage the public in determining the best approach. Specifically, the reaction of the Catholic community would have to be sought. It would not be appropriate to declare at the outset that constitutional amendment is on or off the table. However, it would be appropriate to argue that the nineteenth-century compromise is out of step with the realities of Canadian society in the twenty-first century and that a new compromise is needed.

A governing party could initiate such a process at any time. An opposition party would likely have to make the issue part of its electoral platform. Either way, careful thought would have to be given to how this would be presented. The lesson of the 2007 Ontario election is that any firm up-front declaration on the preferred outcome is to be avoided. For any consultation to be genuine, it must be seen as genuine.

The risk, of course, is that the outcome of a consultation would be unpredictable. However, the lesson from Newfoundland is that the views of special interests, including those of the Catholic leadership, are less important than, and may well be at odds with, those of the public at large, including the Catholic population. In that case, it took a couple of years of unproductive negotiation with church leaders before the government went more directly to the people. It found, perhaps to its own surprise, that the public broadly opposed the mechanisms of church control but supported a continued religious presence in schools. Decisive wins in two referenda and a provincial election cemented the consensus.

The importance of this issue would warrant that the consultation be done by a royal commission or other high-level public inquiry, led by someone of high public credibility and no obvious political bias. It would be appropriate to keep the main focus on the principles at hand rather than on ancillary issues such as cost or consolidation, although these would inevitably become part of the agenda at some point. A careful agenda for public consultations would have to be devised, including the usual calls for submission, public meetings, document review and, of critical importance, well-designed surveys. A compelling argument can be made that the status quo is inconsistent with modern Canadian diversity and with the Charter. The significant question is how to resolve this inconsistency.

The main political obstacle to this approach is likely to be a perception on the part of political leaders that a vocal and activist minority within the protected class could vote as a bloc while the broader public would be relatively indifferent to the issue. Bloc voting, even by small groups, can often influence election results, especially in constituencies where the bloc is strongly represented. That was a concern in Newfoundland in the two referenda. It would have been much more difficult for government to act had it been clear that Catholic or Pentecostal adherents voted as a bloc against the constitutional change proposals.

It would take an act of political courage for any party to bring such a proposition to the electorate. Nevertheless, a properly framed argument focusing on removing discrimination and accommodating religion in schools, and based on broad consultation, could be an attractive electoral proposition.

A consultative body would be able to conduct more focused surveys than those that currently exist. The broad question is whether religion has any place in schools and, if so, what form should that take. More specific questions would also need to be asked about support for the mechanisms of church control within the separate system; these include student selection, teacher employment, school board elections, school locations, and funding. Also requiring investigation is the extent to which permeation is, in practice, a core feature of Catholic teachings in separate schools, especially as they move towards recruiting non-Catholic students.

Questions on parent choice, sex education, religion in schools, and access to schools by religious groups would also be required, perhaps in the form of responses to specific scenarios related to ongoing controversies. More specifically, all the options discussed in this chapter could be canvassed directly. Surveys should include breakdowns by religion, with smaller religious groups over-sampled to give accurate results.

This brings us to the question of a referendum. While referenda have their limitations, especially when highly complex issues are at stake, this form of consultation can be useful when the issue at hand is narrowly defined. A lesson can be drawn from the two Newfoundland referenda. The first was based on a complex proposition designed to retain an element of church control of some schools and the second on a simple and unambiguous proposition to establish a single non-denominational school system. While both propositions received majority support, the second was more in accord with public opinion, including that of the Catholic population. Lessons might also be drawn from recent provincial referenda on electoral reform, where the change options appeared to be too vague or poorly understood, leaving the status quo as the default. For these reasons, a referendum would be useful only after the range of options has been narrowed down. Ideally, a single change option would be presented and defended by government.

On a practical note, there would almost certainly be some concern that radical change to the governing structure might lead to significant disruption to students and teachers. The general answer to that is that the shift to secular systems in Newfoundland and Quebec proceeded without much such disruption. In both cases, the initial changes were at the school board and not the school level. Students and teachers simply remained in their existing schools. While considerable school consolidation occurred in Newfoundland in the years following the reform, that was driven as much by declining enrolment as by the reforms. Local challenges to school board decisions on school closings were dealt with under existing rules. This occasionally required court intervention, but only to ensure that due process was followed. Fears that all traces of the religious history of schools would be erased by zealous new school boards were addressed by regulations prohibiting school name changes or altering other heritage features over the objection of the denominations. Also, the province agreed to return any church land on which schools had been built once the school was no longer needed. In practice, this proved not to be as much of an issue as anticipated. Only in one case was there a significant issue of cost. In that case, Catholic authorities successfully argued that a particular school was owned by an order of nuns, who had paid for the school through their teacher salaries. The outcome was that the province was required to "buy out" the order's financial interest in the school.

Some lessons might also be learned from Ontario's decision to extend Catholic rights to the secondary level in the 1980s. That change required that many public schools be transferred from public to Catholic school boards. However, regulations were introduced to ensure that existing students could remain in their own schools. Ten-year protections were also offered to non-Catholic teachers in schools that were transferred. Such measures allowed for a gradual shift of status. A shift in jurisdiction from Catholic to public would, in fact, be simpler as this would require no screening of either students or teachers.

Finally, it is worth reiterating that the question of separate schools by religion remains an issue of public debate only in the three provinces where such systems exist. However, the broader issue of the place of religion in schools is relevant to all jurisdictions. While the issue is perhaps high on the agenda for only a few activists on both sides, it does represent an unresolved matter of principle. It is extremely difficult to argue that the status quo accurately reflects the diversity of Canadian society. The only options consistent with contemporary reality are a fully secular public system or equal accommodation for all who desire a religious basis in schooling. Though controversial, the first is straightforward, as Newfoundland and Quebec have shown. However, going fully secular does not resolve any unease about the need to understand and accept religious differences and whether schools have any role in promoting such understanding. Indeed, recent events in Quebec may illustrate the consequence of extreme secularity.

The most significant issue is to determine the level of religious accommodation that might be most acceptable and whether parents should have any say in the matter at a local school level. The main proposition advanced here, that of access to schools for religious activities outside the school program, is relatively easy to defend, helps resolve the issues of discrimination and parent choice in religion, and adds little complexity or cost. However, comprehensive consultations would likely result in other ideas and could certainly allow for a more fully developed model.

Notes

Introduction

1 Government of Canada. Constitution Act 1982, Canadian Charter of Rights and Freedoms, Section 29. https://laws-lois.justice.gc.ca/eng/const/page-15.html.

Chapter 1. Philosophical and Legal Foundations

1 *Syndicat Northcrest v. Amselem*, 2004 2 S.C.R. 551.
2 *Syndicat Northcrest v. Amselem*, 2004 2 S.C.R. 551.
3 J. A. Buckingham, *Fighting over God: A Legal and Political History of Religious Freedom in Canada* (Montréal and Kingston: McGill-Queen's University Press, 2014).
4 Buckingham, *Fighting over God*, 73.
5 C. Taylor, *A Secular Age* (Cambridge, MA: The Belknap Press of Harvard University Press, 2007).
6 G. Bouchard and C. Taylor, *Building the Future: A Time for Reconciliation* (Quebec: Government of Quebec, 2008).
7 Taylor, *A Secular Age*.
8 United Nations Universal Declaration on Human Rights, (1948), http://www.un.org/en/universal-declaration-human-rights/.
9 United Nations Convention on the Rights of the Child, (1959), http://www.un.org/Docs/asp/ws.asp?m=A/RES/1386%20(XIV.
10 *R v. Jones*, 1986 2 S.C.R. 28.

11 For a concise statement of the Catholic philosophy on schooling see J. Michael Miller, "Five Essential Marks of Catholic Schools," in *The Holy See's Teachings on Catholic Schools* (Atlanta: Sophia Institute Press, 2006): 17–63, http://www.catholiceducation.org/en/education/philosophy-of-education/five-essential-marks-of-catholic-schools.html.
12 The struggle and success of minority francophone populations in achieving the right to education in their own language is fully documented in M. Behiels, *Canada's Francophone Minority Communities: Constitutional Renewal and the Winning of School Governance* (Montréal and Kingston: McGill-Queen's University Press, 2005).
13 J. Berglund, *Publicly Funded Islamic Education in Europe and the United States* (New York: Brookings Institute, 2015).
14 F. A. Cranmer, J. Lucas, and R. M. Morris, *Church and State: A Mapping Exercise* (London: Constitution Unit, University College London, 2006).
15 United Kingdom, *Human Rights Act* (1998), http://www.bl.uk/collection-items/human-rights-act-1998.
16 United Kingdom, *Equality Act* (2010), http://www.legislation.gov.uk/ukpga/2010.
17 Constitution of the United States, *Amendments: Article I (First Amendment)*. (Washington, DC: US Government Publishing Office, 2007).
18 *McCollum v. Board of Education Dist. 71*. The Oyez Project at IIT Chicago-Kent College of Law. 12, http://www.oyez.org/cases/1940-1949/1947/1947_90; *Engel v. Vitale*, The Oyez Project at IIT Chicago-Kent College of Law, http://www.oyez.org/cases/1960-1969/1961/1961_468; *Murray v. Curlett*, 374 U.S. 203 (1963), The Oyez Project at IIT Chicago-Kent College of Law, http://www.oyez.org/cases/1960-1969/1962/1962_142; *Abington School District V. Schempp*. The Oyez Project at IIT Chicago-Kent College of Law, http://www.oyez.org/cases/1960-1969/1962/1962_142.
19 United States Department of Education, *Guidance on Constitutionally Protected Prayer in Public Elementary and Secondary Schools* (2003), http://www2.ed.gov/policy/gen/guid/religionandschools/prayer_guidance.html.
20 Constitution of France, October 4, 1958, http://www.conseil-constitutionnel.fr/conseil-constitutionnel/english/homepage.14.html.
21 "France – Education System Overview," (n.d.), https://education.stateuniversity.com.
22 Dutch Eurydice Unit, *The Education System in the Netherlands* (The Hague: Ministry of Education, Culture and Science, 2005).
23 Dutch Eurydice Unit, *The Education System in the Netherlands*, 8.
24 Constitution of the Kingdom of the Netherlands, (2008). http://www.government.nl/documents-and-publications/regulations/2012/10/18/the-constitution-of-the-kingdom-of-the-netherlands-2008.html.

25 Statistics Netherlands, *Statline* (2012), http://statline.cbs.nl/Statweb/publication/?DM=SLEN&PA=03753eng&D1=a&D2=1,6-7,10,13-14&D3=a&D4=a&D5=l&LA=EN&HDR=G4,G1,T,G2&STB=G3&VW=T.
26 *Constitution of Australia,* Section 116, http://www.aph.gov.au/About_Parliament/Senate/Powers_practice_n_procedures/~/~/link.aspx?_id=6ED2CAE61E7742A1B2C42F95D4C05252&_z=z.
27 Government of Australia, *Australian Education Act* (2013), https://www.legislation.gov.au/Details/C2014C00806.
28 Australian Bureau of Statistics, *Schools Australia* (2014), http://www.abs.gov.au/AUSSTATS/abs@.nsf/DetailsPage/4221.02014?OpenDocument.
29 M. Harrington, *Australian Government Funding for Schooling Explained* (Canberra: Parliament of Australia: Parliamentary Library, 2011), http://www.aph.gov.au/binaries/library/pubs/bn/sp/schoolsfunding.pdf.
30 Protestant separate school boards still exist in Penetanguishene, Ontario, and St. Albert, Alberta.

Chapter 2. Historical Context

1 R. Magnuson, *Education in New France*. (Montréal and Kingston: McGill-Queen's University Press, 1980).
2 C. P. Lucas, ed., *Lord Durham's Report on the Affairs of British North America* (Oxford: Clarendon Press, 1912).
3 J. H. Putman, *Egerton Ryerson and Education in Upper Canada* (1912). https://www.scribd.com/book/187518385/Egerton-Ryerson-and-Education-in-Upper-Canada.
4 Egerton Ryerson, *Report on a System of Public Elementary Instruction for Upper Canada*. (1846). Full text digitized by the Library of the Ontario Institute for Studies in Education, University of Toronto, 2008, https://archive.org/details/reportonsystemofooryeruoft.
5 *Canada and Its Provinces*; Vol 14, Atlantic Provinces, II, p. 153. Cited in Sissons, *Church and State,* 513.
6 The Douay version of the Bible is a translation first published in France in 1582 to promulgate a Catholic perspective in the face of the Protestant Reformation.
7 New Brunswick, *Parish Schools Act, 1858, Section VIII.* Cited in K. F. C. MacNaughton, *The Development of the Theory and Practice of Education in New Brunswick, 1784–1900: A Study in Historical Background* (Fredericton: University of New Brunswick, 1947), 169. (Digital Edition, 2010), https://educationhistory.lib.unb.ca/.
8 New Brunswick, *Parish Schools Act, 1858, Section VIII.*
9 *The Quebec Resolutions,* (1864), https://www.collectionscanada.gc.ca/confederation/023001-7104-e.html.

10 Canada, *Constitution Acts, 1867 to 1982,* https://laws-lois.justice.gc.ca/eng/const/page-4.html.
11 British Columbia, *An Act Respecting Public Schools* (1872), https://www2.viu.ca/homeroom/content/topics/statutes/1872act.htm.
12 *Manitoba Act,* (1870), Section 22(1). http://www.solon.org/Constitutions/Canada/English/ma_1870.html.
13 Northwest Territories, *The School Assessment Ordinance* (1901), http://www.qp.gov.sk.ca/documents/english/statutes/historical/ONWT-1901-CH-30.pdf.
14 *Alberta Act, 1905,* http://www.justice.gc.ca/eng/rp-pr/csj-sjc/constitution/lawreg-loireg/p1t121.html. (The Saskatchewan Act is identical).
15 *British North America Act, 1949 – Enactment No. 21* (1949). *Term 17 of the Terms of Union of Newfoundland with Canada,* http://www.justice.gc.ca/eng/rp-pr/csj-sjc/constitution/lawreg-loireg/p1t212.html.
16 *Board of Trustees of the Roman Catholic Separate Schools of the City of Ottawa v R. Mackell and others* (1916), http://www.bailii.org/uk/cases/UKPC/1916/1916_92.html
17 J.A. Hope, *Report of the Royal Commission on Education in Ontario,* (Toronto: King's Printer, 1950). https://www.worldcat.org/title/report-of-the-royal-commission-on-education-in-ontario-1950/oclc/1052549588
18 Ontario Separate School Trustees Association. *Equal Opportunity for Continuous Education in the Separate Schools of Ontario* (Toronto, 1969) 5.
19 Cited in R. Dixon, "William Davis and the Road to Completion in Ontario's Catholic High Schools, 1971–1985," *Canadian Catholic Historical Association. Historical Studies* 69 (2003): 7–33.
20 Cited in R. Dixon, "William Davis and the Road to Completion," 7–33.
21 *Living and Learning: The Report of the Provincial Committee on Aims and Objectives of Education in the Schools of Ontario* (Toronto, 1968).
22 *Living and Learning.*
23 Dixon, "William Davis."
24 Detailed historical accounts of English Catholic education in Quebec up to the 1980s are given by N. Henchey and D. Burgess, *Between Past and Future: Quebec Education in Transition* (Calgary: Detselig Enterprises, 1987), and R. Magnuson, *A Brief History of Quebec Education* (Montréal: Harvest House, 1980).
25 *Michael Hirsch and Other v. The Protestant Board of School Commissioners of the City of Montreal and Others* (1928), http://www.bailii.org/uk/cases/UKPC/1928/.
26 A full account of the development of Jewish education in Quebec is found in D. Fraser, *Honorary Protestants: The Jewish School Question in Montreal 1867–1997* (Toronto: University of Toronto Press, 2015).
27 P. Gallagher, "Power and Participation in Educational Reform," *McGill Journal of Education* 7, no. 2 (1972): 149–165.

28 Royal Commission of Inquiry on Education in the Province of Quebec (Parent Commission) (1963). *Part 1, The Structure of the Education System* (Québec City, 1963).
29 *Official Languages Act*, Statutes of Quebec 1974, Chapter 6, Section 1.
30 *Charter of the French Language*, Statutes of Quebec 1977, Chapter C-11. Section 73.
31 H. Milner, *The Long Road to Reform, Restructuring Public Education in Quebec* (Montréal and Kingston: McGill-Queen's University Press, 1986).
32 E. G. Hudon, "Church, State and Education in Canada and the United States: A Study in Comparative Constitutional Law," *Les Cahiers de droit* 21, no. 2 (1980): 461–484.
33 Milner, *The Long Road to Reform*, 57–59.
34 G. Pelletier and C. Lessard, *La population Québecoise face à la restructuration scolaire* (Montréal: Guérin, 1981). Cited in Milner, *The Long Road to Reform*, 58.
35 Ministère de l'Éducation du Québec, *The Quebec School – A Responsible Force in the Community* (Québec City, 1982).
36 *Attorney General of Quebec. v. Greater Hull School Board*, 1984 2 S.C.R. 575.
37 *Attorney General of Quebec. v. Greater Hull School Board*, 1984 2 S.C.R. 575.
38 Although Quebec has never signed on to the 1982 constitution, it is binding on that province.
39 K.F.C. MacNaughton, *The Development of the Theory and Practice of Education in New Brunswick, 1784–1900: A Study in Historical Background* (Fredericton: University of New Brunswick, 1947). (Digital edition, 2010), 193, https://educationhistory.lib.unb.ca/.
40 *Henry Maher v. The Town Council of the Town of Portland*, 1874–1883, http://www.bailii.org/uk/cases/UKPC/1874/1874_83.pdf.
41 Sissons, *Church and State*, 238.
42 *Manitoba School Act, 1890. Sections 6–8*. Cited in *The City of Winnipeg v. Barrett (Manitoba)*, http://www.bailii.org/uk/cases/UKPC/1892/1892_42.html.
43 *Barrett v. the City of Winnipeg*, 1891 19 S.C.R. 374.
44 *Barrett v. the City of Winnipeg* and *Logan v. the City of Winnipeg*, http://www.bailii.org/uk/cases/UKPC/1892/1892_42.html.
45 *Re Statutes of Manitoba relating to Education*, 1894, 22 S.C.R. 577.
46 *Brophy and others v. The Attorney General of Manitoba (Canada)*, http://www.bailii.org/uk/cases/UKPC/1895/1895_1.html.
47 A more complete account of the Manitoba Schools Question is found in Paul E. Crunican, *Priests and Politicians: Manitoba Schools and the Election of 1896* (Toronto: University of Toronto Press, 1974).
48 O. J. Skelton, (1921). Cited in L. Clark, *The Manitoba School Question: Majority Rule or Minority Rights*. (Toronto: Copp-Clark, 1968), 211.

49 Pope Leo XIII, (1897). *Encyclical Affari vos On the Manitoba School Question*, http://faculty.marianopolis.edu/c.belanger/quebechistory/docs/manitoba/1897-5.htm.
50 *Regina Public School District v. Gratton Separate School District*, 1915 S.C.R. 58.
51 *The City of Regina and others v. J. McCarthy*, 1918, http://www.bailii.org/uk/cases/UKPC/1918/1918_79.html.
52 Province of Alberta, *Report of the Royal Commission of Education* (Edmonton: Queen's Printer, 1959), 270.
53 *Calgary (City) Board of Education v. Alberta (Attorney General)*, 1979 ABQB 1187.
54 *Calgary Board of Education v. Alberta (Attorney General)*, 1981 ABCA 29.
55 *Public School Boards' Association of Alberta v. Alberta (Attorney General)*, 1988 ABCA 94.
56 *Public School Boards' Association of Alberta v. Alberta (Attorney General)*, 2000 SCR 409 SCC 45.
57 Royal Commission on Education and Youth (P. J. Warren, Chair), *Report of the Royal Commission on Education and Youth* (St. John's: 1967).
58 House of Commons Debates, 33rd Parliament, 2nd Session: Vol. 6, June, 1987.

Chapter 3. The 1982 Constitution and Impact of the Charter

1 Government of Canada. *Constitution Act 1982, Canadian Charter of Rights and Freedoms*, Section 2. https://laws-lois.justice.gc.ca/eng/const/page-15.html.
2 Government of Canada. *Constitution Act 1982*, Section 15.
3 Government of Canada. *Constitution Act 1982*, Section 29.
4 Government of Canada. *Constitution Act 1982*, Preamble.
5 Former Prime Minister Jean Chrétien and former Newfoundland Premier Brian Peckford have written memoirs describing their part in the negotiations, especially around the so-called Kitchen Accord. Neither commented explicitly on Section 29.
6 R. J. Romanow, "Reflections on the Kitchen Accord," *University of Alberta Constitutional Forum* 21, no.1 (2012), https://journals.library.ualberta.ca/constitutional_forum/index.php/constitutional_forum/issue/view/1363.
7 R. Graham, *The Last Act: Pierre Trudeau, The Gang of Eight and the Fight for Canada* (Toronto: Penguin Random House, 2012).
8 *Reference re an Act to Amend the Education Act*, 1986 2863 ONCA.
9 *Reference re Bill 30, An Act to Amend the Education Act (Ont.)*, 1987 1 S.C.R. 1148.
10 *Adler v. Ontario*, 1982 ONSC.
11 *Adler v. Ontario*, 1996 3 S.C.R. 609.

12 *Report of the United Nations Human Rights Committee*, Sixty-Seventh Session, October 18–November 5, 1999, http://www.worldcourts.com /hrc/eng/decisions/1999.11.03_Waldman_v_Canada.htm.
13 United Nations, *International Covenant on Civil and Political Rights*, Article 50, https://treaties.un.org/doc/Publication/UNTS/Volume%20 999/volume-999-I-14668-English.pdf.
14 *Good Spirit School Division No. 204 v. Christ the Teacher Roman Catholic Separate School Division No. 212*, 2017 SKQB.
15 *Good Spirit School Division No. 204 v. Christ the Teacher Roman Catholic Separate School Division No. 212*, 2017 SKQB, para. 474(3).
16 *Saskatchewan v. Good Spirit School Division No. 204*, 2017 SKCA 34.
17 Revised Regulations of Ontario, *Regulation 262, Section 28*, 1980.
18 *Zylberberg et al. and Director of Education of Sudbury Board of Education*, 1986 ONSC.
19 *Zylberberg v. Sudbury Board of Education (Director)*, 1988 ONCA.
20 *Singh-Multani c. Commission scolaire Marguerite-Bourgeois*, 2002 QCCS.
21 *Commission Scolaire Marguerite-Bourgeoys v. Singh Multani*, 2004 QCCA.
22 *Multani v. Commission scolaire Marguerite-Bourgeoys*, 2006 1 S.C.R. 256, SCC 6.
23 *S.L. v. Commission scolaire des Chênes*, 2012 1 S.C.R. 235, SCC 7.
24 *E.T. v. Hamilton-Wentworth District School Board*, 2016 ONSC 7313.
25 *Bonitto v. Halifax Regional School Board*, 2014 NSSC 311.
26 *Bonitto v. Halifax Regional School Board*, 2014 NSCA 80.
27 Province of Alberta, *School Act, RSA 2000*, Chapter S-3. Section 50(1) (b).
28 Northwest Territories, *The School Ordinance* (1901), Chapter 29, Section 137.
29 *R. v. Jones*, 1986 2 S.C.R. 2.
30 *Loyola High School v. Courchesne*, 2010 QCCS 2631.
31 *Quebec (Attorney General) v. Loyola High School*, 2012 QCCA 2139.
32 *Loyola High School v. Quebec (Attorney General)*, 2015 SCC 12, 1 S.C.R. 613.
33 *Ross v. New Brunswick School District No. 15*, 1996 1 S.C.R. 825.
34 *Ross v. New Brunswick School District No. 15*, 1996 1 S.C.R. 825.

Chapter 4. Constitutional Amendment: Newfoundland and Quebec

1 G. Galway and D. Dibbon, "A Perfect Storm: Conceptualizing Educational (Denominational) Reform in Newfoundland and Labrador," in *Education Reform: From Rhetoric to Reality*, ed. G. Galway and D. Dibbon (London, ON: The Althouse Press, 2012), 13–35.
2 Archdiocese of St. John's, *Report of the Archdiocesan Commission of Enquiry into the Sexual Abuse of Children by Members of the Clergy* (St. John's, NL: Author, 1990).

3   P. J. Warren, "The Politics of Educational Change: Reforming Denominational Education," in *Education Reform*, 37–69.
4   Royal Commission of Inquiry into the Delivery of Programs and Services in Primary, Elementary and Secondary Education (Williams Commission), *Our Children Our Future* (St. John's: Government of Newfoundland and Labrador, 1992).
5   Williams Commission, 219.
6   Williams Commission, Recommendation 1, 221.
7   Williams Commission, Recommendation 2, 221.
8   The full legal opinion is found in Williams Commission, 437–465.
9   Ministerial statement by Premier Clyde Wells to the House of Assembly, March 1993.
10 This document seems no longer to be available from public sources. The summary was sourced from the author's personal files.
11 Government of Newfoundland and Labrador, *Adjusting the Course: Restructuring the School System for Educational Excellence* (St. John's: Author, 1993).
12 The results of this poll were made public but appear not to have been preserved in documents available to the public. The account given here was drawn from the author's personal files.
13 The full text of the 1996 amendment is found at https://www.solon.org/Constitutions/Canada/English/Proposals/Bill-C-xxx_1996.html.
14 Proceedings of the Newfoundland House of Assembly (*Hansard*), Vol. XLII, Nos. 36–46, October 16–31, 1995.
15 The account of this debate was drawn from the House of Commons and Senate Debates (*Hansard*) various days from May 31 to December 4, 1996.
16 Senate of Canada, Standing Committee on Legal and Constitutional Affairs, *Amendment to the Constitution of Canada Term 17 of the Terms of Union of Newfoundland with Canada* (1996), http://www.parl.gc.ca/content/sen/committee/352/lega/rep/t17-e.htm.
17 House of Commons Standing Senate Committee on Legal and Constitutional Affairs, *Amendment to the Constitution of Canada Term 17 of the Terms of Union of Newfoundland with Canada* (1997), http://www.parl.gc.ca/content/sen/committee/352/lega/rep/t17-e.htm.
18 Newfoundland, *Education Act*, (1996).
19 Newfoundland, *Schools Act*, (1996).
20 *Hogan v. School Boards for Ten Districts*, 1997 NL SCTD.
21 The full text of the 1997 amendment is found at https://www.solon.org/Constitutions/Canada/English/cap_1997nfa.html.
22 Brian Tobin, Speech to the Newfoundland House of Assembly, September 4, 1997.

23 Parliament of Canada, *Report of the Special Joint Committee on the Amendment to Term 17 of the Terms of Union of Newfoundland* (December 8, 1997), http://www.parl.gc.ca/Content/SEN/Committee/411.
24 The account of these debates was drawn from the House of Commons and Senate Debates (Hansard) various days from December 8–18, 1997.
25 *Hogan et al. v. Newfoundland (Attorney General) et al.*, 1998 NL SCTD.
26 *Hogan et al. v. Newfoundland (Attorney General) et al.*, 1998 NL SCTD.
27 *Hogan et al. v. Newfoundland (Attorney General)*, 1999 NL SCTD.
28 *Hogan v. Newfoundland (Attorney General)*, 2000 NFCA.
29 *Robert Hogan, et al. v. Attorney General of Newfoundland, et al.* (by leave), 2001, http://www.scc-csc.ca/case-dossier/info/dock-regi-eng.aspx?cas=27865.
30 B. Hodder, "The Impact of Educational Reform on Religious Education and Religious Observances," in *A Perfect Storm*, 175–189.
31 Quebec, *Education Act*, S.Q. 1988, Chapter 84.
32 *Reference re: Education Act (Que.), 1993* 2 SCR 511.
33 Commission for the Estates General on Education, *The State of Education in Quebec* (Québec City: Author, 1996), 131.
34 Commission for the Estates General on Education, *Renewing Our Education System: Ten Priority Actions*, Final Report (Québec City: 1996), 85.
35 Resolution of the Quebec National Assembly authorizing an amendment of Section 93 of the Constitution Act, 1867, http://www.saic.gouv.qc.ca/documents/positions-historiques/positions-du-qc/part3/Document33_en.pdf.
36 *An Act to Amend the Education Act, the Act Respecting School Elections and Other Legislative Provisions*, S.Q. 1997, Chapter 47.
37 Section 33 of the Canadian Charter and Section 52 of the Quebec Charter.
38 This account is drawn from *Hansard*, House of Commons 36th Parliament, 1st Session, April–December 1997.
39 This account is drawn from the *Report of the Special Joint Committee to Amend Section 93 of the Constitution Act, 1867 Concerning the Quebec School System* (October, 1997). http://publications.gc.ca/pub?id=9.510694&sl=0.
40 Catholic Committee of the Superior Council on Education, quoted by Senator John Lynch-Staunton, Senate Hansard, December 9, 1997.

Chapter 5. Catholic Schools in Canada

1 Calgary Catholic School District, *Permeation of Catholicity: Instructional Programming and School Culture*, 2014, https://www.cssd.ab.ca/administrative-procedures.

2 Ontario Catholic School Trustees Association. *Our Catholic Schools 2006–07 A Discussion on Ontario's Catholic Schools & Their Future*, (2007), https://www.ocsta.on.ca/resources/our-catholic-schools-kit/.
3 Pew Research Center, *Canada's Changing Religious Landscape*, (2012), https://www.pewforum.org/2013/06/27/canadas-changing-religious-landscape/.
4 D. E. Eagle, "Changing Patterns of Attendance at Religious Services in Canada, 1986–2008," *Journal for the Scientific Study of Religion* 50, (1) (2011): 187–200.
5 Ontario Ministry of Education, *Quick Facts: Ontario Schools, 2016–17*, http://www.edu.gov.on.ca/eng/general/elemsec/quickfacts/2016_2017.html.
6 Alberta, *Student Population Statistics, 2014–2018*, https://www.alberta.ca/student-population-statistics.aspx.
7 Statistics Canada, *Number of Students in Elementary and Secondary Schools, by School Type and Program Type: Saskatchewan*, https://www150.statcan.gc.ca/t1/tbl1/en/tv.action?pid=3710010901&pickMembers%5B0%5D=1.9.
8 C. Alphonso, "In Push for Funding, Ontario Catholic Boards Look Beyond Faith to Enrol More Students," *Globe and Mail*, February 13, 2018.
9 *Globe and Mail*, Editorial, "Protecting Public Schools," February 14, 2018.
10 "Registration," Calgary Catholic School District, https://www.cssd.ab.ca/Parents/Registration/Pages/default.aspx.
11 "Student Registration," Regina Catholic School Division, https://www.rcsd.ca/Schools/StudentRegistration/Pages/default.aspx#/.
12 "Registrations," Ottawa Catholic School Board, https://www.ocsb.ca/register/.
13 "Registration," Hamilton-Wentworth Catholic District School Board, https://www.hwcdsb.ca/onlineregistration/.
14 Michelle McQuigge, *Toronto Star*, June 13, 2017.
15 J. Coleman, S. N. Hoffer, and S. Kilgore, *High School Achievement: Public, Catholic and Private Schools Compared* (New York: Basic Books, 1982).
16 Todd Elder and Christopher Jepsen, "Are Catholic Primary Schools More Effective than Public Primary Schools?," *Journal of Urban Economics* 80 (2014): 28–38.
17 Fraser Institute, *School Performance: Elementary and Secondary School Rankings*, (n.d.), https://www.fraserinstitute.org/school-performance.

Chapter 6. Religion and Private Schools

1 Bernard Shapiro, *Report of the Commission on Private Schools* (Toronto: Ontario Ministry of Education, 1985).
2 Shapiro, *Report of the Commission on Private Schools*, 34.
3 Shapiro, *Report of the Commission on Private Schools*, 35.
4 D. J. Allison, S. Hasan, and D. Van Pelt, *A Diverse Landscape: Independent Schools in Canada* (Vancouver: Fraser Institute, 2016).

5 D. N. Van Pelt, J. Clemens, B. Brown, and M. Palacios, *Where Our Students Are Educated: Measuring Student Enrolment in Canada* (Vancouver: Fraser Institute 2015).
6 These estimates are rough because the population proportions are individuals while the school numbers are schools. If, as seems likely, private schools are on average smaller than public schools, the true proportions are lower than the estimates.
7 Statistics Canada, "Elementary–Secondary Education Survey for Canada, the Provinces and Territories, 2016–2017," *The Daily*, November 2, 2018, https://www150.statcan.gc.ca/n1/daily-quotidien/181102/dq181102c-eng.htm.
8 Nova Scotia, *Education Act*, 1995–96, Section 130 (3).
9 British Columbia, *Independent School Act, 1996*, Chapter 216. Schedule, Section 2 (a) (ii).
10 Saskatchewan, *Education Act, Independent School Regulation* (x).
11 Canada Revenue Agency, *Tuition Fees and Charitable Donations Paid to Privately Supported Secular and Religious Schools*. Bulletin # IC75-23, http://www.cra-arc.gc.ca/E/pub/tp/ic75-23/ic75-23-e.html.
12 See, for example, http://www.ourkids.net/; https://www.cais.ca/.
13 *R. v. Jones*, 1986 2 S.C.R. 284.
14 *Adler v. Ontario*, 1996 S.C.R. 609.
15 *Loyola High School v. Courchesne*, 2010 QCCS 2631.
16 M. Frenette and P. C. W. Chan, *Academic Outcomes of Public and Private High School Students: What Lies Behind the Differences?* (Ottawa: Statistics Canada, 2015).
17 Organisation for Economic Co-operation and Development (OECD), *Private Schools: Who Benefits? PISA in Focus 7* (Paris: Author, 2011).

Chapter 7. The Churches, the Federal Government, and Indigenous Education

1 Truth and Reconciliation Commission of Canada, *Canada's Residential Schools: The History, Part 1* (Montréal and Kingston: McGill-Queen's University Press, 2015).
2 Truth and Reconciliation Commission, 15.
3 R. Magnuson, *Education in New France* (Montréal and Kingston: McGill-Queen's University Press, 1980).
4 Canada, *An Act to Amend and Consolidate the Laws Respecting Indians*, (Statutes of Canada, 1876), Chapter 18.
5 Canada, *An Act to Amend*, Chapter 18.
6 Canada, *An Act to Amend*, Chapter 18.
7 Truth and Reconciliation Commission, 153.

8   N. F. Davin, *Report on Industrial Schools for Indians and Half-Breeds (1879)*, Cited in Truth and Reconciliation Commission, Volume 1, 452.
9   Truth and Reconciliation Commission, 198.
10 Truth and Reconciliation Commission, 204.
11 Truth and Reconciliation Commission, 208.
12 K. S. Coates, *Best Left as Indians: Native-White Relationships in the Yukon Territory, 1840–1973* (Montréal and Kingston: McGill-Queen's University Press, 1991), 112.
13 Coates, *Best Left as Indians*, 112.
14 Coates, *Best Left as Indians*.
15 S. E. Gray, *Methodist Indian Day Schools and Indian Communities in Northern Manitoba, 1890–1925* (Winnipeg: Manitoba Historical Society, 1995).
16 P. H. Bryce, *Report on the Indian Schools of Manitoba and the North West Territories* (Ottawa: Government Printing Bureau, 1907), https://archive.org/stream/reportonindianscoobryc/reportonindianscoobryc_djvu.txt.
17 P. H. Bryce, *The Story of a National Crime: An Appeal for Justice for the Indians of Canada* (Ottawa: James Hope & Sons, 1922).
18 Truth and Reconciliation Commission of Canada, *Canada's Residential Schools: The History, Part 2* (Montréal and Kingston: McGill-Queen's University Press, 2015) 3.
19 Truth and Reconciliation Commission of Canada, *Canada's Residential Schools*, 19.
20 Truth and Reconciliation Commission of Canada, *Canada's Residential Schools*.
21 Truth and Reconciliation Commission of Canada, *Canada's Residential Schools*, 61.
22 *Statement of the Government of Canada on Indian Policy (The White Paper)*. Presented to the First Session of the 28th Parliament by the Honourable Jean Chrétien, Minister of Indian Affairs and Northern Development. (1969), http://www.aadnc-aandc.gc.ca/eng/1100100010189/1100100010191.
23 Truth and Reconciliation Commission, *History Part 2*, 105.
24 National Indian Brotherhood/Assembly of First Nations, *Indian Control of Indian Education* (Ottawa: 1972), http://www.oneca.com/IndianControlofIndianEducation.pdf.
25 *Indian Control of Indian Education*, 23–24.
26 *Report of the Royal Commission on Indigenous Peoples*, 1996, http://www.collectionscanada.gc.ca/webarchives/20071211055641/http://www.ainc-inac.gc.ca/ch/rcap/sg/sg28_e.html#100.
27 *Report of the Royal Commission on Indigenous Peoples*, Volume 1, Chapter 10,
28 The Missionary Oblates of Mary Immaculate of Canada, *An Apology to the First Nations of Canada by the Oblate Conference of Canada*, 1991, http://www.cccb.ca/site/images/stories/pdf/oblate_apology_english.pdf.

29 Anglican Church of Canada, *Apology for Residential Schools*, 1993, https://www.anglican.ca/tr/apology/.
30 *The Confession of the Presbyterian Church as Adopted by the General Assembly*, 1994, http://caid.ca/PresChuApo1994.pdf.
31 *United Church Apology to Former Students of United Church Indian Residential Schools and to their Families and Communities*, 1998, (http://caid.ca/UniChuApo1998.pdf).
32 *Statement of Apology by the Catholic Bishops of Canada to the Indigenous Peoples of this Land*, (2021), https://www.cccb.ca/letter/statement-of-apology-by-the-catholic-bishops-of-canada-to-the-indigenous-peoples-of-this-land/
33 *Canada's Catholic Bishops Welcome Pope Francis' Apology to Indigenous Peoples*, (2022), https://www.cccb.ca/media-release/canadas-catholic-bishops-welcome-pope-francis-apology-to-indigenous-peoples.
34 Truth and Reconciliation Commission, *History Part 2*, 561–563.
35 Truth and Reconciliation Commission, *History Part 2*, 569.
36 *Cloud v. Canada (Attorney General), 2004 73 O.R. (3d) 401.*
37 *Attorney General of Canada, et al. v. Marlene Cloud, et al. (by leave)*, http://www.scc-csc.ca/case-dossier/info/dock-regi-eng.aspx?cas=30759.
38 Indian Residential Schools Settlement Agreement, (2006), http://www.residentialschoolsettlement.ca/IRS%20Settlement%20Agreement-%20ENGLISH.pdf
39 The full text of the apology is available at http://www.aadnc-aandc.gc.ca/eng/1100100015644/1100100015649.
40 *McLean v. Canada*, 2019 FC 1074.
41 Assembly of First Nations, Chiefs Assembly on Education, *A Portrait of First Nations and Education*, (2012), https://www.afn.ca/uploads/files/events/fact_sheet-ccoe-3.pdf.
42 Assembly of First Nations, *First Nations Control of First Nations Education* (Ottawa: Author, 2010), https://www.afn.ca/uploads/files/education/3._2010_july_afn_first_nations_control_of_first_nations_education_final_eng.pdf.
43 Government of Canada, "Government of Canada and Assembly of First Nations Announce New Policy and Funding Approach for First Nations K-12 Education on Reserve," news release, September 21, 2019, https://www.canada.ca/en/indigenous-services-canada/news/2019/01/government-of-canada-and-assembly-of-first-nations-announce-new-policy-and-funding-approach-for-first-nations-k-12-education-on-reserve.html.
44 Assembly of First Nations, *First Nations Control of First Nations Education.*
45 *Servatius v. Alberni School District No. 70*, 2020 BCSC 15.

Chapter 8. The Contemporary Debate

1. Province of Ontario, *Accepting Schools Act. Section 1(1).* (2012).
2. Province of Ontario, *Accepting Schools Act,* Section 303.1(1)(d).
3. Province of Ontario, *Accepting Schools Act,* Section 303.1(2).
4. Assembly of Ontario Catholic Bishops, *Statement on Accepting Schools Act, Bill 13* (2012), https://slmedia.org/blog/assembly-of-catholic-bishops-of-ontario-responds-to-bill-13-and-14.
5. Ontario Catholic School Trustees Association, *Respecting Differences* (2012), http://www.ocsta.on.ca/ocsta/wp-content/uploads/2013/04/PDF-RespectingDifference-FINAL-Jan.26.2012.pdf.
6. Toronto Catholic District School Board, "Minutes of Public Meeting," May 23, 2013.
7. Transcript of an interview between CBC reporter Matt Galloway and Angela Kennedy, chair of the Toronto Catholic District School Board, December 2, 2015, http://www.cbc.ca/news/canada/toronto/programs/metromorning/angela-kennedy-1.3346791).
8. Parents as First Educators, May 23, 2013, http://www.p-first.com/.
9. Kevin O'Dwyer, president of the Ontario Catholic Teachers' Association, quoted in the *National Post,* March 14, 2012.
10. Assembly of Catholic Bishops of Ontario, *The Human Person, Love and Sexuality* (Toronto: Author, 2016), https://catholicintelligenceblog.files.wordpress.com/2019/11/the-human-person-love-and-sexuality-2016.pdf
11. Toronto Catholic District School Board, "Minutes of Public Meeting," June 11, 2015
12. Halton District Catholic School Board, "Minutes of Public Meeting," June 2, 2015.
13. "Protesting Parents Ask Wynne to Scrap New Sex-Ed Curriculum," *Globe and Mail,* April 14, 2015.
14. *Elementary Teachers' Federation et al v. Her Majesty,* 2018 ONSC 6318.
15. Alberta, Bill 10, *An Act to Amend the Alberta Bill of Rights to Protect our Children.*
16. Alberta, Bill 10, *An Act to Amend.*
17. Alberta Catholic School Trustees' Association, "Statement Regarding the Passing of Bill 10, March 11." (2015), http://www.acsta.ab.ca/news/2015/3.
18. D. King, "Separate School System at Odds with Modern Democracy," *Edmonton Journal,* February 2, 2016.
19. D. King "Here Are My Six Objections to Separate School Education," http://www.ouridea.ca/blog. November 17, 2017.
20. Parents for Choice in Education, *Bill 10 and Alberta Education Guidelines Petition,* http://parentchoice.ca/bill-10-petition/.
21. Frederick Henry, "Totalitarianism in Alberta III," https://www.catholicculture.org/culture/library/view.cfm?recnum=11148.

22 Legislative Assembly of Alberta, Third Session, 29th Legislature, *Bill 24: An Act to Support Gay-Straight Alliances.*
23 Jason Kenney, "Accusations that Party Wants to Out LGBT Kids Are 'Ridiculous,'" https://globalnews.ca/news/ November 12, 2017.
24 Alberta Catholic School Trustees Association, *Review of Bill 24*, http://www.acsta.ab.ca/content/file/ACSTA_Review_Bill_24_Final.pdf.
25 Education Act, *Statutes of Alberta, 2012*, Chapter E-0.3, (September, 2019).
26 National Assembly of Quebec, *An Act Respecting the Laicity of the State.* http://m.assnat.qc.ca/Media/Process.aspx?MediaId=ANQ.Vigie.Bll.DocumentGenerique_143925en&process=Default&token=ZyMoxNwUn8ikQ+TRKYwPCjWrKwg+vIv9rjij7p3xLGTZDmLVSmJLoqe/vG7/YWzz
27 Ibid. Schedule 2, Paragraph 10.
28 CTV News Montreal, "Teachers, Students Gather against Quebec's Bill 21 after Hijab Wearing Teacher Forced from Classroom," December 15, 2021, https://montreal.ctvnews.ca/teachers-students-gather-against-quebec-s-bill-21-after-hijab-wearing-teacher-forced-from-classroom-1.5709267
29 Hak c. Procureur général du Québec, 2021 QCCS 1466.
30 D. Hart and A. Kempf, *Public Attitudes Toward Education in Ontario: The 19th OISE Survey of Educational Issues* (Toronto: Ontario Institute for Studies in Education, 2018).
31 Forum Research, *News Release and Poll Results* (2015), http://poll.forumresearch.com/data/ON%20Sex%20Ed%20News%20Release%20%282015%2002%2028%29%20Forum%20Research.pdf.
32 Forum Research, *Majority Continue to Oppose Public Funding for Catholic Schools* (2016), http://poll.forumresearch.com/post/2473/levels-steady-since-last-summer/).
33 Mainstreet Research, (2016), http://www.mainstreetresearch.ca/progress-alberta-poll/.
34 One Public Education Now, (n.d.), https://open.cripeweb.org/about Open.html.
35 One Public Education Now, (n.d.), https://open.cripeweb.org/about Open.html.
36 Andrea Gordon, "Grassroots Group Plans Legal Challenge against Separate School Funding," *Toronto Star*, June 5, 2017.
37 W. J. Phillips, *Public and Catholic School Merger Study* (Federation of Urban Neighbourhoods of Ontario, 2012), https://urbanneighbourhoods.files.wordpress.com/2010/11/ingsfromthemergerofontariopublicandseparateschoolsystems.pdf.

Chapter 9. The Way Forward

1 Commission on Reform of Ontario's Public Services, *Public Services for Ontarians: A Path to Sustainability and Excellence* (Toronto: Queen's Printer, 2012).
2 The full text of that report appears not to be publicly available. However, various summaries and media reports support the conclusion that the review was silent on the separate school issue.
3 *Every Child Learns. Every Child Succeeds,* Report and Recommendations of Alberta's Commission on Learning (Edmonton: Author, 2003).
4 Manitoba, *Public Schools Act*, S. 84(8) 2021.
5 *Constitution Amendment Proclamation, 1997 (Newfoundland Act)* https://www.solon.org/Constitutions/Canada/English/cap1997nfa.html.
6 Alberta Education, *School and Authority Index.* https://education.alberta.ca/alberta-education/school-authority-index/everyone/school-authority-information-reports/.

Bibliography

Alberta Act. 1905. http://www.justice.gc.ca/eng/rp-pr/csj-sjc/constitution/lawreg-loireg/p1t121.html.
Alberta. Bill 10, *An Act to Amend the Alberta Bill of Rights to Protect Our Children*, 2014.
Alberta. Bill 24, *An Act to Support Gay-Straight Alliances*, 2017.
Alberta Commission on Learning. *Every Child Learns. Every Child Succeeds.* Edmonton, 2003.
Alberta. Education Act, Statutes of Alberta 2012, c. E-0.3. September 2019.
Alberta. *Report of the Royal Commission of Education*. Edmonton: Queen's Printer, 1959.
Alberta. *School Act*, Statutes of Alberta 2012.
Alberta. *School Act, RSA* 2000, c. S-3.
Alberta. *Student Population Statistics, 2014–2018.* https://www.alberta.ca/student-population-statistics.aspx.
Alberta Catholic School Trustees Association. 2016. http://www.acsta.ab.ca/.
Alberta Catholic School Trustees Association. *Review of Bill 24*. n.d. http://www.acsta.ab.ca/content/file/ACSTA_Review_Bill_24_Final.pdf.
Alberta Catholic School Trustees' Association. *Statement Regarding the Passing of Bill 10*. March 11. 2015. http://www.acsta.ab.ca/news/2015/3.
Alberta Conference of Catholic Bishops. *The Parent and the Catholic School: Pastoral Letter from the Bishops of Alberta on Catholic Education*. Edmonton: Author, 2006. http://www.acsta.ab.ca/content/file/Pastoral_Letter-Education.pdf.
Alberta Catholic School Trustees Association. *Statement in Response to Guidelines for Best Practices*. 2016. http://www.acsta.ab.ca/.

Allison, D. J., S. Hasan, and D. Van Pelt. *Diverse Landscape: Independent Schools in Canada*. Vancouver: Fraser Institute, 2016.

Alphonso, Caroline. "Saskatchewan Ruling on Catholic Schools Could Have Far-reaching Consequences." *Globe and Mail*, April 21, 2017.

Alphonso, Caroline. "In Push for Funding, Ontario Catholic Boards Look Beyond Faith to Enrol More Students." *Globe and Mail*, February 13, 2018.

Anglican Church of Canada. *Apology for Residential Schools*. 1993. https://www.anglican.ca/tr/apology/.

Archdiocese of St. John's. *Report of the Archdiocesan Commission of Enquiry into the Sexual Abuse of Children by Members of the Clergy*. St. John's, 1990.

Assembly of First Nations, Chiefs Assembly on Education. *A Portrait of First Nations and Education*. 2012. https://www.afn.ca/uploads/files/events/fact_sheet-ccoe-3.pdf.

Assembly of First Nations. *First Nations Control of First Nations Education*. Ottawa: Author, 1972. https://www.afn.ca/uploads/files/education/3._2010_july_afn_first_nations_control_of_first_nations_education_final_eng.pdf.

Assembly of Catholic Bishops of Ontario. *Statement on Accepting Schools Act, Bill 13*. 2012. http://acbo.on.ca/download/inclusive-education/.

Assembly of Catholic Bishops of Ontario. *The Human Person, Love and Sexuality*. Toronto: 2016. http://acbo.on.ca/download/human-person-love-sexuality/.

Australian Bureau of Statistics. *Schools Australia*. 2014. http://www.abs.gov.au/AUSSTATS/abs@.nsf/DetailsPage/4221.02014?OpenDocument.

Behiels, Michael. *Canada's Francophone Minority Communities: Constitutional Renewal and the Winning of School Governance*. Montréal and Kingston: McGill-Queen's University Press, 2005.

Berglund, Jenny. *Publicly Funded Islamic Education in Europe and the United States*. New York: Brookings Institute, 2015.

Bernard, H. C. *Education and the French Revolution*. Cambridge: Cambridge University Press, 2009.

Bolger, Francis William Pius. "Prince Edward Island and Confederation, 1863–1873." *Canadian Catholic Historical Association Report* 28 (1961): 25–30.

Bouchard, Gérard, and Charles Taylor. *Building the Future: A Time for Reconciliation*. Quebec: Government of Quebec, 2008.

British Columbia. *An Act Respecting Public Schools, 1872*. https://www2.viu.ca/homeroom/content/topics/statutes/1872act.htm.

British Columbia. *Independent School Act*. Victoria, British Columbia: Queen's Printer, 1996.

British Columbia. *Précis of the Report of the Royal Commission on Education*. Victoria, 1960.

British North America Act, 1949 – Enactment No. 21. *Term 17 of the Terms of Union of Newfoundland with Canada,* 1949. http://www.justice.gc.ca/eng/rp-pr/csj-sjc/constitution/lawreg-loireg/p1t212.html.

Bryce, Peter Henderson. *Report on the Indian Schools of Manitoba and the North West Territories.* Ottawa: Government Printing Bureau, 1907. https://archive.org/stream/reportonindianscoobryc/reportonindianscoobryc_djvu.txt.

Bryce, Peter Henderson. *The Story of a National Crime: An Appeal for Justice for the Indians of Canada.* Ottawa: James Hope & Sons, 1922.

Buckingham, Janet Epp. *Fighting over God: A Legal and Political History of Religious Freedom in Canada.* Montréal and Kingston: McGill-Queen's University Press, 2014.

Calgary Catholic School District. *Mission and Vision Statements.* n.d. https://www.cssd.ab.ca/AboutUs/MissionVisionStatements/Pages/default.aspx.

Calgary Catholic School District. *Permeation of Catholicity: Instructional Programming and School Culture.* 2014. https://www.cssd.ab.ca/AboutUs/DistrictGovernance/Regulations/Documents/IHAL1.pdf.

Calgary Catholic School District. "Registration." https://www.cssd.ab.ca/Parents/Registration/Pages/default.aspx.

Canada. *An Act to Amend and Consolidate the Laws Respecting Indians* (*Indian Act*), Statutes of Canada 1876, c. 18.

Canada. *Constitution Act 1982. Canadian Charter of Rights and Freedoms,* s. 2. https://laws-lois.justice.gc.ca/eng/const/page-15.html.

Canada. *House of Commons Debates,* 2nd sess., 33rd Parliament, vol. 6, June 1987.

Canada. House of Commons Standing Senate Committee on Legal and Constitutional Affairs. *Amendment to the Constitution of Canada Term 17 of the Terms of Union of Newfoundland with Canada.* 1997. http://www.parl.gc.ca/content/sen/committee/352/lega/rep/t17-e.htm.

Canada Revenue Agency. *Tuition Fees and Charitable Donations Paid to Privately Supported Secular and Religious Schools.* Bulletin # IC75-23. http://www.cra-arc.gc.ca/E/pub/tp/ic75-23/ic75-23-e.html.

Canadian Conference of Catholic Bishops. *Statement by the National Meeting on Residential Schools.* 1991. http://www.cccb.ca/site/images/stories/pdf/apology_saskatoon.pdf.

Canadian Conference of Catholic Bishops. *Statement of Apology by the Catholic Bishops of Canada to the Indigenous Peoples of this Land.* 2021. https://www.cccb.ca/letter/statement-of-apology-by-the-catholic-bishops-of-canada-to-the-indigenous-peoples-of-this-land/.

Catholic Independent Schools of British Columbia. "History of Our Schools." Undated. http://fisabc.ca./who-are-we/history/.

Catholic Insight, May 27, 2013. http://catholicinsight.com/gay-straight-alliance-and-the-distortion-of-truth/.

Census of Canada. *Religions of the People.* 1861. http://library.queensu.ca/data/census-1665-1871-uc.
Chalmers, John W. *Schools of the Foothills Province.* Toronto: University of Toronto Press, 1967.
Clark, Lowell. *The Manitoba School Question: Majority Rule or Minority Rights.* Toronto: Copp-Clark, 1968.
Coates, Ken S. *Best Left as Indians. Native-White Relationships in the Yukon Territory, 1840–1973.* Montréal and Kingston: McGill-Queen's University Press, 1991.
Coleman, James, Thomas Hoffer, and Sally Kilgore. *High School Achievement: Public, Catholic and Private Schools Compared.* New York: Basic Books, 1982.
Colony of British Columbia. *An Ordinance to Establish Public Schools Throughout the Colony of British Columbia.* 1869. https://www2.viu.ca/homeroom/content/topics/statutes/1869ord.htm.
Commonwealth of Australia. *Constitution.* n.d. http://www.aph.gov.au/About_Parliament/Senate/Powers_practice_n_procedures/~/~/link.aspx?_id=6ED2CAE61E7742A1B2C42F95D4C05252&_z=z
Commonwealth of Australia. *Australian Education Act 2013.* https://www.legislation.gov.au/Details/C2014C00806
Constitution of Canada. *Alberta Act 1905.* http://www.justice.gc.ca/eng/rp-pr/csj-sjc/constitution/lawreg-loireg/p1t121.html.
Constitution of Canada, 1982. *Canadian Charter of Rights and Freedoms.* https://laws-lois.justice.gc.ca/eng/const/page-15.html.
Constitution of France, 1958. http://www.conseil-constitutionnel.fr/conseil-constitutionnel/english/homepage.14.html.
Constitution of the Kingdom of the Netherlands, 2008. http://www.government.nl/documents-and-publications/regulations/2012/10/18/the-constitution-of-the-kingdom-of-the-netherlands-2008.html
Constitution of the United States. *Amendments: Article I (First Amendment).* Washington: US Government Publishing Office, 2007.
Commission for the Estates General on Education. *The State of Education in Quebec.* Québec City, 1986.
Cranmer, Frank A., John Lucas, and Robert M. Morris. *Church and State: A Mapping Exercise.* London: Constitution Unit, University College London, 2006.
Crocker, Robert, and Victor Glickman. *Jurisdictional Profiles and Achievement Equity.* Toronto: Council of Ministers of Education, 2013.
Davin, Nicholas Flood. *Report on Industrial Schools for Indians and Half-Breeds.* In Truth and Reconciliation Commission, Volume 1 (1879): 452.
Dawson, William. *Fifty Years of Work in Canada.* London and Edinburgh: Ballantyne, Hanson & Co., 1901. https://archive.org/stream/fiftyyearsworkioodawsgoog/fiftyyearsworkioodawsgoog_djvu.txt
Dictionary of Canadian Biography, Volume IV (1771–1800). http://www.biographi.ca/en/bio/smith william_1728_93_4E.html.

Dixon, Robert. "William Davis and the Road to Completion in Ontario's Catholic High Schools, 1971–1985." *Canadian Catholic Historical Association. Historical Studies*, 69 (2003): 7–33. http://www.cchahistory.ca/journal/CCHA2003/Dixon.htm.

Dutch Eurydice Unit. *The Education System in the Netherlands*. The Hague: Ministry of Education, Culture and Science, 2005.

Eagle, David E. "Changing Patterns of Attendance at Religious Services in Canada, 1986–2008." *Journal for the Scientific Study of Religion* 50, no. 1 (2011): 187–200.

Edmonton Catholic School District. *Student Registration Form 2016–17*. https://www.ecsd.net.

Elder, Todd, and Christopher Jepsen. "Are Catholic Primary Schools More Effective than Public Primary Schools?" *Journal of Urban Economics* 80, no. 1 (2014): 28–38.

Evans, William, and Robert M. Schwab. "Finishing High School and Starting College: Do Catholic Schools Make a Difference?" *Quarterly Journal of Economics* 110, no. 4 (1995): 947–974.

Forum Research. *News Release and Poll Results*, 2015. http://poll.forumresearch.com/data/ON%20Sex%20Ed%20News%20Release%20%282015%2002%2028%29%20Forum%20Research.pdf.

Forum Research. *Majority Continue to Oppose Public Funding for Catholic Schools*. 2016. http://poll.forumresearch.com/post/2473/levels-steady-since-last-summer/.

France. *Education System Overview*. http://education.stateuniversity.com.

Fraser, David. *Honorary Protestants: The Jewish School Question in Montreal, 1867–1997*. Toronto: University of Toronto Press, 2015.

Fraser Institute. *School Performance: Elementary and Secondary School Rankings* n.d. https://www.fraserinstitute.org/school-performance.

Fraser, John James. *Report on Bathurst Schools, 1893*. http://www.lib.unb.ca/Texts/NBHistory/Commissions/ES29/pdf/es29r0.pdf.

Frenette, Marc, and Ping Ching Winnie Chan. *Academic Outcomes of Public and Private High School Students: What Lies Behind the Differences?* Ottawa: Statistics Canada, 2015.

Gallagher, Paul. "Power and Participation in Educational Reform." *McGill Journal of Education* 7, no. 2 (1972): 149–165.

Galway, Gerald, and David Dibbon. "A Perfect Storm: Conceptualizing Educational (Denominational) Reform in Newfoundland and Labrador." In *Education Reform: From Rhetoric to Reality*, edited by Gerald Galway and David Dibbon, 13–35. London, ON: The Althouse Press, 2012.

Galway, Gerald. "The Economics of Educational Reform." In *Education Reform: From Rhetoric to Reality*, edited by Gerald Galway and David Dibbon, 95–116. London, ON: The Althouse Press, 2012.

Gee, Marcus. "Toronto Needs a Single, Secular School System." *Globe and Mail,* June 9, 2017.

Gidney, Robert. *From Hope to Harris: The Reshaping of Ontario's Schools.* Toronto: University of Toronto Press, 1999.

Globe and Mail, Editorial. "Protecting Public Schools." February 14, 2018.

Gordon. Andrea. "Grassroots Group Plans Legal Challenge against Separate School Funding." *Toronto Star,* June 5, 2017.

Government of Alberta. *Decisions to Make: A Framework for Funding School Boards in the Province of Alberta.* 1994. https://archive.org/stream/decisionstomakefooalbe/decisionstomakefooalbe_djvu.txt

Government of Canada. *Gathering Strength: Canada's Aboriginal Action Plan.* Ottawa, 1997.

Government of Canada. *Report of the Royal Commission on Bilingualism and Biculturalism.* Ottawa: Queen's Printer, 1967.

Government of Canada. *Statement of Apology to Former Students of Indian Residential Schools.* 2008. http://www.aadnc-aandc.gc.ca/eng/1100100015644/1100100015649.

Government of Newfoundland and Labrador. *Adjusting the Course: Restructuring the School System for Educational Excellence.* St. John's, 1993.

Graham, Ron. *The Last Act: Pierre Trudeau, the Gang of Eight and the Fight for Canada.* Toronto: Penguin Random House, 2012.

Grant, Agnes. *No End of Grief: Indian Residential Schools in Canada.* Winnipeg: Pemmican Publications Inc., 1996.

Gray, Susan E. "Methodist Indian Day Schools and Indian Communities in Northern Manitoba, 1890–1925." *Manitoba Historical Society,* no. 30 (Autumn 1995).

Greene, John. *Between Starvation and Damnation.* Montréal and Kingston: McGill-Queen's University Press, 1999.

Gregor, Alexander, and Keith Wilson. *The Development of Education in Manitoba.* Dubuque, IA: Kendall/Hunt, 1984.

Haig-Brown, Celia. *Resistance and Renewal: Surviving the Indian Residential School.* Vancouver: Tillacum Library, 1988.

Halton District Catholic School Board. *Minutes of Public Meeting.* June 2, 2015.

Hamilton, W. "Society and Schools in Nova Scotia." In *Canadian Education: A History,* edited by Donald Wilson, Robert Stamp, and Louis-Philippe Audet. Scarborough, ON: Prentice-Hall, 1970.

Hansard, House of Commons. 33rd Parliament, 2nd Session, June, 1987.

Hansard, Senate. 36th Parliament, 1st Session, December, 1997.

Hansard, Senate. 36th Parliament, Catholic Committee of the Superior Council on Education, quoted by Senator John Lynch-Staunton. December 9, 1997.

Hamilton-Wentworth Catholic District School Board. "Registration." https://www.hwcdsb.ca/onlineregistration/.

Harrington, Marilyn. *Australian Government Funding for Schooling Explained*. Canberra: Parliament of Australia, Parliamentary Library, 2011. http://www.aph.gov.au/binaries/library/pubs/bn/sp/schoolsfunding.pdf.

Hart, Doug, and Arlo Kempf. *Public Attitudes Toward Education in Ontario: The 19th OISE Survey of Educational Issues*. Toronto: Ontario Institute for Studies in Education, 2018.

Henchey, Norman, and Donald Burgess. *Between Past and Future: Quebec Education in Transition*. Calgary: Detselig Enterprises, 1987.

Henry, Frederick. *Totalitarianism in Alberta III*. https://www.catholicculture.org/culture/library/view.cfm?recnum=11148

Hodder, B. "The Impact of Educational Reform on Religious Education and Religious Observances." In *Education Reform: From Rhetoric to Reality*, edited by Gerald Galway and David Dibbon, 175–189. London, ON: The Althouse Press, 2012.

Hodgins, John George. *The Establishment of Schools and Colleges, in Ontario, 1792–1910* (Vol. 3). London: Forgotten Books, 2013. First published 1910 by King's Printer.

Houston, Susan E., and Alison Prentice. *Schooling and Scholars in Nineteenth Century Ontario*. Toronto: Government of Ontario, Ontario Historical Studies Series, 1988.

Hudon, Edward G. "Church, State and Education in Canada and the United States: A Study in Comparative Constitutional Law." *Les Cahiers de droit*, vol. 21, no. 2 (1980):461–484.

Indian Chiefs of Alberta. *Citizens Plus: A Presentation by the Indian Chiefs of Alberta to the Right Honourable P. E. Trudeau, Prime Minister and the Government of Canada*. Edmonton: The Indian Association of Alberta, 1970.

Jackson, Robert W. B. *Implications of Declining Enrolment for the Schools of Ontario*. Toronto: Queen's Printer, 1978.

Johnson, F. Henry. *A History of Public Education in British Columbia*. Vancouver: University of British Columbia, 1964.

Jones, Robert Alun. "Elementary Forms of the Religious Life." In *Émile Durkheim: An Introduction to Four Major Works*. Beverly Hills, CA: Sage Publications, 1986.

Kennedy, Angela. "Interview with Angela Kennedy, Chair of the Toronto Catholic School Board." By Matt Galloway. *CBC Metro Morning*. December 15, 2020. https://www.cbc.ca/news/canada/toronto/programs/metromorning/angela-kennedy-1.3346791.

Kenney, Jason. "Jason Kenney: Accusations that Party Wants to Out LGBT Kids Are 'Ridiculous'." By Vassy Kapelos. The West Block, Global News, November 12, 2017. https://globalnews.ca/news/ November 12, 2017.

King, David. "Separate School System at Odds with Modern Democracy." *Edmonton Journal*, February 2, 2016.

King, D. *Here Are My Six Objections to Separate School Education*. November 17, 2017. http://www.ouridea.ca/blog.

Lewis, Charles. "Ontario Catholic School Groups Divided Over Accepting Gay-Straight Alliances on Campus." *National Post*, March 14, 2012.

Lopez, Jeanylin. "Protesting Parents Ask Wynne to Scrap New Sex-Ed Curriculum." *Globe and Mail*, April 14, 2015.

Lucas, Charles P., ed. *Lord Durham's Report on the Affairs of British North America*. Oxford: Clarendon Press, 1912.

Macfarlane, R. O. *Report of the Manitoba Royal Commission on Education*. Winnipeg: Government of Manitoba, 1959.

Mackinnon, Frank. *Church Politics and Education in Canada*. Calgary: Detselig, 1959.

MacNaughton, Katherine F. C. *The Development of the Theory and Practice of Education in New Brunswick, 1784–1900: A Study in Historical Background*. Fredericton: University of New Brunswick, 1947. (Digital Edition, 2010). https://educationhistory.lib.unb.ca/.

Magnuson, Roger. *Education in New France*. Montréal and Kingston: McGill-Queen's University Press, 1980.

Magnuson, Roger. *A Brief History of Quebec Education*. Montréal: Harvest House, 1980.

Mainstreet Research. *Progress Alberta Poll*. 2016. http://www.mainstreetresearch.ca/progress-alberta-poll/

Manitoba Act 1870. http://www.solon.org/Constitutions/Canada/English/ma_1870.html

Manitoba School Act 1890, s. 6-8. Cited in *The City of Winnipeg v. Barrett* (Manitoba) UKPC 42, 1892.

Manley-Casimir, Michael, and Kirsten Manly-Casimir, eds. *The Courts, the Charter and the Schools*. Toronto: University of Toronto Press, 2009.

Martin, Ashley. "Long-Running Theodore Court Case Decides Non-Catholic Students Won't Be Funded to Attend Catholic Schools." *Regina Leader Post*, April 20, 2017.

McCann, P. "From Christian Humanism to Neoliberalism—A Decade of Transition, 1985–1995." In *A Perfect Storm: Education Reform: From Rhetoric to Reality*, edited by Gerald Galway and David Dibbon, 5–93. London, ON: The Althouse Press, 2012.

McGowan, Mark C. *Michael Power: The Struggle to Build the Catholic Church on the Canadian Frontier*. Montréal and Kingston: McGill-Queen's University Press, 2005.

McQuigge, Michelle. "Students Can Opt Out of Religious Classes at Catholic School after Complaint Settled." *Toronto Star*, June 13, 2017.

Miller, J. Michael. "Five Essential Marks of Catholic Schools." 2006. http://www.catholiceducation.org/en/education/philosophy-of-education/five-essential-marks-of-catholic-schools.html.
Milner, Henry. *The Long Road to Reform: Restructuring Public Education in Quebec*. Montréal and Kingston: McGill-Queen's University Press, 1986.
Missionary Oblates of Mary Immaculate of Canada. *An Apology to the First Nations of Canada by the Oblate Conference of Canada*. 1991. http://www.cccb.ca/site/images/stories/pdf/oblate_apology_english.pdf.
Morton, W. L., ed. *Manitoba: The Birth of a Province*. Winnipeg: Manitoba Record Society Publications, 1965.
Murphy, M. "The Modernization of Prince Edward Island Under the Government of W. R. Shaw: The Case of Educational Reform." Master's thesis, Dalhousie University, 2014.
National Indian Brotherhood/Assembly of First Nations. *Indian Control of Indian Education*. Ottawa, 1972. http://www.oneca.com/IndianControlofIndianEducation.pdf.
Newfoundland. *Education Act*. 1996.
Newfoundland House of Assembly (*Hansard*), Vol. XLII, nos. 36–46, October 16–31, 1995.
Newfoundland. *Schools Act*. 1996.
Newfoundland Royal Commission of Inquiry into the Delivery of Programs and Services in Primary, Elementary and Secondary Education (L. Williams, Chair). *Our Children Our Future*. St. John's: Government of Newfoundland and Labrador, 1992.
Newfoundland Task Force on Education. *Improving the Quality of Education, Challenge and Opportunity (Final Report)*. St. John's, 1979.
Noël, Françoise. "The Impact of Regulation 17 on the Study of District Schools: Some Methodological Considerations." *Historical Studies in Education* 24 (2012): 73–91.
Northwest Territories. *Education Act*, Statutes of the Northwest Territories 1996, c. 28.
Nova Scotia. *Education Act* 1995–1996, c. 1.
Nunavut. *Education Act*, Statutes of Nunavut 2008, c. 15.
Ontario. *Accepting Schools Act*. 2012.
Ontario Commission on Reform of Ontario's Public Services. *Public Services for Ontarians: A Path to Sustainability and Excellence*. Toronto: Queen's Printer, 2012.
Ontario Provincial Committee on Aims and Objectives of Education in the Schools of Ontario. *Living and Learning*. Toronto: Author, 1968.
Ontario Royal Commission on Learning. *For the Love of Learning: Report of the Royal Commission on Learning*. Toronto: Publications Ontario, 1994.
Ontario. *Report of the Ontario Royal Commission on Education (Hope Commission)*. Toronto, 1950.

Ontario Catholic School Trustees Association. *Our Catholic Schools 2006-07 A Discussion on Ontario's Catholic Schools & Their Future.* 2007. https://www.ocsta.on.ca/resources/our-catholic-schools-kit/.

Ontario Catholic School Trustees Association. *Respecting Differences.* 2012. http://www.ocsta.on.ca/ocsta/wp-content/uploads/2013/04/PDF-RespectingDifference-FINAL-Jan.26.2012.pdf.

Ontario Ministry of Education. *Quick Facts: Ontario Schools, 2016–17.* http://www.edu.gov.on.ca/eng/general/elemsec/quickfacts/2016_2017.html.

Ontario. *Regulation 262.* 1980. Revised Regulations, Section 28.

Ontario Separate School Trustees Association. *Equal Opportunity for Continuous Education in the Separate Schools of Ontario.* Toronto, 1969.

Organisation for Economic Co-operation and Development (OECD). *Private Schools: Who Benefits? PISA in Focus 7.* Paris: Author, 2011.

Ottawa Catholic School Board. "Registration." https://www.ocsb.ca/register/.

Parents as First Educators. May 23, 2013. http://www.p-first.com/.

Parents for Choice in Education. *Bill 10 and Alberta Education Guidelines Petition.* http://parentchoice.ca/bill-10-petition/.

Parliament of Canada. *Constitutional Amendment Proclamation,* (Newfoundland Act). 1987.

Parliament of Canada. *Report of the Special Joint Committee on the Amendment to Term 17 of the Terms of Union of Newfoundland.* 1997. http://www.parl.gc.ca/Content/SEN/Committee/411.

Parliament of Canada. *Report of the Special Joint Committee to Amend Section 93 of the Constitution Act, 1867 Concerning the Quebec School System.* 1997. http://publications.gc.ca/pub?id=9.510694&sl=0.

Pew Research Center. *Canada's Changing Religious Landscape.* 2012. https://www.pewforum.org/2013/06/27/canadas-changing-religious-landscape/.

Pope Leo XIII. *Encyclical Affari vos On the Manitoba School Question.* 1897. http://faculty.marianopolis.edu/c.belanger/quebechistory/docs/manitoba/1897-5.htm.

Presbyterian Church of Canada. *Confession of the Presbyterian Church as Adopted by the General Assembly.* 1994. http://caid.ca/PresChuApo1994.pdf.

Prince Edward Island, Public Archives and Records Office. *Miscouche Convent School Fonds*: 1927–1930. http://www.archives.pe.ca/peiain/fondsdetail.php3?fonds=Acc3336.

Putman, John H. *Egerton Ryerson and Education in Upper Canada.* Toronto: William Briggs, 1912.

Quebec. *An Act to Amend the Education Act, the Act Respecting School Elections and Other Legislative Provisions,* SQ 1997.

Quebec. *Charter of the French Language,* SQ 1977. c. C-11, s. 73.

Quebec. *Charter of Human Rights and Freedoms,* 1975. http://legisquebec.gouv.qc.ca/en/showdoc/cs/C-12.

Quebec Commission for the Estates General on Education. *The State of Education in Quebec*. Québec City, 1996.
Quebec. *Education Act*, Statutes of Quebec 1988.
Quebec. Ministère de l'Éducation du Québec. *The Quebec School—A Responsible Force in the Community*. Québec City, 1982.
Quebec. *Official Languages Act*, Statutes of Quebec 1974, c. 6, s. 1.
Quebec Resolutions, 1864. https://www.collectionscanada.gc.ca/confederation/023001-7104-e.html.
Quebec. *Resolution of the Quebec National Assembly Authorizing an Amendment of Section 93 of the Constitution Act, 1867*. http://www.saic.gouv.qc.ca/documents/positions-historiques/positions-du-qc/part3/Document33_en.pdf.
Regina Catholic School Division. *Student Registration*. https://www.rcsd.ca/Schools/StudentRegistration/Pages/default.aspx#/.
Report of the Royal Commission on Aboriginal Peoples. 1996. http://www.collectionscanada.gc.ca/webarchives/20071211055641/http://www.ainc-inac.gc.ca/ch/rcap/sg/sg28_e.html#100.
Robertson, Ian R. "Reform, Literacy and the Lease: The Prince Edward Island Free Education Act of 1852." *Acadiensis* 20 (1990): 52–71.
Romanow, Roy J. "Reflections on the Kitchen Accord." *University of Alberta Constitutional Forum* 21, no. 1 (2012): 1–5. https://journals.library.ualberta.ca/constitutional_forum/index.php/constitutional_forum/issue/view/1363.
Rowe, Frederick W. *The Development of Education in Newfoundland*. Toronto: Ryerson Press, 1964.
Royal Commission of Inquiry on Education in the Province of Quebec (Parent Commission). *Part 1, The Structure of the Education System*. Québec City, 1963.
Ryerson, Egerton. *Report on a System of Public Elementary Instruction for Upper Canada*. 1846. Text digitized by the Library of the Ontario Institute for Studies in Education, University of Toronto, 2008. https://archive.org/details/reportonsystemofooryeruoft.
Salton, Herman T. "Unholy Union: History, Politics and the Relationship between Church and State in Modern France." *Review of European Studies* 4, no. 5 (2012): 135–147.
Saskatchewan, *Education Act*, Statutes of Saskatchewan 1995.
Saskatchewan, *Education Act*, Independent School Regulation (x), 1995.
Saskatchewan, *The School Act*, RSS 1930. http://www.qp.gov.sk.ca/documents/english/statutes/historical/1930-CH-131.pdf.
School Assessment Ordinance, Ordinances of the Northwest Territories 1901. http://www.qp.gov.sk.ca/documents/english/statutes/historical/ONWT-1901-CH-30.pdf.
School Ordinance, Ordinances of the Northwest Territories 1901, c. 29, s. 137. http://www.qp.gov.sk.ca/documents/english/statutes/historical/ONWT-1901-CH-30.pdf.

Shapiro, Bernard. *Report of the Commission on Private Schools.* Toronto: Ontario Ministry of Education, 1985.

Sharkey, C. W. "The History of Education in the Province of Prince Edward Island." Master's thesis, Boston University, 1948.

Sissons, C. B. *Church and State in Canadian Education: An Historical Study.* Toronto: Ryerson Press, 1959.

Skelton, Oscar D. *The Life and Letters of Sir Wilfrid Laurier.* Toronto: Oxford University Press, 1921.

Statement of the Government of Canada on Indian Policy (The White Paper). Presented to the First Session of the Twenty-Eighth Parliament by the Honourable Jean Chrétien, Minister of Indian Affairs and Northern Development, 1969. http://www.aadnc-aandc.gc.ca/eng/1100100010189 /1100100010191.

Statistics Canada. *Censuses of Canada 1665–1871.* http://www.statcan.gc.ca/pub /98-187-x/4064810-eng.htm.

Statistics Canada. *National Household Survey.* Ottawa: 2011.

Statistics Canada. *Education Indicators in Canada: An International Perspective.* Ottawa: 2014. http://www.statcan.gc.ca/pub/81-604-x/2014001/ch/chb -eng.htm.

Statistics Canada. "Elementary–Secondary Education Survey for Canada, the Provinces and Territories, 2016/2017." *The Daily*, November 2, 2018. https:// www150.statcan.gc.ca/n1/daily-quotidien/181102/dq181102c-eng.htm.

Statistics Canada. "Employment and Social Development Canada and the Council of Ministers of Education, Canada." *Skills in Canada: First Results from the Programme for the International Assessment of Adult Competencies (PIAAC).* Ottawa: 2013.

Statistics Canada. *Number of Students in Elementary and Secondary Schools, by School Type and Program Type: Saskatchewan.* https://www150.statcan. gc.ca/t1/tbl1/en/tv.action?pid=3710010901&pickMembers%5B0%5D=1.9.

Statistics Netherlands. *Statline.* 2012. http://statline.cbs.nl/Statweb/publicatio n/?DM=SLEN&PA=03753eng&D1=a&D2=1,6-7,10,13-14&D3=a&D4=a&D5 =l&LA=EN&HDR=G4,G1,T,G2&STB=G3&VW=T.

Sweet, Lois. *God in the Classroom: The Controversial Issue of Religion in Canada's Schools.* Toronto: McLelland and Stewart, 1997.

Taylor, Charles. *A Secular Age.* Cambridge, MA: The Belknap Press of Harvard University Press, 2007.

Tetley, William. "Language and Education Rights in Quebec and Canada." *Law and Contemporary Problems* 45, no. 4. (1983): 177–219.

The Guardian. "Religious Education in NSW Schools 'Inappropriate' but Government Vows Support." April 12, 2017.

Thibeau, Patrick W. "Education in Nova Scotia Before 1811." PhD diss., Catholic University of America, 1922.

Tobin, Brian. *Speech to the Newfoundland House of Assembly.* September 4, 1997.

Toronto Catholic District School Board. *Minutes of Public Meeting.* May 23, 2013.
Toronto Catholic District School Board. *Minutes of Public Meeting.* June 11, 2015.
Truth and Reconciliation Commission of Canada. *Canada's Residential Schools: The History, Parts 1 and 2.* Montréal and Kingston: McGill-Queen's University Press, 2015.
United Church of Canada. *Apology to Former Students of United Church Indian Residential Schools and to their Families and Communities.* 1998. http://caid.ca/UniChuApo1998.pdf.
United Kingdom. *Human Rights Act, 1998.* http://www.bl.uk/collection-items/human-rights-act-1998.
United Kingdom. *Equality Act,* 2010. http://www.legislation.gov.uk/ukpga/2010.
United Nations. *Convention on the Rights of the Child.* 1959. http://www.un.org/Docs/asp/ws.asp?m=A/RES/1386%20(XIV).
United Nations. *International Covenant on Civil and Political Rights.* Article 50. https://treaties.un.org/doc/Publication/UNTS/Volume%20999/volume-999-I-14668-English.pdf.
United Nations. *Report of the United Nations Human Rights Committee*, Sixty-Seventh Session, October 18–November 5, 1999.
United Nations. *Universal Declaration on Human Rights.* 1948. http://www.un.org/en/universal-declaration-human-rights/.
United States Department of Education. *Guidance on Constitutionally Protected Prayer in Public Elementary and Secondary Schools.* 2003. http://www2.ed.gov/policy/gen/guid/religionandschools/prayer_guidance.html.
Vancouver Island Colony. *An Act Respecting Common Schools, 1865.* https://www2.viu.ca/homeroom/content/Topics/Statutes/65act.htm.
Van Pelt, Deani N., Jason Clemens, Brianna Brown, and Milagros Palacios. *Where Our Students Are Educated: Measuring Student Enrolment in Canada.* Vancouver: Fraser Institute, 2015.
Warren, P. J. "The Politics of Educational Change: Reforming Denominational Education." In *Education Reform: From Rhetoric to Reality,* edited by Gerard Galway and David Dibbon, 37–69. London, ON: The Althouse Press, 2012.
Wilson, Donald, Robert Stamp, and Louis-Philippe Audet. *Canadian Education.* Scarborough, ON: Prentice-Hall, 1970.
Yukon Act, Statutes of Canada 2002.
Yukon. *Education Act*, Statutes of the Yukon 2002.

Court Cases Cited

Except where otherwise noted, Canadian cases were retrieved from https://www.canlii.org. Cases from the Judicial Committee of the Privy Council were retrieved from http://www.bailii.org/uk/cases/UKPC/.

Abington School District v. Schempp. The Oyez Project at IIT Chicago-Kent College of Law. http://www.oyez.org/cases/1960-1969/1962/1962_142.
Adler v. Ontario, 1982 ONSC.
Adler v. Ontario, 1996 3 S.C.R. 609.
Attorney General of Canada, et al. v. Marlene Cloud, et al. (Ontario) (Civil) (By Leave), 2005.
Attorney General of Quebec. v. Greater Hull School Board, 1984 2 S.C.R. 575.
Barrett v. The City of Winnipeg, 1891 19 S.C.R. 374.
Barrett v. the City of Winnipeg and Logan v. the City of Winnipeg, 1892 UKPC.
Brophy and others v. The Attorney General of Manitoba (Canada), 1895 UKPC 1.
Brothers of the Christian Schools and others v. The Minister of Education for the Province of Ontario and another (Ontario), 1906 UKPC 68.
Board of Trustees of the Roman Catholic Separate Schools of the City of Ottawa v. R. Mackell and others, 1916 UKPC.
Bonitto v. Halifax Regional School Board, 2014 NSSC.
Bonitto v. Halifax Regional School Board, 2015 NSCA 80.
Brothers of the Christian Schools and others v. The Minister of Education for the Province of Ontario and Another (Ontario), 1906 UKPC 68.
Caldwell et al. v. Stuart et al., 1984 2 S.C.R. 603.
Calgary (City) Board of Education v. Alberta (Attorney General), 1979 ABQB.
Calgary Board of Education v. Alberta (Attorney General), 1981 ABCA 29.
City of Regina and others v. J. McCarthy, 1917 127 UKPC.
Cloud v. Canada (Attorney General), 2004 73 O.R. (3d) 401.
Commission scolaire Marguerite-Bourgeoys v. Singh Multani, 2004 QCCA.
Dillon and Catelli Food Products Ltd. (and twenty-two other appeals), 1937 O.R. 114.
Engel v. Vitale. The Oyez Project at IIT Chicago-Kent College of Law. http://www.oyez.org/cases/1960-1969/1961/1961_468.
Epperson v. Arkansas, 1968, 393 U.S. 97. http://www.bc.edu/bc_org/avp/cas/comm/free_speech/epperson.html.
E.T. v. Hamilton-Wentworth District School Board, 2016 ONSC 7313.
Good Spirit School Division No. 204 v. Christ the Teacher Roman Catholic Separate School Division No. 212, 2017 SKQB.
Good Spirit School Division No. 204 v. Christ the Teacher Roman Catholic Separate School Division No. 212, 2017 SKCA.
Henry Maher v. The Town Council of the Town of Portland, 1874-1883 UKPC.
Hogan v. School Boards for Ten Districts, 1997 NL SCTD.
Hogan et al. v. Newfoundland (Attorney General) et al., 1998 NL SCTD.
Hogan et al. v. Newfoundland (Attorney General), 1999 NL SCTD.
Hogan v. Newfoundland (Attorney General), 2000 NLCA 12.
Loyola High School v. Courchesne, 2010 QCCS 2631.
Loyola High School v. Quebec (Attorney General), 2015 SCC 12, 1 S.C.R. 613.
Manitoba Assn. for Rights & Liberties Inc. v. Manitoba, 1992 5 W.W.R. 749, 94 D.L.R. (4th) 678, 82 Man. R (2d) 39.

Mccollum v. Board of Education Dist. 71. The Oyez Project at IIT Chicago-Kent College of Law. 12. http://www.oyez.org/cases/1940-1949/1947/1947_90.
McCarthy v. Regina, 1917 SKCA.
McLean v. Canada, 2019 FC 1074.
Michael Hirsch and Other v. The Protestant Board of School Commissioners of the City of Montreal and Others, 1928 UKPC.
Multani v. Commission scolaire Marguerite-Bourgeoys, 2006 1 SCR 256.
Murray v. Curlett, 374 U.S. 203, 1963. The Oyez Project at IIT Chicago-Kent College of Law. http://www.oyez.org/cases/1960-1969/1962/1962_142.
Public School Boards' Association of Alberta v. Alberta (Attorney General), 2000 2 SCR 409.
Public School Boards' Association of Alberta v. Alberta (Attorney General), 1998 ABCA 94.
Quebec (Attorney General) v. Loyola High School, 2012 QCCA 2139.
R. v. Jones, 2 1986 S.C.R. 284.
Reference re Education Act (Que.), 1993 2 S.C.R. 511 SCC (cases 22112, 22119, 22123, 22124, 22129).
Reference re An Act to Amend the Education Act, 1986 ONCA.
Reference re Bill 30, An Act to Amend the Education Act (Ont.), 1987 1 S.C.R. 1148.
Reference re Education Act (Que.), 1993 2 S.C.R. 511.
Reference re s. 17 of the Alberta Act, 1927 S.C.R. 364.
Regina S. D. 4 Trustees v. Grattan Separate School Trustees, 1914 SKQB.
Regina Public School District v. Gratton Separate School District, 1915 S.C.R. 589.
Robert Hogan, et al. v. Attorney General of Newfoundland, et al., 2001 SCC.
Ross v. New Brunswick School District No. 15., 1996 1 S.C.R. 825.
Saskatchewan v. Good Spirit School Division No. 204, 2020 SKCA 34.
Servatius v. Alberni School District No. 70, 2020 BCSC 15.
Singh-Multani c. Commission scolaire Marguerite-Bourgeois, 2002 QCCS.
S.L. v. Commission scolaire des Chênes, 2012 1 S.C.R. 235.
Statutes of Manitoba relating to Education, 1894 22 S.C.R. 577.
Syndicat Northcrest v. Amselem, 2004 2 S.C.R. 551.
Tiny Separate School Trustees v. The King, 1927 S.C.R. 637.
Zylberberg et al. and Director of Education of Sudbury Board of Education, 1986 ONSC.
Zylberberg v. Sudbury Board of Education, 1988 ONCA.

Education

Series Editors: Nicholas Ng-A-Fook and Carole Fleuret

Our *Education* series seeks to advance thought-provoking research within the broader field of education. Scholarly works in this series examine educational research from a multidisciplinary perspective and address a variety of issues in the field, including curriculum studies, arts-based education, educational philosophy, life writing, foundations in education, teacher education, evaluation, and counselling.

Previous titles in the *Education* Series:

Timothy M. Sibbald and Victoria Handford, eds., *The Academic Sabbatical: A Voyage of Discovery*, 2022.

Joël Thibeault and Carole Fleuret, eds., *Didactique du français en contextes minoritaires : entre normes scolaires et plurilinguismes*, 2020.

Timothy M. Sibbald and Victoria Handford, eds., *Beyond the Academic Gateway: Looking Back on the Tenure-Track Journey*, 2020.

Anne M. Phelan, William F. Pinar, Nicholas Ng-A-Fook, and Ruth Kane, eds., *Reconceptualizing Teacher Education: A Canadian Contribution to a Global Challenge*, 2020.

Michelle Forrest and Linda Wheeldon, *Scripting Feminist Ethics in Teacher Education*, 2019.

William F. Pinar, *Moving Images of Eternity: George Grant's Critique of Time, Teaching, and Technology*, 2019.

Pierre Jean, *Planification de formations en santé : guide des bonnes pratiques*, 2019.

Thomas R. Klassen and John A. Dwyer, *Décrocher son diplôme (et l'emploi de ses rêves !) : comment maîtriser les compétences essentielles menant au succès à l'école, au travail et dans la vie*, 2018.

Timothy M. Sibbald and Victoria Handford, eds., *The Academic Gateway: Understanding the Journey to Tenure*, 2017.

Lise Gremion, Serge Ramel, Valérie Angelucci, and Jean-Claude Kalubi, eds., *Vers une école inclusive : regards croisés sur les défis actuels*, 2017.

For a complete list of the University of Ottawa Press titles, please visit:
www.press.uOttawa.ca

www.ingramcontent.com/pod-product-compliance
Lightning Source LLC
Chambersburg PA
CBHW052017290426
44112CB00014B/2281